MUSIC, SENIOR CENTERS, AND QUALITY OF LIFE

Lisa Lehmberg and Victor Fung present a groundbreaking look at quality of life via the music participation of older adults in diverse US senior centers. The state of musical activities in senior centers pre- and mid-pandemic is elucidated through original research conducted in senior centers across six states. Featured are older adults' stories told in their own words; insights from senior center activity leaders, management, and staff; and data, analyses, and syntheses from the authors' senior center visits and a survey of center managers. The authors document the adjustment process undergone by these centers during the pandemic and leading into a new normal. Recommendations are offered for policy makers, school and community music educators, music activity leaders, older adults, caregivers, and service providers to enhance the quality of life of older adults. The critical role that music plays in supporting their quality of life is emphasized.

LISA J. LEHMBERG is Professor of Music Education at the University of Massachusetts Amherst, USA. She holds a PhD degree in music education and has extensive experience as a school music specialist. Her publications include research- and practice-based books, chapters, and articles, including the book *Music for Life: Music Participation and Quality of Life of Senior Citizens* (coauthored with C. Victor Fung, 2016).

C. VICTOR FUNG is Professor of Music Education at the University of South Florida, USA. He authored *Music for Life: Music Participation and Quality of Life of Senior Citizens* (with Lisa J. Lehmberg, 2016) and *A Way of Music Education: Classic Chinese Wisdoms* (2018). He was a Fulbright researcher in Japan and has given open lectures at over thirty institutions across four continents.

MUSIC, SENIOR CENTERS, AND QUALITY OF LIFE

LISA J. LEHMBERG
University of Massachusetts Amherst

C. VICTOR FUNG
University of South Florida

Shaftesbury Road, Cambridge CB2 8EA, United Kingdom

One Liberty Plaza, 20th Floor, New York, NY 10006, USA

477 Williamstown Road, Port Melbourne, VIC 3207, Australia

314–321, 3rd Floor, Plot 3, Splendor Forum, Jasola District Centre, New Delhi – 110025, India

103 Penang Road, #05–06/07, Visioncrest Commercial, Singapore 238467

Cambridge University Press is part of Cambridge University Press & Assessment, a department of the University of Cambridge.

We share the University's mission to contribute to society through the pursuit of education, learning and research at the highest international levels of excellence.

www.cambridge.org
Information on this title: www.cambridge.org/9781009164351

DOI: 10.1017/9781009164344

© Lisa J. Lehmberg and C. Victor Fung 2023

This publication is in copyright. Subject to statutory exception and to the provisions of relevant collective licensing agreements, no reproduction of any part may take place without the written permission of Cambridge University Press & Assessment.

First published 2023
First paperback edition 2025

A catalogue record for this publication is available from the British Library

Library of Congress Cataloging-in-Publication data
NAMES: Lehmberg, Lisa J., author. | Fung, C. Victor, author.
TITLE: Music, senior centers, and quality of life / Lisa J. Lehmberg, C. Victor Fung.
DESCRIPTION: [1.] | New York : Cambridge University Press, 2023. | Includes bibliographical references and index.
IDENTIFIERS: LCCN 2022030691 (print) | LCCN 2022030692 (ebook) | ISBN 9781009164368 (hardback) | ISBN 9781009164351 (paperback) | ISBN 9781009164344 (epub)
SUBJECTS: LCSH: Music–Social aspects–United States. | Music and older people–United States. | Music therapy for older people–United States. | Senior centers–United States. | Quality of life–United States. | Aging–Social aspects–United States.
CLASSIFICATION: LCC ML3917.U6 L44 2023 (print) | LCC ML3917.U6 (ebook) | DDC 780.84/6073–dc23/eng/20220805
LC record available at https://lccn.loc.gov/2022030691
LC ebook record available at https://lccn.loc.gov/2022030692

ISBN 978-1-009-16436-8 Hardback
ISBN 978-1-009-16435-1 Paperback

Cambridge University Press & Assessment has no responsibility for the persistence or accuracy of URLs for external or third-party internet websites referred to in this publication and does not guarantee that any content on such websites is, or will remain, accurate or appropriate.

To older adults everywhere, and to all who provide services for older adults

Contents

List of Figures	*page* viii
List of Tables	ix
Acknowledgments	x

PART I A NEW SCENE FOR EXPLORATION

1	Social and Musical Responsiveness	3
2	State of Music in US Senior Centers	10

PART II AN EXPERIENTIAL VIEW OF MUSIC IN SENIOR CENTERS

3	A Close-up Look at Senior Centers	41
4	Music across Six Senior Centers	65
5	Older Adults' Perspectives on Music	100
6	Toward Enhanced Quality of Life through Musical Activities in Senior Centers	121

PART III ENTERING A NEW NORMAL

7	Musical Opportunities in US Senior Centers Pre- and Mid-Pandemic	139
8	Lifelong Music Participation and New Considerations	154

Appendices	162
References	191
Index	204

Figures

3.1	Map of six regions of the United States	page 43
5.1	Interviewee numbers by category, with category overlaps	101
5.2	Forms of music participation: Senior center clients	102
5.3	Instruments utilized in music-making by senior center clients	105
5.4	Music participation and nonparticipation across senior center clients and activity leaders	107
6.1	Qualities of desired musical activities	131
6.2	Toward enhanced quality of life	133
7.1	Number of senior center managers reporting their clients' ethnicities	141
7.2	Approximate age group of most center attendees (each center manager could choose up to two age groups)	143
7.3	Number of senior centers offering three types of musical activities in pre- and mid-pandemic periods: Music-making activities (singing, playing of instruments, musical improvisation, or musical composition)	144
7.4	Number of senior centers offering three types of musical activities in pre- and mid-pandemic periods: Dance- or exercise-focused activities in which attendees move to music or exercise-focused activities with music in the background	144
7.5	Number of senior centers offering three types of musical activities in pre- and mid-pandemic periods: Live musical performance events	145
7.6	Senior center managers' plans for musical activities after the pandemic is under control	147
7.7	Ways musical activities might be modified after the pandemic is under control	148

Tables

2.1	Studies reflecting the functions of senior centers in the United States	page 16
2.2	Studies showing characteristics of senior center clients	19
2.3	Senior center clients compared to nonparticipants in senior centers	22
2.4	Sample studies in specific aspects of activity participation in senior centers	26
2.5	Senior center studies that target minority and underrepresented groups	28
2.6	Senior center challenges within four areas, as identified by Cannon (2015)	31
4.1	Musical groups and classes observed and/or discussed with group leaders	69
6.1	Benefits of older adult music participation: Connections between current study and previous research	130
6.2	Quality of life model and related findings on senior center clients' music participation	134
7.1	Distribution of senior center managers who completed the survey	141
7.2	Activity formats at the time of the survey, October 2021	142
7.3	Number of musical activities in relation to availability for beginners or experienced attendees, fee requirement, and paid activity leader	145
7.4	Center managers' responses to the effect of the pandemic on musical activities	146

Acknowledgments

We are forever thankful to those who helped us along the path toward completion of this book. First and foremost, we thank our study participants for their trust and the generous donation of their time. We are extremely grateful for the kindness, openness, and wisdom they offered us. Their stories have been most inspiring, and we wish them well wherever they may be.

Our research could not have been completed without the senior center managers and staff, who warmly welcomed us into their senior center facilities and helped us to connect with their center's older adult clientele. We so appreciate their generosity in providing us with access to center activities and events and supporting our research goals.

We appreciate the anonymous reviewers who provided insightful comments, which helped us to make our book the best it could be. We would also like to express our gratitude to Janka Romero, Commissioning Editor for Psychology, and Rowan Groat, Editorial Assistant, at Cambridge University Press, for their guidance and patience throughout the review and publication process.

We also thank Daniel Albert and Stephen Paparo, our music education colleagues at the University of Massachusetts, for assuming extra responsibilities within the music education program so that our book process could be more expedient, and for providing encouragement throughout this project.

Last but not least, a project of this magnitude could not be accomplished without the inexhaustible support of our families. Lance Lehmberg, Monica Fung, and our children – we love and thank you more than words can express.

PART I

A New Scene for Exploration

CHAPTER 1

Social and Musical Responsiveness

The world is inevitably changing, but music and quality of life remain as "two of the most stable and everlasting human desires" (Fung & Lehmberg, 2016, p. 3). Advancements in many sectors that benefit humans have improved through the years. Global trends show that people are living longer and healthier and are enjoying an overall better quality of life. Older adults are increasingly a larger share of the population (United Nations, 2019). More people have increased opportunities to enjoy music throughout their lives, as music is a medium for all to pursue in an indefinite number of ways. Beyond enjoyment, music is essential in maintaining a social, psychological, physical, and an overall well-being. Music can also serve as a refuge and a safe haven in times of crisis, hardship, and even disaster. For some, music can be the best medium for deep, meaningful experiences. Music is an indestructible medium regardless of how life and the world change. Not only have the chances to take advantage of musical activities increased due to extended lifespans, perspectives of different disciplines have also broadened in recent decades. We are at a juncture where lifelong learning and community music, among other areas, have joined forces in opening up new spaces for reflection, investigation, and practice. These broadened views are not only results of disciplinal development but more importantly results of a heightened awareness of individuals and places long underplayed in literature and in practice.

In this book, we utilize a social psychological approach to explore the musical needs of diverse older adults who make use of places where such needs can be fulfilled – senior centers. Both older adults and senior centers normally fall outside the purview of fields not directly linked to older adults and their service providers, such as music and music education, yet musical activities found in senior centers could be essential and may even be life-changing to participants. We define music participation activities inclusively to encompass all forms of music-making and creating, music listening, and moving to music (Fung & Lehmberg, 2023). These activities show that at the minimum, everyone at any life stage is capable of engaging in music and thus improving their quality of life. To this end, we present our studies to illustrate how older adults, a culturally undervalued population, used senior centers across the United States to engage in music and to provide a glimpse of how such activities are adopting dramatic changes through a global pandemic, which has turned everyone's life into a new normal. We begin this chapter with a contemporary overview of the benefits of older adults' music participation and of the venues available for such activities. Subsequently, we delve into a rationale for carrying out our studies of senior centers presented in the remaining chapters of the book.

1.1 Benefits of Music Participation

A plethora of studies shows that music participation has numerous benefits throughout the lifespan (e.g., Rickard & McFerran, 2012). Although there maybe interpretive issues and inconsistencies across a group of studies finding that music participation improves children's academic achievement (e.g., Blackburn, 2017; Gordon, Fehd, & McCandliss, 2015; Guhn, Emerson, & Gouzouasis, 2020; Sala & Gobet, 2020), evidence of the benefits of music participation for adults is overabundant. Krause, Davidson, and North (2018) identified 562 distinct benefits in their review of 97 studies of predominantly adults and older adults. Since reviews of earlier studies of older adult music participation have been presented elsewhere (Fung & Lehmberg, 2016; Lehmberg & Fung, 2010; Noice, Noice, & Kramer, 2014), we focus here on an overview of studies published since 2016. The mainstays in the benefits of older adults' music participation are (a) social, such as networking, socializing, making friends, and having a sense of community; (b) psychological, such as emotional satisfaction, maintenance and improvement of cognition, and fulfillment through musical learning; (c) physical, such as improved breathing, posture, and health; and (d) overall well-being, including spiritual wellness, life satisfaction, and quality of life. These benefits are distinctive only to some degree; they overlap significantly.

Benefits of music participation are also reported across a wide spectrum of social strata and activities. For example, a sample of homeless adults with mental illness in the United States reported therapeutic and social–emotional benefits from listening to hip-hop pieces and reading their lyrics (Travis, Rodwin, & Allcorn, 2019). Our work with older adults in a predominantly middle-class retirement community revealed five contributors of music participation to lifelong engagement in music and quality of life (Fung & Lehmberg, 2016): (1) social and temporal connections; (2) variety of musical styles and musical activities; (3) meaningful participation to include commitment, socialization, and supportive context; (4) ownership and autonomous learning; and (5) flexibility to enter and re-enter at any time. These findings were so persuasive that they prompted us to take a grassroots approach, that is taking actions and responsibilities at a local, diverse community level, in exploring venues that offer musical opportunities for older adults.

While we do not intend to present a comprehensive literature review on the benefits of older adults' music participation, we see consistent findings in studies across various world regions. In Australia, Joseph and Southcott (2018) identified social connection, a sense of well-being, and musical engagement as the three overarching themes based on an interpretative phenomenological analysis of data from older chorus singers. In an analysis of a sample of 17- to 85-year-olds, Krause, North, and Davidson (2019) found that female music participants were more likely than males to perceive benefits that were associated with autonomous motivation and the social, cognitive, esteem, competency, and relatedness dimensions of well-being. In Canada, David and colleagues (2018) found that enhanced cognitive function, development of meaningful relationships, and improved psychosocial status (e.g., reduction of social isolation) were among the benefits of older adults participating in an intergenerational music program. Increased socialization and uplifted spirits were among the benefits reported by Millett and Fiocco (2021) based on long-term care residents between ages 63 and 95, who participated in a weekly singing and discussion session around a self-selected theme. In the United States, a short-term intense piano training was shown to benefit cognitive performance of 34 older adults with an average age of 70.79 years (Bugos & Kochar, 2017). Drawing from 35 instrumental ensemble participants in Canada and the United States, Barbeau and Mantie (2019) found that biological, psychological, and social benefits outweighed the stress related to performance anxiety. In China (Southcott & Li, 2018), 13 older adults between the ages of 54 and 78 years taking singing lessons at a university for retirees collectively recognized the benefits of emotional well-being, physical well-being, mental well-being, and "learning new things" (p. 283), musical preferences, and sharing music. A four-year study of a community choir in the United Kingdom with singers aged 55–78 (Lamont et al., 2018) highlighted many individual and interpersonal benefits, including musical achievements and the development of social relationships within a supportive community. Pitts and Robinson (2016) interviewed 18 adult current and past music participants, also in the United Kingdom, and concluded that "past experiences of learning music, and particularly of learning an instrument, were seen to have lifelong benefits even for those who no longer played" (p. 344). A large-scale survey (N = 14,265) of adults in Denmark suggested that music activities and music experiences contributed to general health (Ekholm, Juel, & Bonde, 2016). Findings as such across the globe seem to ascertain a high level of universality, in that benefits of music participation are widespread with potential deep impacts. However, differences across nations, societies, and cultures shape different organizations and avenues for older adults to participate in music. While it is hard to compare institutions across nations, we have chosen to explore venues within the local community and supported by the people and the government in the United States. Not to expect parallels worldwide, observations of music participation in such venues may generate global interests and understanding in their function, operation, and benefits.

1.2 Venues for Older Adult Music Participation

Older adults' musical activity occurs in a wide variety of venues, which may be characterized as formal or informal, private or public, government or nongovernment, for-profit or nonprofit, religious or secular, and small or large. These are neither clear-cut nor exclusive categories but ways of viewing their multidimensionality and integrality in the social fabric. For example, a subgroup from a church choir may meet at a singer's home for a weekend private gathering that includes friends, neighbors, and family members, and they may take turns singing along with a guitarist strumming chords; or a jazz instrumental group with a salaried leader and an executive board may rehearse in a government-funded community center for two hours every week and perform an average of ten times per year in schools, hospitals, community centers, churches, and at private parties. While it is impossible to account for all types of musical activities in which older adults engage, it is feasible to identify a study target that is open to the public, where all older adults feel welcome and can take ownership and be intimately connected among themselves and with the local community. This would be an environment open to all older adults to actively engage in music and to make contributions to their own quality of life. It should be a setting that is readily responsive to the social and musical needs of a wide range of older adults; we found it most readily observable in senior centers, which are distinctively different from other communal sites serving older adults, such as assisted living facilities, retirement communities, and nursing homes. While these other sites may offer music activities, they tend to have limited accessibility to the public due to specific qualifying conditions that are financially or health-related. Senior centers do not provide live-in services and are intended as public service hubs that serve mostly independent older adults.

1.3 Studying Music Participation in Senior Centers in the United States

Numerous writers have outlined the history, development, and variety of senior centers, especially those in the United States (e.g., Krout, 1989; National Institute of Senior Centers, 1975; Niles-Yokum & Wagner, 2011; Shollenberger, 1995). While we do not mean to be presumptuous to assume the nonexistence of senior centers outside of the United States, we have to rely on what is available in the literature, which is almost exclusively in and about the United States, and on rare occasions, Canada. Counterpart organizations in other nations are probably conceived, structured, and labeled differently. At appropriate moments throughout this text, we bring forward their global relevance while maintaining a focus on the case in the United States.

The earliest senior centers we could identify were located in New York City (1943) and San Francisco (1947) (Lowy & Doolin, 1990). The numbers of such centers grew exponentially across the country from hundreds in the 1960s to thousands in the 1970s. By the early 2010s, a nationwide network of 11,000 senior centers served over four million older adults annually (Pardasani & Goldkind, 2012). Dal Santo (2009) reported 15,000 centers serving close to 10 million older adults annually when she included large multipurpose senior centers as well as "small nutrition sites run by volunteers that provide only occasional programming" (p. 4). The case of increased support for older adults and the growth of senior centers in the United States shows how the people, the community, and the government have helped to address the global trend of an aging population within a nation. There is much to learn about the effectiveness of music in fulfilling the needs of older adults through senior centers.

While "senior center" seems to be a static term, its transformational development should be considered. The public image of senior centers has been evolving through the decades, from merely reaching out to those who retired and needed a venue to stay connected with others to serving as an "entry point for the aging service network" (Wick, 2012, p. 664). Various editions of *The Aging Networks* between 1999 and 2019 (Gelfand, 1999,

2006; Niles-Yokum & Wagner, 2011, 2015, 2019) provided a context of how senior centers have become situated in the broader evolution of policies, programs, and services available for older adults. Given the changing needs of older adults, a variety of programs are offered through senior centers. Wick (2012, p. 665) outlined 18 types of programs that are frequently available:

- Arts and humanities entertainment
- Caregiver education
- Consumer protection information
- Continuing education
- Emergency and natural disaster refuge or relief
- Financial assistance
- Fitness and exercise
- Health and wellness
- Intergenerational awareness
- Leisure trips and travel
- Library services
- Nutrition and meals
- Service referral
- Social networking
- Tax assistance
- Training for lay leaders, students, and professionals
- Transportation
- Volunteer opportunities in the center or in the community

This list of programs suggests that (a) services offered at senior centers are catered to the needs of contemporary older adults in the United States, which could well be similar to needs in other nations, (b) senior centers carry a heavy and varied load of responsibilities, (c) there is an emphasis on the health and well-being of older adults, (d) music activities fit within the category of arts and humanities entertainment, and (e) music activities may reinforce the program categories of continuing education, fitness and exercise, health and wellness, intergenerational awareness, social networking, and volunteer opportunities in the center or in the community, as well as overall well-being and quality of life.

As senior centers are fluid entities, there is no lack of voices to demand change in specific areas of service through senior centers. Some have advocated for more responsiveness to local community needs (Dal Santo, 2009; Pardasani & Goldkind, 2012). Others have suggested increasing funding and administrative support (Pardasani & Goldkind, 2012).

Furthermore, many writers have revealed the need for more attention to racial and ethnic diversity (Niles-Yokum & Wagner, 2019; Taylor-Harris, 2006), diverse age groups among older adults (Fitzpatrick & McCabe, 2008), and health and well-being (Niles-Yokum & Wagner, 2019; Wick, 2012). Musicians and music educators seem to be tacit in all of these advocacy voices despite the plethora of literature that supports the significant benefits of older adults' music participation. As a way of being socially and musically responsive, studies about music participation in senior centers from various perspectives are necessary, so policy makers and administrators of these centers can partner with the music and music education community and take full advantage of what music can offer to older adults in their neighborhoods to maximize their quality of life.

This book consists of three parts. The remainder of Part I contains a review of the state of music in senior centers (Chapter 2). Part II is an experiential view of music in senior centers across six different regions of the continental US (i.e., Northwest, Western, North Central, Southwestern, Eastern, and Southern) from the perspectives of the center management, the music activity leaders at the centers, and the older adults who may or may not be engaged in music activities in these centers. It is based on field studies of six senior centers in culturally and socioeconomically diverse cities of different sizes. Chapter 3 presents the settings, operations, and features of the six senior center cases, followed by a synthesis and cross-case comparison of musical opportunities in the six centers in Chapter 4. We focus on the older adults' perspectives on music in Chapter 5, followed by the impact of music participation on their quality of life in Chapter 6. Part III presents two chapters that lead into a new normal, containing the report of a survey study of 23 senior centers located in six cities across the six US regions examining mid-pandemic musical opportunities through senior centers in October 2021 in relation to the pre-pandemic period prior to March 2020 (Chapter 7). The final chapter draws on all findings from the six senior center case studies and the survey study for new considerations in music education and older adults' lifelong music participation.

CHAPTER 2

State of Music in US Senior Centers

This chapter is based on the literature found in a wide range of fields, most notably aging studies and gerontology, on studies conducted in senior centers and about their users. Due to the vast differences in the nature and context of the senior centers across the world, we have chosen to focus on the music activities in such centers in one nation, the United States, for consistency, which makes comparisons and synthesis across centers feasible. Furthermore, due to the major shift in the mode of operation of senior centers in the year 2020, we use it as a time mark as we review the literature prior to this time. The three main sections present (a) various aspects of these centers including their clients, benefits, and challenges; (b) music in these centers; and (c) questions that arise in seeking directions for further development.

2.1 Senior Centers and Their Clients

2.1.1 Historical Background

As renditions of historical development of senior centers in the United States are found elsewhere (e.g., Lowy & Doolin, 1990; Niles-Yokum & Wagner, 2011; Pardasani, 2003; Rill, 2011; Weil, 2014), this section reveals some highlights. Although the emergence of peer groups of older adults gathering for social and psychological support could be traced back to 1870 as "clubs for older adults" (Cannon, 2015, p. 10; Gelfand, 1999), the first such publicly funded institution, a senior center, was established in 1943 by the New York City Welfare Department where the idea of these clubs was expanded beyond just a place to meet. Games and refreshments were offered "primarily for low-income and socially isolated older adults" (Cannon, 2015, p. 10). By 1950, "218 senior centers had opened across the country, with most located in cities" (Wick, 2012, p. 664), and that has been a continuing trend.

The Older Americans Act (OAA) of 1965 was "a federal legislation that created the network of community-based services for older adults, [within which] senior centers were envisioned as community focal points" (Pardasani, 2010, p. 49). Via this Act, legislators "carved out funding to support almost 6,000 centers" (Wick, 2012, p. 664), and "the number of senior centers ... increased from 340 in 1966 to over 5,000 in 1975" (Krout, 1984, p. 71). However, due to the decentralized nature of services for older adults, not all senior centers received funding from the OAA (Bobitt & Schwingel, 2017). Regardless of OAA funding, they typically partnered with local organizations, including state, county, city, nonprofit, educational, or private, to provide services for older adults (e.g., see Krout, 1986, 1988b, 1989). Based on a survey of 246 senior center administrators (Krout, 1989), the top reasons for senior centers to work with other organizations were to improve their ability to meet the needs of older adults (82.3%), to increase the number of services (79.7%), to provide services for low-income older adults (78.8%), and to increase the number of older adults served (77.5%).

Based on a study of older adults in the state of New York in the 1970s, Taietz (1976) determined that senior centers were viewed as "social agencies" or "voluntary organizations." A social agency was to "meet the needs of the elderly." This suggests that "the poor and the disengaged were the most likely candidates for participation [in center activities]." Alternatively, senior centers were viewed as organizations that supported the assumption that older adults "who [were] more active in voluntary organizations and who manifest[ed] strong attachments to the community [were] also the ones who ma[d]e use of senior centers" (p. 219). In the 1980s, senior centers were misperceived as "eccentric social service" agencies that were "unique in [their] costumes, sometimes unconventional in [their] approach. The informality of the setting often leads the newcomer to believe that nothing of great importance is happening" (Brandler, 1985, pp. 195–196), which led to a perception of these centers' surface atmosphere but not their nature, function, and intent. It is possible that this misperception may still persist to this day, as is evidenced in the use of the stigmatized name "senior center" in more recent studies (e.g., Cannon, 2015).

Beyond the historic surface perception of the environment, senior centers have been changing with growing demands and diversifying funding sources (Dal Santo, 2009; Lawler, 2011; Pardasani & Goldkind, 2012). Dal Santo (2009) wrote,

> [S]enior centers are required to reflect and respond to the features and needs of the communities they serve. No two communities are identical, and each evolves differently, thereby producing a wide array of variability. To continue to adapt, senior center[s] will have to draw on their strengths, continue their linkages with strategic partners and expand their collaborations with other organizations to become more of a hub linking individuals to a wider array of activities and services in their communities. (p. 2)

Many writers (e.g., Aday, 2003; Lawler, 2011; Weil, 2014) resonated with the idea that senior centers should respond to the needs of their local communities. Lawler (2011) epitomized,

> The older adult population of today is significantly different than [sic] the older adult populations of yesterday and of tomorrow. Senior centers have long been important community resources for older adults and their families but to stay relevant, they must adjust to the changing needs of their customers. (p. 1)

After studying the responses of 187 members of the National Institute of Senior Centers, Pardasani and Thompson (2012) identified six models of operation in senior centers – *community center* for all ages, *wellness center* for those 50 years or older, *lifelong learning/arts center* for working adults 50 years or older, *continuum of care/transitions center* as in neighborhood centers, *entrepreneurial center* that makes use of work skills after retirement, and meal-based *café program* – each with somewhat different client profiles, missions, philosophical foci, program design and offerings, main sources of funding, and identification as "senior centers." Weil (2014) added two more models in the changing landscape: "centers without walls, or virtual centers" and the "Next Chapter model," which combined "elements of learning, social support, with all-aged-networks, and volunteerism" (p. 135). Whereas it is debatable whether these eight models are distinctively identifiable, it is clear that senior centers in the United States are continuing to evolve, from a dual-model view (social agency and voluntary organization) in the 1970s (Taietz, 1976) to the eight models of operation in the 2010s (Pardasani & Thompson, 2012; Weil, 2014). We expect continuous changes in the coming years. The following sections outline the recent and current states of senior centers in the United States with a focus on their nature and functions, center clients, level of involvement, benefits of using the centers, and challenges facing the centers and their clients.

2.1.2 Nature and Functions

In the 2010s, there were 11,000 publicly funded senior centers (National Institute of Senior Centers, n.d.; Pardasani & Thompson, 2012), playing "a vital role in maintaining the health and quality of life of older adults" (Pardasani, 2018, p. 314). "The National Council on Aging estimates 11,400 senior centers serve more than one million senior citizens every day" (Keller, 2017). Current senior centers in the United States could be publicly or privately funded and are characterized as community spaces where local older adults come together to participate in various activities. Based on a survey of 246 senior centers in 48 states (Krout, 1989), 52.7% were stand-alone centers, 15.5% were recreation or community centers, and 10.2% were multiservice agencies. Others were housed in religious organizations (5.7%), housing projects (4.9%), and so forth. Furthermore, 51% of the center facilities were between 3,000 to 9,999 square feet, 28% were under 3,000 square feet, and 21% were 10,000 square feet or bigger. Whereas the diversity of facility type and square footage seems to have continued to this day, the majority were stand-alone centers and under 10,000 square feet.

There has been a substantial body of literature in which authors have studied the nature and function of senior centers. Some suggested that it might be advantageous to make senior centers hubs for social-work services (Brandler, 1985) or counseling services (Grady, 1990). While these services may not have been consistently available on site as core programs across all senior centers, older adults could readily be referred to resources as needed. Krout (1983, 1984, 1985, 1986, 1987, 1988a, 1988b, 1989, 1991, 1994, 1996) and colleagues (Krout, Cutler, & Coward, 1990) conducted a series of studies of senior centers mostly in the 1980s. Others have followed suit (e.g., Pardasani, 2003). These studies provided important points of reference regarding the nature and function of senior centers in the United States.

With a sample of 222 center clients and nonparticipant adults aged 60 or higher (median age = 70.8 years) and 70% identifying as female, Krout (1983) conducted in-depth interviews and found that center clients involved themselves in the center mostly because there was "something to do," they were invited by "friends or others," and they wanted "to be with people" and make friends. Those who did not participate in the centers were mostly "too busy" or "not interested." In the same series of studies, Krout (1984) found that both center clients and nonparticipants were aware of the location of the senior centers, but the participants were more aware of the specific *activities* offered. Very few participants and nonparticipants were aware of the *services* offered except for the "hot lunch" program, which 98% participants and 76% nonparticipants knew about.

In a large-scale study of 755 senior centers across 31 states in the United States, Krout (1985) identified that the examined senior centers offered an average of 17.6 services and 11.1 activities, corroborating with the 18 types of frequently available programs and services included in Wick's (2012) list. More specifically, Krout (1987) found that the number of activities and services were significantly greater for metropolitan centers when compared to nonmetropolitan areas. Krout (1985) enumerated activities in the categories of Recreation, Education and Culture, Volunteering, and Leadership. Within the Education and Culture category, 52.7% of the centers offered activities specific to the performing arts in comparison to 87.0% offering arts and crafts in the same category, and in comparison to activities in the Recreation category (91.0% sedentary, 82.2% parties, 80.4% active, and 61.6% trips). In the state of New York, Pardasani (2004a) found that only 36.5% of senior center activities were in performing arts. Ten years later in New York City, Pardasani and Sackman (2014) identified 34 recreational, 23 health and fitness, 13 social service, and seven continuing education and volunteerism programs across 155 senior centers. Among recreational programs were cultural celebrations (89.0%), dancing (82.5%), choral groups (64.1%), drama performing groups (52.4%), therapeutic arts (40.8%), and piano (32.2%). When the center administrators were asked "what recreational programs would be offered if resources were available, respondents *overwhelmingly* [emphasis added] chose programs from performing arts (drama, choral group, piano) and special programs for the visually- or hearing-impaired adults" (p. 207). The demands for these activities were reflected from 35.9% to 70.8% of the respondents, whereas 29.2% to 64.1% of the respondents stated that they already had these activities in their centers. It becomes evident that music and other performing arts activities have been among the highest demand activities in senior centers regardless of whether they already have these activities in the center.

Pardasani's (2003) analyses of responses from 218 senior center administrators in the state of New York found that the model of operation (center for voluntary participation or as social service agency), level of public funding, geographic location, administrator's education level, number of professional and bilingual staff, age and ethnic distribution of center clients, community linkages, and assessment of client needs had an impact on the number and types of programs and services provided. These results implied that there was a need to diversify center programs to meet the needs of the growing elderly population and to implement new fundraising techniques, develop strategic partnerships, and use formalized needs assessments to remain relevant to the community of older adults.

Recent trends seem to indicate that senior centers are moving toward the direction of increased wellness consciousness, as suggested in a report supported by the American Association of Retired Persons (AARP) Foundation and Caesar's Foundation (Lawler, 2011). In that report, six dimensions of wellness were proposed as orientations for senior centers' programs. The six dimensions were emotional, spiritual, intellectual, social, physical, and occupational and were defined as:

- Emotional: Degree to which one feels positive and enthusiastic about oneself and life
- Spiritual: The development of a deep appreciation for the depth and expanse of life and natural forces that exist in the universe
- Intellectual: Expanding one's own knowledge and skills while discovering the potential for sharing one's gifts with others
- Social: Emphasizes the interdependence of human beings and encourages contribution to one's community and the environment
- Physical: Achieved through good nutrition and regular physical activity
- Occupational: Recognizes personal satisfaction and enrichment in one's life through work (p. 11)

A wide range of activities were showcased, using senior centers in Washtenaw County, Michigan, as examples, to address specific priorities, needs, and histories of local residents. These activities were aligned with target outcomes in health, such as establishing social networks, reducing isolation, improving strength and balance, and maintaining cognitive health, and in the community, such as becoming involved in civic activities (Lawler, 2011). While an extensive list of activities was revealed without specifying any in music, we believe that music can potentially and easily be incorporated among most, if not all, of such activities. For example, socialization and networking in group musical activities, physical activities accompanied by music, learning of musical knowledge and skills, and performing in community events can all be designed to meet these targets.

We identified five studies conducted in different parts of the United States between 1991 and 2017 with senior center directors, participants, or both and with findings that reflect the functions of senior centers (see Table 2.1). Although the number of studies is small, a trend can be traced in that researchers of the earlier studies found that senior centers were

Table 2.1. Studies reflecting the functions of senior centers in the United States

Study	Sample	Purpose	Finding	Function of senior center
Gelfand et al. (1991)	Center directors (n = 48), staff (n = 82), and participants (n = 237) in Maryland	Determine the most important programs and services	• Exercise programs were most important as reported by 65% participants, 35% staff, and 19% directors • Meals at the center were most important as reported by 26% directors, 17% staff, and 8% participants • Exercise programs were reported as most helpful (71% participants, 49% staff, and 40% directors), followed by blood pressure testing and trips	Socialization, exercise, and meals
Havir (1991)	Three senior centers in rural Minnesota (70 interviews with center clients, 42 with nonparticipants, and 94 surveys of participants), also interviews with mayors, council members, city clerks, clergy, media representatives, and social service providers	Examine how centers meet the needs of local elderly and their role in the service delivery system	• Two of three centers were social and recreational centers • Great variability among rural organizations	Voluntary organization with an informal atmosphere for socialization and recreation

Study	Sample	Purpose	Findings	Theme
Eaton & Salari (2005)	Participants (*N* = 30) in three senior centers in the western US	Determine influences of the physical, social, and organizational environments on learning in senior centers	• Need for lifelong learning, leadership, and volunteer service • The fit between the environment (space and facilities) and educational programs is critical • Importance of socialization	Venue for lifelong learning and socialization
Aday et al. (2006)	Women living alone (*n* = 274) and living with spouses (*n* = 171), age 51–96 years (average = 74.4), in the United States	Determine influences of late-life friendship and senior center activities on health and well-being	• Senior center was an excellent environment with supportive friendships • Women living alone participated in center activities more frequently • Center activities were related to better mental health and social support	Support health and well-being
Bobitt & Schwingel (2017)	Senior center directors (*N* = 12) in Illinois	Identify factors impacting the implementation of evidence-based lifestyle programs at regional and community levels	• Senior center programs were driven by clients • Funding and program inflexibility were the main barriers for implementation	Client-driven

primarily venues for socialization, exercise, and meals (Gelfand, Bechill, & Chester, 1991) or for voluntary organizations with an informal atmosphere that facilitated socialization and recreation (Havir, 1991). These findings parallel characteristics described in the two-concept model of senior centers (social agencies and voluntary organizations) (Taietz, 1976). In the 2000s, senior centers evolved into sites for lifelong learning and socialization (Eaton & Salari, 2005) and spaces that support health and well-being (Aday, Kehoe, & Farney, 2006). Notice that socialization has been a staple throughout the evolution of senior centers. Even more recently, with a trend to offer programs and services driven by local clients (Bobitt & Schwingel, 2017), socialization is still within the core function of senior centers. The next section focuses on who participated in these centers.

2.1.3 Senior Center Clients

Numerous researchers have studied US senior center clientele throughout the last few decades. Some specifically focus on those who participated in activities in the senior centers, others compared characteristics between center clients and nonparticipants. Overall, regardless of geographic location in the United States, the majority of senior center clients can be characterized as age in their 70s, mostly females, non-Hispanic White, and in considerable good health sufficient enough to take care of themselves with a high degree of independence. The culture and socioeconomic status of these clients can vary a great deal depending on the community in which they are located, because senior centers tend to attract older adults who live nearby. For senior centers that offer a meal program, the meal program tends to have a very high participation rate and be a major draw to the center. The more information clients know about various center activities, the more likely they are to join the activities.

Table 2.2 presents a summary of the characteristics of senior center clients found in studies published between 1987 and 2014. Not only are they based on a range of sites across different US regions, but they also comprise different levels of specificity, including center clients' number of center activities participated, frequency of participation, and continuation of participation. While quantitative findings across these studies present a broad picture of senior center clients, an ethnographic study of one senior center in New York City (Weil, 2014) offered unique insights in that the "regular" senior center attendees saw themselves as beneficiaries as well as caregivers. While they received social and emotional support at the center,

Table 2.2. *Studies showing characteristics of senior center clients*

Study	Context	Characteristics of senior center clients
Ferraro & Cobb (1987)	48 White adults, average age of 70 years, 73% female, in the state of North Carolina	• Frequent center clients were likely those who were in poorer health and used it as a social agency • Long-term clients with greater participation in center activities were likely those with higher levels of life satisfaction, who did not live alone, and used it as a voluntary organization • Over 90% center clients participated in the lunch meal program • Nearly 80% of center clients used the health maintenance program (e.g., diagnostic screening and preventive health measures)
Cox & Monk (1990)	282 senior center managers in New York State	• Mostly between 65 and 84 years • Mostly White female • 10% clients were described by center directors as frail, and one-third of the frail participants were hearing impaired
Aday (2003)	Adult clients in approximately 20 senior centers in seven states	• Typically aged in the mid-70s • About one-third aged over 80 • Mostly Caucasian White females • Relatively well-educated
Pardasani (2003, 2004a)	Survey of 218 senior center managers in New York State	• 79.95% Caucasian, 8.83% African American, 7.31% Hispanic American, 2.39% Asian American, and 0.97% other • 49.53% at 75–84 years old, 35.35% at 65–74 years old, and 13.70% at 85 years or older
Walker et al. (2004)	Survey of 289 older adults in an 11 county area in Texas (50% from rural low-income communities, 14% self-identified as minority)	• Average age was 77.45 years old (mode = 77) • 63% women, 36% men • 47% lived with significant other • 52% had family living within 50 miles • 96% had friends living within 50 miles • 94% lived within 10 miles from the senior center, average distance to senior center was 3.71 miles (mode = 2) • Average of 1.52 types of transportation available (mode = 1) • Participated in an average of 84.39 faith-based activities per year (mode = 52) • Attended senior center on an average of 170.51 times per year (mode = 260) • Average of attending 2.73 activities per senior center visit (mode = 2)

Table 2.2. (*cont.*)

Study	Context	Characteristics of senior center clients
		• Average knowledge of 6.35 activities at the center (mode = 5) • Preferred an average of 6.35 participants per activity (mode = 4) • Did not have significant problems in activities of daily living (ADL) (walking, dressing, bathing, and feeding) • Expressed interest in music programs at the senior center (e.g., country and western and southern gospel) • Likely participated in faith-based activities, preferred smaller group activities, and knowledgeable in number of center activities and types of transportation available
Pardasani & Sackman (2014)	Survey of 155 senior center managers in New York City	• Majority at age 70 years or older, nearly 40% older than 80 years • 44.5% Caucasian, 21.7% Hispanic, 18.5% Black, 15.1% Asian • 5.2% self-identified as gay, lesbian, bisexual, or transgender
Weil (2014)	Ethnographic study of a senior center in New York City	• Average age at 75 years, 70% female, and 89% non-Hispanic White • 50% lived within a few blocks of the center and traveled to the center on foot, 32% by carpool, 14% on public transportation, and 4% in the center's van • Health problems were expected but did not greatly affect participation in center activities • Looked to senior center for emotional support • Understood being an active member of the senior center was a crucial part of quality of life and identity • Saw social interaction with others at the senior center as pleasurable as a way to help with instrumental tasks, such as transportation, meal preparation, and financial matters • Saw choice of activities at the senior center as essential • Believed social interaction with others at the center as a way to ward off mental decline • Saw themselves as helpers of others, not helpless or vulnerable

they were helpers of others, such as preparing for meals and offering assistance in transportation. They were *not* helpless or vulnerable.

Some researchers explored reasons why potential older adult clients *did not* participate in center activities or use their services. Lack of transportation, time, interest, and need were identified as reasons for nonparticipation in senior center activities, services, and events (Krout, 1983, 1986; Pardasani, 2004a, 2010). Furthermore, Krout (1986) found that "lack of transportation" and "lack of time" were the *biggest* barriers for participation in these centers. These findings corroborated findings of a later study in the state of New York in that the "lack of transportation" and "lack of interest" were the most significant obstacles for senior center participation (Pardasani, 2004a). Also, home and work responsibilities (Ralston & Griggs, 1985) and self-perceived poor health (Jirovec, Erich, & Sanders, 1989) served as barriers to attend center activities. When asked what types of programming might attract them to senior centers, older adult non-participants identified "educational courses, performing arts/drama, choral music, fitness programs, evidence-based health programs, nutritional education, and health screenings" as potential attractions (Pardasani, 2010, p. 61). It is important to keep in mind, though, that most research on senior center clients has focused on White older adults; knowledge of barriers for minority older adults is spotty, with a lack of data for certain ethnic and cultural groups (Ralston, 1991b).

Other researchers made direct comparisons between senior center clients and those who *did not* participate in center activities or use their services. Since socialization has been a core function of senior centers, older adults who lived alone tended to participate in center activities more so than those who lived with others. Having "something to do" in the center only scratched the surface of what senior centers provided. Deeper meanings of participating in senior center activities might be associated with social and psychological benefits found in socialization. There was even evidence of lower incidence of depression (Hanssen et al., 1978) and better quality of life (Kirk & Alessi, 2000). At the same time, center clients might be at a higher risk of depression (Schneider et al., 2014). These contradictory findings regarding depression should be interpreted with caution, because studies by Hanssen et al. (1978) and Schneider et al. (2014) were conducted in different types of locations (a senior center and community in Burbank, California, versus in public housing with senior center on premise in New York City), using different methodologies (structured interview versus phone survey), and at different times (1978 versus 2014). Table 2.3 presents a summary of studies published between 1978 and 2014 that made

Table 2.3. *Senior center clients compared to nonparticipants in senior centers*

Study	Context	When compared to nonparticipants in senior centers
Hanssen et al. (1978)	39 center clients, 30 nutrition site users, 30 former participants, and 30 nonparticipants aged 60 years and above, in structured interviews in Burbank, California	• More likely learned about center activities from friends • Had higher levels of social activities • Had lower depression score • Had more out-of-home activities • Had fewer passive activities
Krout (1983)	222 adults (50% over 70 years of age, 70% female, 60% married, and one-third lived alone)	• Less mobility limitations due to health • Had lower incomes • Saw friends more often • More female, not married, and live alone • 1.5 years less education • Desired more contact with their children • Reported the senior center as "something to do," "invitation from friends or relatives," and "desire for company or to make friends" • Participated in lunch program as a "social activity" rather than a nutritional need
Krout (1984)	250 adults aged 60 and older, 70% female, 58% married, 34% lived alone	• Aware of more senior center activities and services • More females • More non-Whites in metro central city • Less income in metro central city and nonmetro urban
Ralston & Griggs (1985)	110 adults aged 65 and older (median age = 71) living in a medium-sized community in the Midwestern US	• Blacks were significantly more committed than Whites to attend senior center programs
Ishii-Kuntz (1990)	1,051 women aged 65 and higher averaged at 73.2 years, 74% White, 70% retired, 62% widowed, 25% married	• Higher income • Lifelong single and widowed more than married or divorced or separated women • Younger, more Blacks • Self-perceived as healthier • Self-perceived as lonely

Table 2.3. (cont.)

Study	Context	When compared to nonparticipants in senior centers
Krout, Cutler, & Coward (1990)	National sample of 13,737 adults aged 60 years and older (13.7% senior center clients and 86.3% did not use a senior center in the past year)	• Had more social interaction with others • Not the youngest or oldest within the age range of above 60 years • Lower family income • Lived alone • Not the lowest or highest educational attainment • More competent in activities of daily living (ADL) (e.g., walking, dressing, and bathing) and instrumental ADL (e.g., shopping, managing finances and communication) • More females • Lived in noncentral city and nonfarm communities
Calsyn & Winter (2000)	4,903 households with an elderly person aged 60 or above in the state of Missouri	• Older • More active socially • Lived in a less urban area • Had fewer days their mental health was not good • Had fewer problems in daily living activities • Aware of more agencies • Had used formal agencies in seeking service information • Used more older adult services • Had no difference in income
Kirk & Alessi (2000)	275 adults between 64 and 93 years (average = 75.9) in rural Louisiana; 34% men, 66% women; 79% White, 20% African American, and 1% Hispanic; 55% widowed, 29% married, 10% divorced, 6% never married	• Lived alone more often • Lived with son or daughter more often • Had more frequent social contact • Less lonely • Had better quality of life
Pardasani (2010)	1,283 adults (722 center clients and 561 nonparticipants) in northwest Indiana	• More Caucasian females • Lived alone more often • Had lower income • More unlikely to be disabled • More often had minimal caregiving or work responsibilities • Lived alone more often

Table 2.3. (cont.)

Study	Context	When compared to nonparticipants in senior centers
Schneider et al. (2014)	Phone survey of 1,036 residents aged 65 or older living in public housing with senior center on premise under New York City Housing Authority; 31.3% reported using the senior center at least once in the past 3 months	• Higher risk of depression • Frequent attendance (i.e., a few days per week or more) at the center was more common for Spanish-speaking Hispanics

comparisons between center clients and nonparticipants. They tended to use a quantitative approach with larger samples.

2.1.4 Level of Involvement

Studies on senior center clients' level of center involvement covered a spread of foci, from new recruits to specific activities to regular long-term activity participants. One study (Xaverius & Mathews, 1999) examined the effect of publicly posted announcements on recruiting new participants for creative writing and painting activities in a senior center in a small Midwestern city. Bright yellow 3' x 8' banners and 8 ½" by 11" bright color cardboard were used at the entrance of the senior center and next to the driver in each of the center's eight buses, respectively, for specified periods. They found that clients were more likely to join these groups during, or immediately following, the public postings of information about these groups. This study demonstrated the importance of getting the information about center activities across to potential activity participants, and that this was vital to their participation rate.

Instead of simply investigating participants versus nonparticipants in senior centers, Krout (1988a, 1991) advocated for a more specific approach to investigate participation by examining the stability of center activity attendance, number of center activities, frequency of participation, and duration of participation, because they tended to be related to different variables. For example, health condition was related to stability, frequency, and duration of center clients' participation in various activities (Krout, 1988a). In addition, participating in higher numbers of activities was related to Whites and to those with more contact with friends. More frequent participation was also related to Whites and to those with reported higher levels of morale and contact with friends, but a longer duration of participation was related to those who were older and lived closer to the centers (Krout, 1991). Some of Krout's (1988a, 1991) findings were in line with other studies, but the distinction across senior center clients' different aspects of activity participation warranted our attention. Krout's (1991) analysis confirmed that senior center activity participation was multidimensional: number of activities, frequency of participation, and duration (in years). He also found that simple linear correlation and multiple regression analysis yielded different results in relation to various sociodemographic, access, health, morale, social contact, and attitudinal variables. Table 2.4 highlights a sample of studies that went into some of the specific aspects of activity participation in US senior centers.

Although studies of senior centers usually focused on clients' participation in activities or usage of services, volunteerism is a form of participation that rarely receives sufficient attention. Pardasani (2018) focused on 172 older adults' motivation to volunteer in a large senior center located in New York City. Findings indicated that 64.7% had prior volunteering experience, only 22.4% were volunteers at the time, and 30.8% were interested in volunteering at or through the senior center. Along with the focus group interviews of 68 older adults in the senior center, results showed that the motivation to volunteer was due to the "prospect of 'giving back' to the community" and the "desire to help those 'in need'" (p. 324). Center clients also noted the perceived benefits of volunteering, such as increased connection with others, reduced social isolation, and fun. Findings show that center clients had more interest in volunteering for single events or projects than for a long-term commitment. Although Pardasani's (2018) study focused on volunteerism with a high level of specificity, its findings corroborated with Weil's (2014) in that center clients were both beneficiaries of and contributors to the centers.

Another aspect of participation in senior center activities was to focus on minority and underrepresented groups. This is vital to the United States, which is among the most diverse nations ethnically, culturally, and economically. It is essential to ensure equity and equality in public activities and services. Senior centers, among other service agencies, have an obligation to provide support for diverse older adults and their descendants. Table 2.5 presents a summary of such studies of a range of underrepresented groups. They suggested that there is no one-size-fits all; activities

Table 2.4. *Sample studies in specific aspects of activity participation in senior centers*

Study	Context	Specific aspects of activity participation in senior centers (i.e., frequency, number, and duration)
Ferraro & Cox (1987)	1 senior center in southeastern North Carolina	• Frequent participants used the center primarily as a social agency • Long-time participants with greater involvement in activities used the center primarily as a voluntary organization • Adults in poorer health were more likely than those in good health to attend the center frequently and to participate in the lunch program • Health maintenance services were more likely used by the poorly educated than the highly educated, and by those who lived alone • Number of activities and duration of participation were related to life satisfaction, being married or lived with someone, and socially active
Krout (1991)	8 senior centers in western New York	• Higher number of center activity participation was related to living in urban areas, seeing more problems at the center, race (White), and rating higher in morale • Higher frequency of center attendance was related to living closer to the senior centers, having more contact with friends, and seeing a higher impact of center activities
Ralston (1991a)	623 center clients from 15 senior centers in a county in a Midwestern state	• Frequent center attendees felt that the meal program was important to daily food intake and lived closer to the center • Longer-term attendees tended to be older • Participants who had higher educational levels tended to have a higher level of involvement in center activities • Clients using more center services were less mobile, made friends at the senior center and had higher life satisfaction
Miner et al. (1993)	Secondary analysis of a national sample of 1,720 adults at age 60 years or older	• Clients using senior centers more frequently tended to be older and have lower income and lower education • The most frequent clients of senior centers were more socially involved, which seemed to be related to volunteering at the center

Table 2.4. (cont.)

Study	Context	Specific aspects of activity participation in senior centers (i.e., frequency, number, and duration)
Sabin (1993)	Secondary analysis of a national sample of 1,781 adults at age 60 years or older	• Clients using senior centers frequently tended to be older, less educated, and non-White • Participation in meal programs was related to frequent participation in other center activities • More socially active adults tended to participate in center activities more frequently than did less socially active adults

and services offered at senior centers should be catered specifically for the needs of the local communities and neighborhoods. An open and welcoming ambience, in ways that are communicable to the local and nearby people, is highly desirable. Activities that embrace diverse intercultural interaction and those that address needs of specific groups should be available.

2.2 Benefits of Using the Centers

Although studies in various aspects of senior centers provided a kaleidoscope-like view of many combinations of changing variables, there seemed to be consistency regarding benefits to center clients. Based on data from 734 senior center clients from seven states in the United States, Aday (2003) reported the contributions of senior centers to the physical and mental well-being of center clients. For example, 90% reported their health to be the same or better than the previous year. There were also reports of feeling less lonely (46%), less stress (48%), more satisfied with life (43%), more energetic (22%), less worried (23%), and more independent (28%). Socially,

> over 90% indicated that they have developed very close friendships at their senior center and the majority do engage in social activities outside of the center with friends made at the center; about 85% reported that the friends they have made at the senior center provide them with a sense of emotional security and someone they can depend on when needed; approximately 85% said they provide some type of assistance to senior center friends ...;

Table 2.5. *Senior center studies that target minority and underrepresented groups*

Underrepresented group	Study	Findings
Hispanic (national sample)	Farone et al. (2005)	• Senior center clients experienced lower levels of psychological stress than did center nonparticipants
Korean older adults in New York City	Kim (2000)	• Koreans attending Korean-specific senior centers participated with lower frequency and for a shorter duration but were involved more in center activities compared to those attending "mainstream" senior centers • Koreans attending "mainstream" centers were older, had higher educational level, resided longer in the neighborhood and in the United States, and had relatively better English skills than those attending Korean-specific centers • Koreans attending Korean-specific centers had more social interactions, volunteered more at the center, lived with other persons, spent longer time traveling to the center, and felt that they were accepted more at the center than Koreans attending "mainstream" centers
Haitian older adult immigrants in southeast Florida	McCaffrey (2008)	• Through an integration program designed for Haitian immigrants held at the senior center, center clients felt accepted, welcomed, and valued in a new community, giving them hope for a good life in a new place
Black older adults in Davenport and Waterloo, Iowa	Ralston (1984)	• Older adults with higher frequencies of social contact with family and friends were less likely to need and use senior centers than those with less frequent social contact with family and friends
Black older adults from a senior center in Atlanta, Georgia	Taylor-Harris & Zhan (2011)	• Clients received four benefits (physical, psychological/emotional, social, and meaning in life) that contributed to a new self-identity
Multiple groups in New York City	Giunta et al. (2012)	• Clients who attended diverse senior centers showed greater risk of social isolation, received less family support, and more likely sought medical care than attendees of relatively homogeneous senior centers

Table 2.5. (cont.)

Underrepresented group	Study	Findings
Senior center administrators (86.2% Caucasian, 7.5% Black, 0.9% Asian; 75.2% spoke only English, 23.4% bilingual) and staff (77.7% Caucasian, 22.2% minority) from New York State	Pardasani (2004b)	• Senior centers with administrators from non-Caucasian backgrounds were almost twice as likely to have an ethnically diverse clientele than those with Caucasian administrators • Among senior center administrators with fluency in a language other than English, 45.8% offered programs in more than one language, but only 14.6% of the administrators not fluent in a second language offered programs in non-English languages
Low-income older adults in Detroit	Jirovec et al. (1989)	• Music performances ranked at the top as reasons for center nonparticipants (28.3%) to choose to use the senior center, followed by financial assistance (26.4%), legal assistance (26.4%), tax assistance (24.5%), and free transportation (20.8%). Ranked further lower were arts and crafts (17.0%), exercises (13.2%), dancing (9.4%), and ethnic/cultural activities (5.7%)

[and] senior center friends call each other on the average of 2.7 times each week just to check on each other. (p. 5)

It is clear that benefits of activities and services offered at the centers extend beyond the purview of the centers. Rill (2011) grouped similar benefits into social (making new friends, belonging to a group, and maintaining friendships), psychological (bereavement support, relaxation, support with problems, and improvement of mental health), physical (improvement of physical health, staying physically active, and eating healthy meals), activities (learning new ideas/skills, having fun, having someplace to go, and keeping busy), and spiritual ([religious] spirituality). Turner (2004) put senior center benefits into the categories of nutrition, socialization, and program activities. These benefits of senior center participation (Aday, 2003; Rill, 2011; Turner, 2004) resonate with findings in many other studies with specific foci, such as factors that influence perceived benefits (Fitzpatrick et al., 2006), neighborhood factors (Friedman et al., 2012), aging women living alone (Aday et al., 2006), grandparents raising grandchildren (Rhynes et al., 2013), African American, or Black, older adults (Taylor-Harris & Zhan, 2011), social network factors (Ashida & Heaney, 2008; Litwin, 1999), rural senior centers (Kirk & Alessi, 2002), effects of a happiness-and-humor group (Mathieu, 2008), and the use of a mental restorative perspective on senior centers (Rosenbaum, Sweeney, & Massiah, 2014). A mental restorative perspective refers to (a) being away: taking respite from responsibilities and entering a world of light-hearted, nonobligatory adult play, (b) fascination: engaging in rich and meaningful social interaction, and (c) compatibility: feeling comfortable, welcomed, safe, secure, respected, and having a safety net.

2.3 Challenges of Senior Centers

With such great benefits, senior centers are not without challenges. Some researchers addressed them as challenges (Fitzpatrick & McCabe, 2008) and barriers (Felix et al., 2014; Krout, 1996); others as educational needs (Ralston, 1981) and difficulties (Salamon & Trubin, 1983). Common challenges included lack of funding and space to serve the needs of local communities. Aday (2003) pointed to the need to motivate younger clients in their 50s and 60s to provide leadership and volunteer services, as center load expectations increase due to the growing older adult population. Based on this phenomenon and the data hitherto, Aday (2003) listed nine specific challenges of senior centers, most of which were related to the lack of financial and human resources. The list also included the need to rectify public misconceptions about senior center programs and services. Marketing strategies were needed to promote a more professional image of the centers that truly reflected the full range of activities and services they offered. Another challenge was the need to deliver more off-site programs or to take services to the older adults, such as operating satellite programs in shopping malls and other nontraditional venues. Furthermore, there was the challenge of recognizing differences in programming of urban and rural centers and also a need to enhance accessibility to programs in rural centers.

More recent data show that these challenges still persist but with a more updated perspective. Based on a case study of five senior centers in Portland, Oregon, Cannon (2015) identified challenges in the four areas of (a) participation and community engagement, (b) administrative structure and funding, (c) transportation and physical environment, and (d) programming, activities, and services. Table 2.6 shows the specific challenges that were inherent in each area.

Table 2.6. *Senior center challenges within four areas, as identified by Cannon (2015)*

Area	Area-specific challenges
Participation and community engagement	• Lack of diversity (e.g., culture, ethnicity, socioeconomic status, gender, and sexual orientation) • Sustainability of volunteers (e.g., lack of continuity) • Barriers to participation (e.g., lack of awareness, not being social, health issues, lack of transportation, not identifying with the center) • Increasing poverty, illness, and disability among participants • Marketing (e.g., lack of funding for marketing) • Siloing (e.g., need to connect with other senior centers) • The term *senior center* (e.g., the term was stigmatizing and often a deterrent)
Administrative structure and funding	• Increased demand for services • Political and public pressure (e.g., lack of public support) • Lack of control (e.g., associated with budget and service cuts from government entities) • Limited staff • Lack of overlap between organizations • Cutbacks in government funding • Need for more external funding sources • Reliance on donations
Transportation and physical environment	• Lack of transportation options • Lack of space • Challenges associated with aging in place for nearby residents (e.g., rising costs of neighborhood housing)
Programming, activities, and services	• Services cut or eliminated due to lack of funding • Providing programming that the community sees as unique, attractive, and relevant to future older adults (e.g., competition with residential facilities)

Again, these challenges were similar to those identified by others and were associated with a combination of (a) the lack of funding, human resources, and space; (b) the need to attend to specific local and diverse needs; (c) the increasing demand due to the aging population; (d) the need for marketing campaigns to present an appropriate image of "senior centers" and their programs; and (e) social–environmental factors outside of the control of the senior centers, such as rising housing costs in the neighborhood and the need to include and serve nongregarious older adults.

In the context of senior centers in New York City, Pardasani and Saackman (2014) pointed out the challenge of the need for professional development for administrators. They made seven recommendations "to advance a data-informed plan for social action advocacy that included the programmatic and policy changes necessary for the future sustainability of senior centers" (pp. 212–213). These consisted of the following:

1. Ensure adequate funding.
2. Engage older adults in senior center service planning.
3. Create outcome measures.
4. Renovate and remodel existing senior centers for adequate space, facility maintenance, upgrades, and capital campaigns.
5. Provide workforce development in the form of professional development for senior center administrators serving diverse older adults and in the areas of fundraising, marketing, program evaluation, political advocacy, aging issues, management skills, and leadership development.
6. Promote social action and advocacy.
7. Design and support innovative senior center models with flexible budget management and regulatory relief.

These recommendations, once again, were in line with the aforementioned challenges.

2.4 Innovative Models for the Future

Senior centers were designed to support the aging population through the provision of social, nutritional, and health services, as well as recreational activities. Historically, two basic senior center models were shown to achieve these goals: (a) a *social service agency model* that provides basic services to older adults of lower socioeconomic status and (b) a *voluntary organization model* that provides social and recreational offerings to better educated, socially active older adults (Pardasani, 2004a).

However, increasing diversity across the aging population, as well as flagging interest of the upcoming population of older adults (e.g., baby boomers) (Marken, 2005; Pardasani & Thompson, 2012) have caused senior centers to be "at unique crossroads in their evolution" as social service organizations. "Although a few senior centers have redesigned and reconceptualized their organizations to meet the challenges of the new millennium, there are limited data on new, promising, thriving, and innovative models of senior centers across the nation" (Pardasani & Thompson, 2012, p. 53).

2.4.1 Multipurpose Senior Centers

In recent years, *multipurpose senior center models* have evolved, which combine the offerings of social service agency and voluntary organization models (Pardasani, 2004a). Marken (2005) identified four themes representing perceived desirable and important qualities of new multipurpose senior centers: "context, positive activity attributes, healthy aging, and intergenerational contact" (p. 73). Older adults preferred easily accessible, colorful, vibrant center spaces with abundant natural light, large exercise spaces, and a noninstitutional feel (i.e., desired *context*). Activities needed to sustain older adults' interest over time by having good leadership and being interesting yet challenging and purposeful and sophisticated, with noticeable outcomes (i.e., *positive activity attributes*). A variety of health and wellness activities should be available, including some vigorous and youth-oriented activities such as aerobics, basketball, tennis, and line dancing (i.e., *healthy aging*). Activities should also bring generations together, for the social and psychological benefit of clients of all ages (i.e., *intergenerational contact*).

Via a multiple case study sponsored by The National Institute for Senior Centers (Pardasani & Thompson, 2012), a New Models Task Force (NMTF) composed of senior center directors and administrators across the United States identified six emerging models of innovative, multipurpose senior centers (in this case, centers that offered an array of services and recreational opportunities, excluding nutrition sites and senior clubs) that could attract younger senior cohorts moving forward. These attempt to address critical challenges relative to senior center sustainability, including (a) effectively serving the current constituency of older center clients while attracting baby boomers in their 60s, (b) responding to differences between older and younger older adult age groups regarding education, political positions, recreational and social needs, and attitudes about retirement, (c) tackling the negative stigma associated with senior centers and participation therein, (d) attractiveness and currency of facilities, and (e) new avenues to increase funding. Criteria for selection as an innovative center included (a) expansiveness or breadth of innovation, (b) cooperation and involvement of stakeholders, (c) utilization of material and nonmaterial resources, (d) innovation impact on center participation, (e) potential for replication in other senior centers, and (f) potential for feasibility and sustainability. The six models and their main foci are as follows:

- *Community Center (CC)*: multiage center for children, adolescents, adults, and active older adults under one roof
- *Wellness Center (WC)*: Focus on health and wellness of older adults aged 50 and above
- *Lifelong Learning/Arts Center (LLA)*: Growth via learning experiences postretirement
- *Continuum of Care/Transitions Center (CC)*: Gradual continuum of services for aging adults
- *Entrepreneurial Center (EC)*: Older adult productivity for postretirement income
- *Café Program (CP)*: Nonage-segregating, inclusive community gathering space for active older adults

For additional characteristics of these models, we recommend a table created by Pardasani and Thomson (2012) that provides information on the program offerings, hours of operation, service sites, location types, and sources of funding for each model type. It is notable that most avoid the use of the term *senior center* because of its negative connotations (Pardasani & Thompson, 2012). Additionally, it is worth noting that all six models are inclusive of music participation in the form of active music-listening opportunities via center performances. We believe that regular music participation of various sorts can be part of any of the six models as musical activities are inherently multifarious and relevant to everyday life. Obviously, music is regarded as a valued element as senior centers strive to include younger cohorts of older adults.

2.5 Music in the Centers

Over the last few years, research on older adults' musical involvement has grown across various music fields (Fung & Lehmberg, 2016; Krause, et al., 2018). Research studies since the year 2000 have focused on instrumental (e.g., Barbeau & Mantie, 2019; Smith, 2012) and choral groups (e.g., Hillman, 2002; Joseph & Southcott, 2018; Lamont et al., 2018); identity formation (e.g., Dabback, 2008; Woody et al., 2019); music learning, creativity, and cognition (e.g., Bugos, 2014; Creech, 2019); music activities specifically for older adults (e.g., Coffman, 2009; Laes, 2015; Li & Southcott, 2012, 2015; O'Shea, 2012; Southcott & Li, 2018); intergenerational music activities (e.g., Kruse, 2013); and therapeutic uses of music (e.g., Solé et al., 2014). Many studies identified health and wellness as key factors contributing to senior citizens' quality of life (e.g., Grau-Sánchez et al., 2017; Hallam et al., 2012, 2014; Jenkins, Storie, & Purdy, 2017; Johnson, Louhivuori, & Siljander, 2017; Varvarigou et al., 2012) as well as the benefits of music participation for quality of life (e.g., Fung & Lehmberg, 2016; Hallam et al, 2012; Hillman, 2002). Closer examinations reveal that participation in music, when present, is integral to older adults' quality of life. These studies involve a wide range of contexts, such as home, retirement communities, or facilities with a range of care levels. However, at the time of this writing, the body of research on music participation within senior centers was quite limited, and research on music in US senior centers was practically untraceable.

2.5.1 Musical Activities

Among the variety of activities offered at senior centers, musical activities are frequent and popular choices. A few studies on musical activities for active, independent adults have been conducted outside the United States, and we describe them briefly here, as our main focus is on research conducted in senior centers within the United States. Via two studies published over a span of three years, Li and Southcott (2012, 2015) examined music participation in community facilities that appeared to share some similarities with US senior centers, in that they served as gathering spaces for active, older adults: a senior citizens' club for Chinese Australians (in the 2012 study), and a "university" (i.e., community education space) in China for older adults interested in lifelong learning (in the 2015 study). Findings were similar across the two studies. The former found that music participation via singing contributed positively to emotional well-being, connection with the past, shared interests, and mental and physical well-being. The 2015 study found that keyboard learning experiences similarly contributed to emotional and physical well-being, and also helped older adults to experience lifelong learning and realize achievement through music performance. We found one additional study by Steinmayr and Gritsch (2019), who explored a project for older adults featuring music rituals, transposition, and interviews, conducted in two Austrian senior centers.

Very few research studies on musical activities for older adults have been conducted in US senior centers, and there appears to be a large gap in the years in which these studies were conducted. Three dissertations from the 1980s (Janowitz, 1986; Patchen, 1986; Tatum, 1985) explored music in senior centers.

Tatum (1985) completed a descriptive analysis of music programs in retirement residencies and senior centers in the southeastern US and found that (a) music held a position of importance in senior centers; however, more emphasis was placed on music-listening than music-making activities, (b) larger centers were more likely to have professional or trained musicians as activity leaders or participants, (c) the most popular musical activities involved singing, (d) centers that did not offer musical activities were interested in doing so, (e) center administrators were most aware of the social, recreational, and therapeutic benefits of music participation and were interested in providing quality programming, and (f) the philosophies of center administrators and persons responsible for programming were critical in determining whether music programs existed as well as types of musical experiences offered. It is notable that the finding concerning the popularity of singing activities was supported more than 20 years later in research conducted outside the United States (e.g., Li & Southcott, 2012; Southcott & Li, 2018).

Via a survey of older adult senior center clients in Indiana, Patchen (1986) examined relationships between current activity level, musical experience, childhood home musical environment, expressed musical values, and availability of musical activities within senior centers, along with client demographics. Findings indicated that (a) musical activities involving listening, singing, and dancing were most frequently offered within senior centers, (b) participants valued music in their daily lives, (c) older adults who valued music were more likely to participate in center musical activities, and (d) older adult center clients tended to participate in music and dance activities that were similar to those in which they had participated in earlier life. Again, these findings are supported in current research, including our own (Fung & Lehmberg, 2016).

Finally, a dissertation by Janowitz (1986) examined the use of selected variables affecting the use of individualized general music learning activity packages with older adult participants in Philadelphia area senior centers. Most findings surrounded the use of the packets, which appeared to be successful, but are outdated compared with today's standards because they utilized older technology for teaching and learning (e.g., cassette tapes and players, printed lesson materials).

We were very surprised to find only one recent study examining musical activities in senior centers in the United States. It was notable that this study occurred 26 years later than the dissertations previously described. This chronological gap warrants further thought and investigation. Smith (2012), a self-identified baby boomer, conducted a long-term ethnographical study in the role of a participant-observer in a senior center band. He found that (a) all band members began playing their instruments in school bands earlier in life, (b) leaders were career music education professionals, (c) over time, age-related physical and cognitive changes caused challenges for band members, (d) death of friends was a part of life for band members, and (e) positivity was an important quality of senior center band leaders. Similar findings concerning music participation of older adults being similar to that of their earlier years, challenges of age-related changes, and death being a part of life have surfaced in other research from the past 20 years (e.g., Fung & Lehmberg, 2016).

2.6 Questions Arise

Revisiting the fact that not many studies of music activities have been conducted in senior center settings, a gap in research is clearly evident, leading to the research described in this book. Questions arise about the current state of music activities in senior centers, specifically concerning their nature, management, participants, impacts, and further development. The purpose of this research was to determine the *role of music participation* in the quality of life of older adults who utilize senior centers, and the *role of music itself* within these centers. In this study, we adopted Flanagan (1978, 1982) and Burckhardt and Anderson's (2003) model of quality of life, involving the dimensions of material well-being; physical well-being; relationships with other people; social, community, and civic activities; personal development and fulfillment; recreation; and independence. Also considered are our additions of spirituality and a dynamic drive to be better, which are extensions of the dimensions of personal development and fulfillment, and two new dimensions of free choices and supportive context.

PART II

An Experiential View of Music in Senior Centers

CHAPTER 3

A Close-up Look at Senior Centers

As evidenced in Chapter 2, the literature on senior centers is dominated by a wide range of center-provided activities and services that fulfill basic survival needs (such as shelter, meals, and health care), how older adults benefit from them, the different types of challenges senior centers face, projected directions for the future, and the diversity of center clientele (e.g., ethnicity, culture, health, and socioeconomic strata). Very few studies explore specific senior center activities, such as musical activities, that enrich quality of life beyond the fulfillment of basic survival needs.

Our previous work on music participation of older adults and quality of life (Fung & Lehmberg, 2016) suggests that music is critical to the quality of life of those who participate. However, this research was limited to a middle-class, largely White, senior living community in the southeastern US, and we were interested to see if findings would be similar across more diverse populations in locations with different characteristics. Using senior centers as a focal point, we intended to fill a gap in research on older adult music participation within activities offered in their local communities.

This chapter and subsequent chapters provide an in-depth, pre-pandemic look at music in senior centers that serve culturally and socioeconomically diverse populations of older adults, within cities of different sizes across different regions of the United States. We use a broad-to-specific structure to present a sense of context for each senior center, within which information on musical activities and the stories of center clients are cohesively situated.

The stage is set in this chapter as we share the story of our path toward this research and introduce readers to the context of our study: six different senior centers across the United States. We provide figurative snapshots of each of these centers constructed from our in-person observations and interviews and also share commonalities we discovered across centers. In Chapter 4, we narrow down to explore the forms of *music participation* in these senior centers, with an in-depth examination of music-making activities witnessed at close range during our in-person observations. Chapter 5 zooms in even further to share the colorful words and stories of senior center clients regarding their own music participation. In Chapter 6, we take a broader view once again to synthesize findings presented in Chapters 3–5, to elucidate the *role of music in the quality of life* of older adult clients of the senior centers we visited.

3.1 Shaping the Research

We decided to gather information via a naturalistic inquiry design (Patton, 2015), which for this study meant gathering data on musical activities as they occurred naturally in senior centers, with no intervention. Our proposed *modus operandi* was to visit and "hang out" at selected senior centers for extended periods of time during their hours of operation, observe musical and nonmusical activities, have informal conversations with center clients who happened to pass by, and interview as many people as possible in each center. We were interested in learning more about musical opportunities within these senior centers. We also wished to connect with independent, older adults who participated in musical activities in these senior centers, to learn more about their experiences and delve further into the role of music participation in their quality of life. In this case, the term *independent* functions as a health- and community-oriented descriptor of most individuals who frequent senior centers and can be defined as *the ability to do for oneself* (Burckhardt & Anderson, 2003), including making one's own decisions and being in control of one's own life. To present a more complete picture of quality of life and the varied elements that contribute to it, we also hoped to connect with, and learn from, senior center clients who *were not* music participants at the time. Furthermore, we believed that the information we collected would be richer and deeper if it came from multiple sources, so we explored the topics of music participation and quality of life of center clients from the perspectives of center musical activity leaders, center directors and managers, and other center staff as well. Appendix A presents a detailed description of our research purpose, design, and methods.

Our first step was to identify the senior centers we wished to study. We sought to gather data that were rich, deep, and representative of the different regions of the United States; however, as is common in many research fields, we faced constraints. As much as we would have enjoyed visiting senior centers in Alaska, Hawaii, and US territories such as Puerto Rico or the US Virgin Islands, time and limited funding necessitated that

Figure 3.1 Map of six regions of the United States
Credit: Image by Clker-free-vector-images from Pixabay
Note: This image was edited by the authors.

we gather data only within the continental US. We further limited our research to government-funded senior centers that offered daytime services for culturally and socioeconomically diverse populations of older adults. This way, we could address a sector that was more socially responsible, grassroot, and community-based. In addition to ensuring diversity and connecting with participants who fell below middle-class socioeconomic status, we believed these criteria would help us to make more valid comparisons across the centers we studied. Since we are members of the music professoriate, it was convenient to utilize the geographical membership regions of the National Association for Music Education (NAfME). Figure 3.1 illustrates our division of the United States into six regions: Eastern, North Central, Northwest, Southern, Southwestern, and Western. Within these six regions, we identified and visited a representative sample of centers in small, mid-sized, and large cities. We visited one center per region for a total of six senior centers.

As we searched online for senior centers, we immediately ran into difficulties in locating centers that met our study criteria. We quickly discovered that music-making, music-composition, and music-production activities and opportunities were either not available at all or only available on a limited basis in most government-funded senior centers that served culturally and socioeconomically diverse populations of older adults. Most centers offered only services that had been *shown in empirical research* to benefit the health and well-being of older adults. We also soon learned that most of this empirical research did not include arts-related research. A majority of centers provided services that satisfied basic needs related to meals, shelter, and health care. Some centers did offer sporadic music-making activities such as monthly or quarterly drum circles or karaoke events. Likewise, several offered opportunities for center clients to enjoy live music via concerts by local musicians or special holiday events featuring local musical groups. Many also offered dance or exercise classes in which attendees deliberately and purposefully moved to music, as well as other types of classes during which participants passively listened to music that played in the background.

Despite the limited availability of musical activities in most centers aside from listening or exercising to music, we eventually identified, selected, and arranged to visit one senior center that met our criteria in each of the six regions. Each of us was assigned three senior center sites, with the goal of visiting the centers, observing activities, and talking with center clients, leaders, and managers. These senior centers are described in the next section. Note that pseudonyms are used throughout this book to protect the privacy and anonymity of center clients and staff.

3.2 The Six Senior Centers

Our goal in relating information on these six sites is to provide enough detail so readers can vividly "see" each center in their minds. We present the context for each center first, and then share several distinct commonalities we discovered across the centers.

3.2.1 Sunnyside Senior Center (Lisa Lehmberg, Researcher)

Sunnyside Senior Center was located in a culturally and socioeconomically diverse neighborhood of a mid-sized city of approximately 650,000 residents in the Northwest region of the United States. The metro area surrounding the city had a population of approximately 2,000,000 residents (Macrotrends, 2010–2021). The median household income in the city was approximately $70,000, with a poverty level of approximately 14%. Approximately 13% of the city's residents were aged 65 or older. The overall White population of the city was approximately 70% (U.S. Census Bureau, 2019); however, the center was located in a neighborhood that was home to residents of Russian, Vietnamese, Latino, and Black descent (U.S. Census Bureau, 2019).

3.2.1.1 *First Impressions*

At first glance, the Sunnyside Senior Center storefront was reminiscent of a 1960s strip mall: an old, plain-looking red brick building with plate glass windows and a recessed entry way with a metal-framed glass door. Some smaller windows across the top of the plate glass windows provided a hint of the neighborhood's "hippie vibe" and were painted in opaque, textured-pastel green and blue. Two of the smaller windows had surprisingly large, painted portraits of the faces of older adult women. A senior center sign hung straight out, high over the sidewalk and perpendicular to the small plate glass windows. The sign looked welcoming in orange sunburst with a white background and the senior center's name. Adjacent to the center was the Humble Boutique thrift store, which was run by center volunteers. It offered "gently used" and handmade items for sale, with all profits going to the senior center.

Upon entering the center, I saw a reception desk immediately to the left (staffed by an older adult volunteer) in front of a large cubicle office area with some small private offices behind it. To the right was a small seating area with a sofa and three chairs. Shelves were close at hand with books and brochures that composed the center's "library." Straight ahead was a large multipurpose room with round tables and chairs, with a small, elevated stage at the back. To the right were two modern-looking classrooms and a large kitchen. There was a ramp leading to a storage room off the stage and a small hall across the back that led to a parking lot, restrooms, and another small room used for health and other services. The center appeared small for the number of clients it served.

Right away, I noticed how friendly the staff and attendees seemed to be. On this day most center clients were White, with two Asian attendees in evidence. Dress was quite casual and comfortable. One older female attendee who appeared to be of Eastern European ethnicity stood out from the other clients because she wore a mid-calf length dress, babushka, and pink and gray argyle knee socks. She was sitting in the entryway library area looking through brochures and books and had brought a handful of individually wrapped coffee candies to the volunteer receptionist. I noted one physically disabled attendee: a White man in a wheelchair.

It was early in the day when I arrived for my first visit and center attendees were sitting and conversing at tables in the multipurpose room.

I met Wendy (center coordinator) and Tina (kitchen staff). Tina was very friendly and appeared to have some sort of disability in that her speech was thick and difficult to understand. She seemed quite narrowly focused on her responsibilities, which I discovered included making sure I had a pitcher of water with the correct number of plastic cups available in Classroom B during interviews with study participants. A dietician came into the multipurpose room and asked if anyone wanted nutrition counseling. The ages of attendees looked to be from the 60s on up. At first, I wasn't quite sure why they were all sitting around the tables, because no special activity appeared to be going on. I later learned that this particular day was a "gleaning day" and also a Meals on Wheels day, so attendees were sitting around talking, playing games, knitting, and waiting for those events to happen. On Gleaning Day (every Monday from Spring through November), the Farmers Market Gleaning Program brought fresh produce from local farmers to the center for attendees to take home at no cost. Meals on Wheels also provided lunch for a suggested donation of three dollars.

I noticed several brochures and flyers on bulletin boards around the periphery of the multipurpose room. These advertised services such as support groups for family caregivers of Alzheimer's patients and for grandparents who were raising grandchildren, a medical equipment loaner program, volunteer programs to help older adults *age in place* (defined by the Centers for Disease Control and Prevention [2009] as "the ability to live in one's own home and community safely, independently, and comfortably, regardless of age, income, or ability level"), Medicare assistance, help with lawn care, Meals on Wheels, computer tutoring, an acupuncture clinic, a personal safety program, a workshop series on living well with chronic conditions, and social services for veterans. Flyers also advertised recreation activities and classes such as ukulele groups, Tai Chi, an arthritis exercise class, Tuesday night Bunco dice games, a class in which older adult clients wrote down their life stories, and a Riders Club in which groups of older adults traveled by van or bus to local cultural activities. Handwritten thank-you cards from second-grade students who had recently visited the center were also prominently displayed. Also visible was a policy statement that the center was a "harassment and violence free zone."

I was given a copy of the monthly newsletter, which was distributed in hard copy at the center and via an email listserv. The newsletter's calendar listed anywhere from four to 13 scheduled activities per day on weekdays, with an average of nine activities per day. Musical activities included two ukulele group rehearsals per week. I was told that some of the center's exercise groups utilized music for movement or in the background.

3.2.1.2 *Delving Deeper*

Over several visits to Sunnyside Senior Center, I was able to meet individually with the center's three full-time paid staff members: Brooke (executive director), Tracy (outreach and development coordinator), and Wanda (center coordinator). I learned that other center staff comprised a few part-time caseworkers and approximately 60 volunteers who together spent an average of 1,033 hours per month in the center. The center's focus was on wellness. Its goal was to offer as much as possible for free to its clients; hence, most activity leaders donated their time. If it was not possible to find a volunteer leader for an activity of interest, then a leader was hired, and participants paid a small fee. The state in which this center was located only funded instructors of classes and leaders of activities shown by empirical evidence to improve older adults' health or well-being (e.g., Tai Chi, exercise groups for arthritis, etc.).

Hours and Clientele. At the time of my visit, Sunnyside Senior Center was open on weekdays from 8:30 a.m. to 4:30 p.m. but was also designated as a nondenominational space that community groups could rent after hours and on weekends. There were approximately 200 attendees per day from all over the county. Some came to the center multiple times per week, but there were approximately 1,300 unduplicated clients each month. One reason for the large number of daily attendees was that mass transit made the center easily accessible. Other businesses were close to the center, so it was convenient for attendees to meet some of their other needs as well when they were in the area. Services were available to clients aged 60 and older; however, those aged 50 and above were welcome to attend events at the center. The average age of center clients was 73.

Though the center was located in a culturally diverse area of the surrounding city and served attendees of Russian, Vietnamese, Latino, and Black ethnicities, a majority of its clients were White. To encourage people of color to use the center, it offered a bilingual "coffee table group," where older adult attendees told stories of their lives and wrote them down to pass on to future generations.

Center clients were mostly independent but lived in different types of housing situations (i.e., alone, with family, etc.). Although they represented a range of incomes, a majority were of lower income with less of a support system than their higher-income peers. I was told that people of higher socioeconomic status who lived in senior living communities generally did not use the center unless there was a specific connection. For example, Wanda reported that Center Board of Directors members who were older adults "don't always attend center activities. Some of them want something more upscale."

Support. Sunnyside Senior Center was a designated County Senior Center. Funding came from the US Older Americans Act, the county government, an endowment, and an Annual Appeal. In addition to supporting within-center and in-home services, this funding helped to pay for transportation for older adults in the form of Lyft rides, taxis, and so forth. This center also had a partnership with the local chapter of the Alzheimer's Association, which held monthly support groups at the center as well as classes for people with Alzheimer's and their caregivers. A partnership also existed with the local Vietnamese Association. Its members used the center for karaoke with music and poetry on Saturdays and for Lunar New Year celebrations. A third partnership with the Urban League helped the center to access the neighborhood Black community.

Challenges. One of the center's biggest challenges was a lack of resources. According to Brooke (executive director), there was not enough funding to fully serve the demographic. Older adults were often an afterthought and not prioritized in competitions among local organizations for community funding. Space was another problem. A bigger facility would have allowed for more services. Brooke, Tracy, and Wanda agreed that there simply were not enough resources to meet the needs of center clients and older adults in the surrounding community. The center was under contract with the county to provide in-home services via case managers, but unfortunately, there had been a substantial decrease in funding for these over the years. Brooke emphasized the need for a stronger investment from the county to move policy forward to stabilize and provide more resources that were relevant to the current constituency of older adults.

Additional challenges mentioned by Wanda were that (a) almost everything at the center had to be done by volunteers and it was difficult to recruit a sufficient number of volunteers, (b) it was difficult to attract baby boomers to the center, yet critical to the center's survival to do so, and (c) there was a need to network to access the large neighborhood Latino community. Unfortunately, the center attracted few Latinos. Wanda, a Latina herself, described this as "a cultural thing. They aren't joiners. Their culture is all about their family, so they stay home."

3.2.2 Better Living Senior Center (Victor Fung, Researcher)

Better Living Senior Center was located in a culturally and socioeconomically diverse large city in the Western region of the United States. The actual population of the city was close to 900,000 at the time of my visit; however, the metro area in which the city was located had over 3,300,000 residents. The median household income in the city was approximately $112,000, with a poverty level of approximately 10%. Over 15% of the city's residents were aged 65 or older. The overall White population was slightly over 45%, with approximately 34% of residents identifying as Asian (U.S. Census Bureau, 2019).

3.2.2.1 First Impressions

Better Living Senior Center operated out of a large two-story building of over 5,000 square feet with multiple rooms. The building formerly housed a police academy. In front of the senior center was a bus stop, at which two older adults were waiting when I arrived at the center. A small parking lot was almost hidden at the back of the building. It appeared to be fully parked with well-maintained cars of Japanese and German makes. Further exploration of the grounds around the center uncovered seven sections of cordoned-off rectangular flower and vegetable gardens, allocated for two-year periods via a drawing to older adults who loved to garden but had no garden space at home.

Upon entering the senior center, I found myself in an open common area immediately inside the front entrance, set up with seven square tables with four to six chairs at each. Four White women were playing cards at one of the tables. Other tables appeared to be used for casual conversations and meetings. A computer was set up in the corner, but I did not see anyone using it during my visit. A sign communicated that wifi was available for center clients without the need for a password.

The center appeared to have multiple rooms, large and small. In addition to the common area, the ground floor contained a ballroom used for dance and larger classes, an exercise room with two exercise bikes, a bingo room, and a kitchen. A mezzanine level contained a small room with no door, utilized for ceramics classes and guitar jams. The upper level of the center contained an art room; a smaller activity room; a common room with bookshelves, a computer, and some tables and chairs; another kitchen; and two office areas. Bulletin boards throughout the center were filled with announcements of various activities. One could easily find the center's schedule of activities and individual flyers with information on specific class activities, parties and other special events, meetings, birthdays, and so forth.

Overall, the center appeared to be quite busy, and I noticed that everyone seemed to have a purpose for being there. Clients were serious-looking and appeared to know what they wanted and needed. I seldom saw anyone who appeared to be there to just "hang around." Looking at the schedule, I saw that musical activities included a guitar jam, a chorus, two karaoke groups, and a ukulele group. There were also exercise classes, such as low-impact Zumba and aerobics, as well as a round-dance class that utilized music.

3.2.2.2 *Delving Deeper*

I visited Better Living Senior Center on a few different days and was able to interview Robert, the facility coordinator, who was the only full-time employee at the center. He had worked there for 15 years. Prior to that time, there were three full-time staff members. Three part-time staff helped with registration and maintained daily operations (e.g., setting up coffee service, arranging tables and chairs, etc.). Other volunteers included Senior Center Council members and older adults who wrote condolence, get well, and birthday cards to center clients. Ninety-five percent of the center's activities and classes were led by volunteers, with others hired to run specific classes (such as Zumba) that required expertise that lay outside that of the current pool of volunteers. The center's activities included physical fitness, art, jewelry making, music, bridge, and bingo. Activities were divided into four sessions throughout the year: 17 weeks in the Fall, 10 weeks in the Winter, 10 weeks in the Spring, and 11 weeks in the Summer. The varying durations were due to the need to coordinate with holidays and other special events in the community.

The center's goal was to support the education, physical fitness, and social and intellectual health of older adults. Though the center had two kitchens, it did not provide meals on site. Furthermore, it did not provide transportation for clients. Most arrived at the center via public buses, paratransit or van services (for attendees with disabilities), taxis, or by driving themselves independently to the center.

Hours and Clientele. Better Living Senior Center's hours of operation were 9:00 a.m. to 5:00 p.m. Monday through Friday, and 10:00 a.m. to 4:00 pm on Saturdays and Sundays (to accommodate clients who were still working on weekdays). Exceptions were made for special events or holiday weekends. The center served approximately 200 to 500 older adults on weekdays and 100 to 250 on weekends. The total number of clients was approximately 1,000. All activities were open to older adults aged 55 and older. At the time of my visit, one attendee was over 100 years old and 36 attendees were aged 90 or older.

Though the center did not track client demographics, I learned from Robert that 85–90% of the center's clientele were of Asian ethnicity (mostly Chinese). There was further diversity among the group of Asian clients; for example, Mandarin-speaking and Cantonese-speaking, native-born and foreign-born, and various Asian nationalities such as Japanese, Filipino, Indian, and Chinese from Myanmar, Indonesia, and Korea. Other clients were White (including Russians), Latino (Spanish-speaking), and Black. Most center clients were women; the center had a ratio of 20:1 female to male clients. Amid substantial cultural diversity, the majority of center clients were middle class and in good health.

Support. Better Living Senior Center did not receive funding from the state legislature, but contracted staff were funded by the city in which the center was located. The city was also responsible for expenses associated with vendors who serviced the center, as well as the operation of the center building and its elevator. Additionally, a membership fee of $20 per client supported hospitality services and parties. Registration fees for individual classes covered expenses such as hired models for art classes and materials for jewelry classes. The senior center partnered with a variety of cultural groups, mainly for organizing and promoting relevant events such as fiestas and lunar new year. While these partnership events were regular, there was not necessarily any formal partnership agreement.

Challenges. According to Robert, the center's main challenges surrounded the needs of individual attendees, particularly their physical needs. For example, someone might forget to take their blood pressure or anxiety pills, or someone might have an accident before they could get to the toilet.

3.2.3 Good Hope Senior Center (Lisa Lehmberg, Researcher)

Good Hope Senior Center was located in a culturally and socioeconomically diverse neighborhood of a culturally diverse, large city in the North Central region of the United States, with a population nearing 900,000 (U.S. Census Bureau, 2019), located within a surrounding metro area of approximately 1.5 million (Macrotrends, 2010–2021). The median household income in the city was approximately $54,000, with a poverty level of almost 20%. Approximately 10% of the city's residents were aged 65 or older. The overall White population of the city was slightly over 55%, with approximately 30% of residents identifying as Black or African American (U.S. Census Bureau, 2019).

3.2.3.1 First Impressions

The center itself was in a nondescript, 1960s-style strip mall with tan-colored brick walls (like those found in many older public school buildings) and large plate glass windows in the storefronts. The sign on the center was confusing because it read "Good Hope Recreation Center" but upon entry, I discovered that the center was without a doubt a senior center. I learned from Nicole, the center manager, that only two dedicated senior centers currently existed in this large city. The rest had been converted to multigenerational centers, which appeared to be the new trend for community centers there.

Good Hope Senior Center's main entrance was on the south side of the building, facing the strip mall parking lot. Upon entering, I saw a multipurpose room immediately to the right and a reception area on the left with a long, curving counter that had room for several volunteers to sit behind it. Behind the reception area counter was a suite of offices. Down the hallway to the left was a large fitness room with a sign on the door reminding attendees to complete their exercise programs at least 15 minutes before the center closed. Other policies posted in the fitness room required that members have a signed physician's medical form and that they complete an initial training program with one of the center's personal trainers. The fee for a fitness center membership was $10.00 per personal training session or $40.00 per year for individual use. Inside the fitness room were elliptical machines, weight machines, stationary bicycles, and several treadmills. The room had a clean, uncluttered look, with light gray walls on which a large mirror and a medium-sized painting in cool hues hung. There was plum-colored indoor–outdoor carpet on the floor. Further down the same hallway was an arts and crafts room (where the music classes and ensembles met) with seven folding melamine tables, chairs, and storage rooms; and a health services examination room with a small waiting area. Down the hall to the right of the reception area was a large game room, a classroom, and an additional multipurpose room. Going straight down the hall from the reception area without turning either left or right, I came to a large, open multipurpose dining/auditorium/stage area with a kitchen at one end. Lunch was served in this room and performances and other large events also took place there. Bulletin boards were hung from one end to the other of every hallway in the center. Posted on these were multiple flyers advertising activities, events, and services offered at and through the center. Activities and events during the month I visited included, but were not limited to, a poetic circle, euchre club, walking for fun group, bingo, veteran's roundtable discussion group, summer cookout, "live truth" series, volunteer lunch, birthday and anniversary parties, Broadway music concert, aerobic exercise training sessions, global fitness club, woodcarving program, street hockey, as well as classes in sewing, line dancing, tap dancing, basketry, fitness ball yoga, and quilting. Musical activities (other than the Broadway concert and dance or exercise activities that utilized music) included a harmonica club, a chorus, and a guitar class. An upcoming trip sponsored by the center was to be a tour of farmers' markets in nearby cities. Health and other services offered through the center included a mobile medical and wellness center, health behavior monitoring for multiple sclerosis, individual and family insurance assistance, transportation, dietician services, hospice services, low-income water and sewer discounts, assisted living help, rehabilitation services, and home care services. Signs and flyers on the bulletin board also announced special donations that had been made to the center, such as the provision of fitness equipment by the local 50+ Center and the Recreation and Parks Department. Photos were posted of attendees who had birthdays that month, clients who had recently died, and other life milestones and newsworthy items and events. Bulletin boards also displayed attendees' artwork, including watercolor paintings and scale drawings of quilt squares.

On the first day I visited the center, the receptionist and all front desk staff were White. On my second visit, all were Black. Attendees also seem to be Black, White, or biracial. I was told that the center had clients of other ethnicities, but I did not notice any. The older adults who attended the center appeared independent and socialized with each other within classes, in the lunchroom, and in the hallways. I was struck by how friendly everyone was! The staff seemed to know attendees well and called each by name. They were friendly to all center clients, but particularly appeared to respect and celebrate center attendees of advanced age, especially a 101-year-old Black man referred to as "Mr. Noah." The staff also appeared to like each other. I frequently heard them teasing each other in fun and laughing together. They were very helpful when I needed assistance to find an interviewee or a place to conduct interviews. The overall feel of the center was welcoming and inclusive.

3.2.3.2 *Delving Deeper*

At this center, I was able to meet with two staff members: Nicole (senior center manager) and Nick (office manager and guitar instructor). I learned that the center generally had seven to eight staff members, four of whom worked full-time at the center (director, assistant director, office manager, and recreation director). Many volunteer hours were utilized. For example, the front desk was run totally by older adult volunteers who also participated in the center's activities on days when they were not working at the front desk. The center's focus was recreation, and it had a wellness center. There were only two contracted classes at the center: conversational Spanish and line dancing. For other classes, enrollees paid a fee and then the center paid instructors from the collected fees.

Hours and Clientele. Good Hope Senior Center was open 53.5 hours per week, on Mondays from 8:00 a.m. to 9:00 p.m., on Tuesdays, Thursdays, and Fridays from 8:00 a.m. to 5:00 p.m., and on Wednesdays from 8:00 a.m. to 9:30 p.m. It served approximately 200 older adults per week at a rate of 35 attendees per hour of operation. The minimum age to join the center was 50; however, members' spouses under the age of 50 were also allowed to use the center. At the time of my visit, the ages of clientele ranged from 50 to 101, with an average of 80. According to Nicole, the center used to serve only an older population, but "now is about 50/50 younger and older seniors." She went on to explain that when it opened in 2005, the center had a largely White clientele, but it had become more culturally diverse over the years. Nicole had worked at another senior center in 2005 but visited this center shortly after it opened and did not feel welcome as a Black person. Later she was transferred to her current position at this center and noted that things were much different by then. Nicole shared that some of the same staff who were unfriendly when she visited earlier were still employed at the center but had gotten to know her and were nicer now. For Nicole, the center was "more about family than ethnicity. That is the change in the center. It has become more diverse and friendly." At the time of my visit, there was a substantial population of Black clientele. An Asian population attended the center for line dancing and ballroom dance activities but attended no other center activities. The center was located in a Latino area of town but there were few Latino clients.

Support. Good Hope Senior Center was funded in part and regulated by the government of the large city in which it was located. Remaining (and sometimes substantial) expenses were covered by the center's Senior

Center Council, which purchased items such as a copier, televisions, and furniture. However, according to Nicole, the city's contributions toward expenses had increased over time. Unlike some senior centers, this center did not directly provide transportation to and from the center. A local bus line provided transportation by reservation only. Vehicles for special center trips were provided by the city's Parks and Recreation Department. This center also had partnerships with other senior centers and organizations to help both center attendees and homebound older adults access community services. These included Meals on Wheels; appointments in the center with nurses, dieticians, speech and hearing specialists; a hospital mobile unit; lawyers; and realtors who came to the center to present programs on downsizing in preparation for assisted living.

Challenges. According to Nicole, the biggest challenge was that "the center is in the middle of the U.N. [located in an ethnically diverse neighborhood]. Language barrier is the biggest challenge. It is difficult to find people to volunteer as translators – everyone wants to be paid for their services." Neighborhood residents were immigrants from Somalia, Eritrea, Indonesia, Sri Lanka, and Latino countries, in addition to native-born Blacks and Whites. The center needed interpreters who were willing to volunteer their services. Another challenge was the small size of the center facility. The limited space made it difficult for Nicole to incorporate the programming she wanted to offer. Nick was of a different opinion and believed the biggest challenge at the center concerned the mental faculties of center clients. He remarked that people often forgot to pay for activities or lunches, but he tried to treat everyone with respect regardless of the situation. Nick also mentioned that center attendance had decreased over the years. "The newer generation of seniors don't [sic] accept the idea of a senior center."

3.2.4 *Mountain View Senior Center (Victor Fung, Researcher)*

Mountain View Senior Center was located in a small-sized city of approximately 140,000 residents in the Southwestern region of the United States. The median household income in the city was approximately $60,000, with a poverty level of almost 16%. Around 11% of the city's residents were aged 65 or older. The White population of the city was approximately 60%, with almost 25% of residents identifying as Hispanic or Latino (U.S. Census Bureau, 2019).

3.2.4.1 *First Impressions*

Upon arrival at the center, I entered through the front door into an open foyer where I saw 10 older adults sitting at multiple square tables, relaxing and chatting. A receptionist and two volunteer office staff were stationed nearby at the front desk. There were two carts that were filled with loaves of bread donated by a local grocery store. I later learned that center clients were allowed to take up to two loaves home. The center was approximately 15,000 square feet in size, built on one level, and contained a library with a computer for use by attendees, a fitness center, a conference room, a multipurpose room with pool tables and an area used for chair volleyball, and a craft store that sold crafts and other items that were handmade by center clients. The center's library contained many books with most being works of fiction. Bookshelves stretched across three walls and there were also three double-sided rolling book carts. A large number of bulletin boards were spaced on walls throughout the center, advertising a huge variety of activities and classes, including some intergenerational activities (e.g., kayaking). Musical activities offered in the center included a choir, a jazz band, and beginner and advanced concert (New Horizons) bands. Some exercise classes also utilized music. The center appeared to be very busy, with people coming and going constantly.

3.2.4.2 *Delving Deeper*

At this center I was able to meet with Jack (center manager), who had worked at the center for 22 years. I learned that there were three full-time staff, including the center manager, and two part-time staff, including a receptionist who worked 27.5 hours at the front desk and a recreation coordinator who worked 20 hours per week. Most activity leaders were paid. The center also had approximately 110 volunteers who each worked 50 hours or more per year.

Hours and Clientele. Mountain View Senior Center operated Monday through Friday from 8:00 a.m. to 9:00 p.m. and Saturday from 9:00 a.m. to 1:00 p.m. Approximately 260 older adults were served in the center each day, and it had a total of around 1,500 members. A large number of nonmembers also used the center facility, making a total of 2,500–3,500 older adults served yearly by the center.

A majority of clients were White, which I surmised was predominantly due to the center's location in a White neighborhood; however, I also noticed some Black and Latino attendees. Ages of clientele ranged from 50 to 99 years, with an average age of 75 years. Most were lower-middle to middle class. A few were wealthy, but not many. Center attendees were required to be capable of taking care of themselves. As Jack stated, "If seniors cannot take care of themselves, they can't be here. This is not a care facility."

Support. Mountain View Senior Center was funded by the city in which it was located, with monetary support coming from city taxes and property funds. The center was also funded in part by membership fees of $10 per local resident client and $15 per nonlocal client. Remaining funding came from program fees, sponsorships, and fundraisers. The center also had an advisory council of approximately 17 members who helped to raise funds and make decisions about center programming. Similar to Good Hope Senior Center, this center did not provide transportation for its attendees. Instead, they arranged for their own transportation via family or friends, by driving independently, or by contracting with special transportation services for older or disabled citizens.

Challenges. According to Jack, the biggest challenge was that "every day is different. There is a broad range of ages and interest levels. Meeting the needs of everyone is a challenge." Jack also mentioned that safety was critical and gave the example of a need for more accessible parking slots in the center lot, which unfortunately meant fewer spots for regular parking. Food was another issue at this center; for example, what to provide and how often to provide it.

3.2.5 Center for Healthy Aging (Lisa Lehmberg, Researcher)

The Center for Healthy Aging was located in a low-income neighborhood of a small, culturally and socioeconomically diverse city of slightly over 40,000 residents in the Eastern region of the United States. The median household income in the city was approximately $41,000, with a poverty level of almost 30%, one of two highest poverty levels of the six cities we visited. Approximately 14% of the city's residents were aged 65 or older. The White population of the city was slightly over 40%, with almost 54% of residents identifying as Hispanic or Latino (U.S. Census Bureau, 2019).

3.2.5.1 First Impressions
I noticed right away that the Center for Healthy Aging was quite new and had a bright, airy feel, with expansive windows that allowed light and sunshine to come through. It was bustling with a large population of attendees. There was a large, free parking lot outside with roomy parking spots, wide aisles for traffic, and several accessible parking spots. Upon entering the center, I found myself in a sizeable open reception area where

attendees were required to sign in and out as they entered and left the building. On the periphery of the reception area were staff offices, a library, an exercise room, a small café, and a large lunchroom-auditorium with a small stage. At the top of the stairs to the second floor was a clean, carpeted, open area with tables and chairs and pool tables. A large multi-purpose room, meeting rooms, and some small offices were also located on the second floor. The center's musical groups (a concert band, a polka band, and a German band) rehearsed in the multipurpose room, which was also used for painting and exercise classes (some of which also utilized music). The room was carpeted and the walls were painted in bright colors, with large, sunlit windows. There was a grand piano and a rack of free weights on one side. Overall, the center was spacious and the staff were very friendly, cheery, and helpful. I was struck by the number of people coming and going. It was a bright and very busy place!

3.2.5.2 *Delving Deeper*

I was able to meet with Francine (center assistant manager) and learned that fifteen staff members were employed at the center, including a director, assistant director, two social workers, a few dispatchers, two cooks, two drivers, two maintenance workers, and several kitchen helpers. Volunteers staffed the front desk in groups of three in the morning and afternoon shifts. Anyone who taught a class or led an activity at the center was paid.

Hours and Clientele. The Center for Healthy Aging was open from 8:00 a.m. to 4:00 p.m. Monday through Friday, and Wednesdays from 8:00 a.m. until 6:30 p.m. Approximately 250 older adults were served each day by the center, with 2,000 to 3,000 older adults served per year. Clients were served mainly *within* the center; however, the center also provided transportation to doctor appointments and scheduled social workers to visit homebound older adults. Additionally, the center provided transportation to and from the center. Anyone aged 55 and above could attend activities at the center; however, lunch and transportation were only available to attendees aged 60 and above.

Attendees were mostly independent-living. A majority were White and spoke English as a first language. Some also spoke Polish, Portuguese, or French. There was a growing, Spanish-speaking Latino community at the center as well. Most attendees were of low- to middle-class socioeconomic status.

Support. The Center for Healthy Aging was funded by the local city government. The dollar amount of funding per attendee was based on the number of attendees per month. The city also provided funding and services to bring the center into compliance with city ordinances; for example, the local city council worked to provide more accessible parking at the center. The center was in the process of building a partnership with the local Alzheimer's Association. One of the eventual goals of this partnership was to offer a memory café for older adults with dementia and their caregivers.

Challenges. Challenges that Francine faced in managing the senior center surrounded activity instructors and appropriate activities. She struggled with "finding instructors that stay committed for the long term. Who teaches what? Who attends what? It's challenging to find activities that senior citizens like that don't marginalize them." Additionally, Francine shared that her biggest challenge was just "getting a grasp on everything that goes on at the center."

3.2.6 *The Senior Place (Victor Fung, Researcher)*

The Senior Place senior center was located in a culturally and socioeconomically diverse, mid-sized Southern city of approximately 350,000 residents (U.S. Census Bureau, 2019), within a large metropolitan area of 2.8 million residents (Macrotrends, 2010–2021). The median household income in the city was approximately $41,000, with a poverty level of almost 30%, one of the highest poverty levels of the six cities we visited. Approximately 12% of two city's residents were aged 65 or older. The White population of the city was almost 45%, with approximately 26% of residents identifying as Hispanic or Latino and 24% identifying as Black or African American (U.S. Census Bureau, 2019).

3.2.6.1 *First Impressions*

The Senior Place, which opened in 2008, was housed in a county-owned two-story complex with about 45,000 square feet of indoor space that also housed a branch public library, a small used bookstore with proceeds that benefited the library, and a Head Start facility that provided early childhood education programs for low-income children and families. The senior center occupied about one-third of the building on the ground floor of an entire wing. Adjacent to the senior center was an outdoor medium-sized park and playground with swings and slides. The parking lot had ample parking spaces to serve clients of all facilities in the complex. Within walking distance in about a thousand feet radius were a large residential area, a post office, supermarkets, fast-food chain restaurants, shopping complexes, and a Vietnamese Buddhist temple.

Directly facing the entrance of the senior center was the reception desk hosted by one or two volunteers, depending on the time and day. Everyone who came into the center was required to sign in. There was a variety of rooms packed in the center. The biggest was the multipurpose room where parties, exercise classes, concerts, and other events were held. Smaller rooms were designed for a variety of classes, lunches, pool tables, table games, fitness equipment, and other social activities. There was also a small kitchen. The smallest rooms were the offices of the manager and staff.

Upon entering the center, I was immediately aware of an obvious presence of Spanish-speaking people. I noticed that some center attendees, staff, and volunteers alike, were bilingual in English and Spanish; others were monolingual (English or Spanish). Center attendees seemed to know which activities were bilingual and which were monolingual. For musical activities, the center offered a guitar class, karaoke, a Friday Fiesta that involved dancing to music, a cardio dance fitness class, and other exercise classes that utilized music.

3.2.6.2 *Delving Deeper*

I was able to interview Maria (center manager) and Amber (an activity specialist). I learned that the center had four full-time staff members: one manager, one custodian, and two activity specialists. Activity leaders generally received a small payment for their services. Forty-two volunteers also helped to staff the center, working from one to eight hours per day. A few of the volunteers helped to lead activities, others worked in the kitchen, and still others helped with organizational tasks such as filing of documents. This center had a membership base but no membership fee. Lunch services were available for those 60 years or older with an advance reservation. I learned that typically there was a waiting list for lunches. The center provided a variety of activities, transportation assistance, and financial aid for low-income households. It was accredited through the National Institute of Senior Centers. It was clear that the center targeted low-income older adults in a culturally and socioeconomically diverse neighborhood.

Hours and Clientele. The Senior Place operated Monday through Friday, from 8 a.m. to 5 p.m. It had approximately 1,200 members and served about 210 older adults each day. Most attended the center at least four days per week, and some came to the center twice per day. All clients were served within the center; no in-home services were provided. Transportation was provided for those who lived within a five-mile radius of the center; however, most attendees drove themselves independently to the center. A transportation service (funded by the Older Americans Act) for low-income older adults was also available.

Ages of center clientele ranged from 50 to 99, with most clients being in their 60s and 70s. Approximately 36% were White, 34% were Latino, 3.4% were Asian, less than 1% were Native American, and the rest were of various other ethnicities. There was also a 50/50 split among clients whose careers were or had been professionals and clients who were or had been blue collar workers in their careers. To attend the center, clients were required to be independent.

Support. Funding for The Senior Place came from the Older Americans Act (58%) and the city (42%) in which the center was located. There was a heavy reliance on volunteers in the operation of this center. The center also had a partnership with the surrounding county to provide free lunches via a county nutrition program to older adults aged 60 and above, regardless of income. Older adults were required to apply to the program and there was a long waiting list. If someone ordered a lunch and then did not show up to eat it, no lunch was ordered for them the following day.

Challenges. According to Maria, the biggest challenge was diversity and "trying to please everybody." For example, if a band played only Latin music at a Valentine's dance, White center attendees would ask, "Where is the American music?" Other challenges involved funding. The center was not permitted to fundraise, and there were restrictions on the federal and municipal funding it received.

3.3 Commonalities across the Six Centers

When we finished our respective visits to the six selected senior centers, we merged our multiple forms of evidence to see what conclusions we could make. Using qualitative data analysis techniques and an online data coding application, we carefully reviewed our observation and interview notes, as well as artifacts we had collected (e.g., images of senior center flyers, senior center newsletters and website pages, etc.). Through this process, we were able to identify six qualities and elements that were common to all six senior citizen centers: (1) *accessibility*, (2) *active and welcoming*, (3) *wellness*, (4) *variety and choice*, (5) *extension of services*, and (6) *resources*. Each is explained in the following subsections.

3.3.1 Accessibility

All six senior centers were easily accessible to older adults. Many were in city center locations with other businesses close by, allowing attendees to meet some of their other needs (e.g., buying groceries, visiting a pharmacy, etc.) while in the area. Center attendees used various means to travel to their center, including mass transportation, free or low-cost senior center buses or vans, driving themselves independently, being transported by family members, or walking to their center if they lived in the neighborhood. Within the centers, facilities were accessible for those who were used wheelchairs.

3.3.2 Active and Welcoming

Study participants and researchers alike perceived the senior centers to be busy and friendly. Clients appeared to be quite comfortable within the centers. We were struck by the number of people coming and going, most of whom appeared to have a specific purpose for being at their center (e.g., for activities, services, meals, etc.). The popularity of the senior centers was evidenced in their activity rooms, which were typically full of attendees. In fact, the activities were so popular that we sometimes experienced difficulties in getting attendees to take a moment away to participate in an interview.

One example of a highly popular activity was chair volleyball, which appeared to attract players and fans of different ethnicities:

> On one of my visits, I got talked into participating in a game of chair volleyball. Two games were going on at once and there was a designated referee for each game. It was a hoot! The rules were that players had to keep at least one "cheek" on the chair at all times, which is difficult when you are trying to hit the ball (a beach ball). Once I forgot and accidentally stood up and they laughingly and loudly ribbed me, admonishing, "One cheek on the chair at all times!" (Lisa Lehmberg, research notes)

An example of a very popular music activity was Music Makers, a large chorus that attracted around 150 older adults weekly.

> Each week's gathering had a different theme (e.g., "Now and Then," "Frank Sinatra," etc.) and the songs for the week fit that theme. Songs were chosen from a songbook that contained 684 songs. Each group member had a copy and there were extra copies for any guests who happened to attend. I was told that the group had even made a CD! (Victor Fung, research notes)

Center clients socialized freely throughout activities, and in the lunchroom and in the hallways. They clearly enjoyed being there. One interviewee, Denise (a ukulele group member), described her senior center and its activities as "hugely popular – like a church only there's no religion."

3.3.3 Wellness

A primary focus of all six senior centers was the health and wellness of older adults. All offered a variety of individual and group opportunities to exercise; for example, fitness rooms with weight training circuits, stationary bikes, treadmills, and ellipticals; classes to develop muscle and joint flexibility; dance classes; yoga classes and classes designed to improve physical functioning through ancient techniques (such as Tai Chi); and low-impact sports such as chair volleyball. Wellness activities also included personal safety programs, spiritual wellness series, and workshops on living well with chronic health conditions.

The six centers also provided numerous services by health and wellness professionals who met with attendees regularly within the centers. These included, but were not limited to, Alzheimer's support groups; medical clinics focusing on blood pressure, foot care, speech and hearing, and diet; programs for home care and aging in place; hospice services; and social services for veterans.

Several centers also offered programs to lessen food insecurity, including free or low-cost meals and free food pantries accessible to center clients. One center had a one-day-a-week gleaning program from Spring through November in which the local farmer's market brought fresh produce to the center for older adults to take home at no cost.

3.3.4 Variety and Choice

All six senior centers offered a large number of activities and services. Musical activities are discussed in the next chapter; however, the most popular nonmusical activities included arts and crafts, exercise and wellness activities, special-interest clubs, games, low-impact sports, and special events such as trips, book sales, movies, parties, and anniversary and birthday celebrations. If a meal program was offered, it was among the most popular programs at the center also. The range of nonmusic-specific activities was quite broad across the six centers.

We discovered that the ability to choose from a wide range of activities was quite important to center attendees, allowing individuals to find an activity that was a perfect fit for them. As Mr. Noah (a 101-year-old Black chorus member) advised, older adults should participate in "whatever they feel comfortable doing."

3.3.5 Extension of Services

Most senior center services were offered within the center; however, a few were offered in clients' homes. These included Meals on Wheels, assistance for aging in place and maintaining independence, counseling services, and visits by social workers.

3.3.6 Resources

The biggest challenge for the centers was a lack of resources, including inadequacies of funding, space, connection with diverse populations, and human resources. Diversity also led to challenges regarding communication and connection with native speakers of non-English languages, attracting clientele, and procuring volunteer staff. Furthermore, it was difficult to retain volunteer activity instructors.

3.4 Further Thoughts

Though the challenges faced by senior centers were weighty and ever-present, the benefits and services they made accessible to older adults were numerous and critical. They obviously made an enormous and positive difference in center clients' quality of life. As mentioned earlier, most of the programs offered by senior centers were supported by non-arts-related empirical research that showed benefits of these activities for the health and well-being of older adults. The question then arises as to whether a future goal of arts professions and other disciplines should be to grow the body of empirical research that shows the *benefits of arts activities* for older adults' health and well-being.

CHAPTER 4

Music across Six Senior Centers

Building on our observations and contextual information provided by senior center staff, we delve more deeply into the structure and community vibe of the music-related activities within each of the six senior centers we visited. Music-related activities generally fell into four categories: (a) passive listening to music, (b) active listening to music, (c) purposeful or deliberate movement to music, and (d) music-making. We begin with a description of the listening activities we discovered and then move on to activities that involved movement to music. The remainder of the chapter is devoted to thick, rich description of the music-making activities we observed, illustrated by the comments of those who participated in them or led them. The words of those involved in the music-making were critical to add a depth of understanding not attainable from observation or conversations with senior center staff alone, thus enabling further reflection on the meaning of these activities for all involved. We close this chapter with insights drawn from a close-range snapshot of music in senior centers, with connections to extant research as appropriate.

4.1 Passive Listening

All six senior centers offered classes in which music was playing in the background and attendees were hearing it but not purposefully or deliberately listening or moving to it (i.e., *passive*, or non-engaged, listening). Brooke (senior center executive director, Sunnyside Senior Center, Northwest region) pointed out examples of these in her center, explaining that "[a]ctivities that utilize [background] music in the center include... arthritis exercise programs, a Tai Chi program, and a meditation program."

Passive listening opportunities were also present when center clients were engaged in activities such as playing cards, working puzzles, or eating meals while music was playing in the background. In one center, a ukulele group rehearsed regularly on the multipurpose room stage, while other attendees passively listened as they played cards, knitted, or worked puzzles at tables on the main floor below the stage. They appeared to enjoy the music – often swaying or tapping a foot to the beat; however, one attendee, Leah, wryly commented that though she enjoyed the group's music, it was "hard to talk over." This uncovered a dilemma for center attendees who enjoyed the music in the background yet had a strong desire to socialize.

4.2 Active Listening

We view *active listening* as purposeful, engaged listening such as one might do when attending a musical performance. The purpose for being there is expressly to listen to the music, as opposed to moving to music (which also involves engaged listening) or participating in a nonmusical activity that happens to have music in the background.

All six senior centers offered opportunities for center clients to listen actively to music. Most centers sponsored performances by local musicians around major holidays and for special events such as monthly birthday celebrations. For example, Christmas shows were big draws at the Good Hope Senior Center (North Central region), with over 200 people in attendance. Additionally, some centers were able to obtain grant or special programming funding to support musical performances. As Tracy (Sunnyside Senior Center outreach and development coordinator) explained,

> Musicians play regularly at the center, funded by a grant from the Musicians Union. The Union sponsors six events per year. Attendance is large – usually 50 or 60 people for each event. There are also NCOA [National Council on Aging] programs that work with the Center and the Musicians Union to get performers into the center. They sponsored six performances last year. (Tracy)

Center clients, musical activity directors, and musical groups also volunteered regularly to provide concerts as listening opportunities for others. One such example was Lulu, a beloved 96-year-old Black female client of Good Hope Senior Center, who had recently learned to play electric bass and regularly performed mini-concerts with a small combo on the center's multipurpose room stage. Large crowds of center attendees gathered to listen to her music. Concerts were also provided by Nick (Good Hope Senior Center office manager and guitar instructor), who had a parallel career as a performer of the hits of "iconic solo male artists of the 50s, 60s, and 70s" (e.g., the music of Elvis Presley, Tom Jones, Neil Diamond, Johnny Cash, etc.). Nick actually looked like an Elvis impersonator, with long sideburns and dark brown hair combed back in a 1950s-style pompadour. He enjoyed performing music of this genre as well as "ballroom-style songs" for center audiences. Good Hope Senior Center also had a chorus that periodically performed patriotic music and music of the 1930s, 1950s, and 1960s in concerts for center clientele.

4.3 Movement to Music

The senior centers we visited also offered classes and other opportunities centering around purposeful and deliberate movement to music, which also necessitated a level of engaged listening. Various types of dance classes were offered, such as line dance, tap dance, round dance, ballroom dance, Latin dance, and Middle Eastern dance. Community social dances were also held as special center events. These sometimes featured a specific genre of music and dance, such as country (line dancing, square dancing, regional dance styles including the Texas two-step), dance band music (swing dancing and ballroom dance), or rock and roll (various styles of dancing). Related to the popularity of specific musical styles at Sunnyside Senior Center, Tracy remarked,

> Sometimes 150 people attend special events such as swing dancing ... There's a stereotypical view that seniors only enjoy dance band music. However, more baby boomers are attending center activities now and they like to "rock out" with events that utilize a DJ. (Tracy)

Senior center staff were sensitive to the fact that not all clients were part of a couple and not all were physically able to dance. As one flyer for a center community dance advertised, "The live bands play at least four line-dance songs [for individual dancers] and one chair dance [for those who have difficulty standing up to dance]." Another center advertised the availability of "dance hosts" to dance with single attendees.

The Senior Place (Southern region) offered an eagerly anticipated "teatime" that provided opportunities for eating, drinking, active listening, and dancing to music. Latin music was performed by an eight-piece combo with an instrumentation of accordion, three guitars, a *charango* (armadillo guitar), maracas, a vocalist, who also played maracas and *guiro* (scraper), and a bongo player, who also played tambourine and cowbell. There was an area with rows of chairs for sitting and listening to the music, an area with tables and chairs where audience members could drink iced tea and eat pizza, and an open area for dancing. Dancing was informal and attendees frequently sang along with the combo as it played. For some of the songs, initially, four to five people (mainly females) got up to dance or clap along. Later, this expanded into groups of more than 10 people dancing together, including a female with a pair of castanets. During one song, even a woman in a wheelchair got up to dance (with help, hands held tightly) after other ladies gravitated toward her! It seemed that the other women knew that the combo was playing her favorite song and that she would like to dance to it. It showed a tight social bonding among them. Teatime ended with several attendees loudly shouting, "*Gracias*!".

Some centers also offered exercise classes that involved deliberate movement to music, such as low-impact aerobics, cardio-dance, and Zumba classes. Mountain View Senior Center (Southwestern region) even offered a chair exercise class in which attendees moved and played maracas to the music. This was quite a spectacle with around 100 pairs of maracas sounding in unison along with the recording!

4.4 Making Music

As mentioned earlier, one of the purposes of our senior center visits was to observe music-making via the musical groups and classes that met in the centers. Fortunately, we were able to observe multiple musical groups and interview many leaders and participants. In some centers we were able to interview leaders of groups or classes that were on hiatus at the time of our visit. In this section, we provide an in-depth look at the music-making activities we discovered, beginning with instrumental activities and progressing to singing activities.

4.4.1 *Instrumental Activities*

Though singing is generally considered to be easily accessible, without the need to purchase or otherwise acquire an instrument, we found it interesting that a majority of the music-making activities offered in the centers we visited were instrumental. These included three concert bands, three ukulele groups, a ukulele class, a jazz band, a polka band, a German band, a harmonica group, two guitar classes, a guitar "jam," and guitar lessons. We noted that most instrumental activities were wind bands or combos with rhythm sections. Stringed-instrument activities involved instruments that were plucked or strummed, such as ukuleles and guitars. Table 4.1

Table 4.1. *Musical groups and classes observed and/or discussed with group leaders*

Group	Location
Choir/Chorus 1*	Good Hope Senior Center, large city, North Central region
Choir/Chorus 2	Better Living Senior Center, large city, Western region
Choir/Chorus 3	Mountain View Senior Center, small city, Southwestern region
Concert Band 1	The Center for Healthy Aging, small city, Eastern region
Concert Band 2	Mountain View Senior Center, small city, Beginner New Horizons Band, Southwestern region
Concert Band 3	Mountain View Senior Center, small city, Advanced New Horizons Band, Southwestern region
German Band	The Center for Healthy Aging, small city, Eastern region
Guitar Class 1*	Good Hope Senior Center, large city, North Central region
Guitar Class 2*	Good Hope Senior Center, large city, North Central region
Guitar Class 3	The Senior Place, mid-sized city, Southern region
Guitar Jam	Better Living Senior Center, large city, Western region
Harmonica Club	Good Hope Senior Center, large city, North Central region
Jazz Band	Mountain View Senior Center, small city, Southwestern region
Karaoke Group 1	Better Living Senior Center, large city, Western region
Karaoke Group 2	The Senior Place, mid-sized city, Southern region
Polka Band	The Center for Healthy Aging, small city, Eastern region
Ukulele Class	Better Living Senior Center, large city, Western region
Ukulele Group 1	Sunnyside Senior Center, mid-sized city, Northwest region
Ukulele Group 2	Sunnyside Senior Center, mid-sized city, Northwest region
Ukulele Group 3	Better Living Senior Center, large city, Western region

An asterisk (*) represents groups or classes that were not observed during our visits but were discussed with their leader(s).

presents an at-a-glance, alphabetical listing of musical groups and classes we observed, discussed, or observed and discussed with their leaders.

The largest instrumental groups we observed were the three concert bands. The rehearsal home of the first was the Center for Healthy Aging (Eastern region). The other two concert bands constituted a beginning band and an advanced band and rehearsed in Mountain View Senior Center (Southwestern region).

4.4.1.1 *Concert Band 1 (The Center for Healthy Aging, Eastern Region)*

Xander, the band's director, described it as "a marvelous community band." The band rehearsed once weekly for two hours at the Center for Healthy Aging. The minimum age for joining the band was 62. Its oldest member was a 94-year-old Portuguese immigrant, who came from a family of professional musicians. According to Xander, very few concert bands for older adults existed in the state in which this senior center was located. This particular band began with 10 members several years ago and rapidly grew to 40 members. In his 60s, Xander was retired from a career as a professional musician. His wife, also a retired musician, was the band's vocalist. The band also had an assistant director who was recently retired from a career as a local high school band director. The band's most prominent performances to date had been at the statehouse in the capital city of the same state.

As with older adult musical groups we had observed in our previous research (Fung & Lehmberg, 2016), members showed their dedication to the group by arriving to rehearsal early, even though they could not warm up because another musical group that rehearsed right before them was still playing on the other side of the room. On the day of observation, Udell, a flute player, was in her seat and ready to go 35 minutes early. The concert band director also arrived quite early and set up the band on the far side of the room, while the previous group, a German band, was finishing rehearsal. As they trickled in, concert band members set up folding music stands they had brought from home.

Udell also seemed to be dedicated to supporting the center's small instrumental combos, even though she was not a member of those. A drummer who had missed a polka band rehearsal earlier in the day poked his head into the rehearsal room and she berated him for his absence, saying several times, "They didn't have a drummer – you're it!"

The rehearsal appeared to be well organized, with the order of musical pieces and announcements posted on a large chart at the front of the room. It was also older adult–friendly in that everyone was sitting for the rehearsal – including the percussionists – except for one bass drummer who stood and leaned on his drum as he played. The director was flexible regarding band members' capabilities with regard to tuning, endurance, and attentiveness.

After the first piece, the band tuned to a B-flat given by the first clarinet. It was sharp in pitch and the tuba was not able to tune to that level of sharpness. No one seemed to mind, and the rehearsal proceeded. Xander, the director, ran through each piece with few stops for corrections or comments, then gave a brief break and said, "Do it again." The second time was generally much better. At the request of band members, Xander lowered the volume of the sound system used by the band's vocalist, which reduced the level of distortion and allowed the instrumentalists to hear more clearly. It was interesting to note that the bassoon player brought knitting for the times she was not playing!

Even though the Center for Healthy Aging served a diverse population, all band members except one were White. Group members appeared to be of varying socioeconomic strata, but this had no effect on their camaraderie or ability to enjoy each other's company. In general, the band members seemed to like joking around with each other. For example, one percussionist wore a silly Halloween hat that the others enjoyed and kidded him about. Other band members were talking as they entered the rehearsal room and asking each other how it was going. One older band member jokingly replied, "The first hundred years are the hardest, then after that..." This remark elicited smiles all around.

4.4.1.2   Concert Bands 2 and 3 (Mountain View Senior Center, Southwestern Region)
Two concert bands, a beginner band and an advanced band, rehearsed in a multipurpose room at Mountain View Senior Center. Both were New Horizons groups, meaning that they were affiliated with the New Horizons International Music Association (NHIMA), an international nonprofit organization whose goals were to (a) expand music-making opportunities for adults, particularly older adults, (b) foster a positive atmosphere for the creation of new adult musical groups, and (c) provide services to Association members and adult musical groups, including, but not limited to, newsletters, information and discounts on adult music camps, communication and visits to other New Horizons groups, and so forth (NHIMA, n.d.).

Elizabeth, the director of the bands, was a member of the music education faculty of a nearby university. At the time of the visit, she had been leading these bands for 19 years. Elizabeth noted that the bands performed infrequently, but she believed the process of learning, the experience of music, and the social aspect of music-making were more important than the product in the form of a performance for an audience. She also shared that she kept leading the bands because she loved people and loved making music with them. She described herself as "a band director at heart."

A majority of band members appeared to be White, even though this senior center served a population of White and Latino users. However, one of the rehearsal assistants was Latino. He was born in Mexico but raised in the United States.

Similar to Concert Band 1 from the Eastern region, members of these two bands in the Southwestern region appeared to have a culture of arriving early to rehearsal. Elizabeth, two assistants, and a few band members arrived at least 25 minutes early to set up for the beginner band rehearsal, which began promptly on time.

The beginner band, had 15 members, rehearsed first and then divided into three groups for lessons. The largest and most advanced group was led by Elizabeth, the band's director, and consisted of 11 players: a mix of 10 players on various woodwinds and one trombonist. This group utilized a commonly used beginning band method book series, and for this rehearsal focused on articulations using half, quarter, and eighth notes and rests, as well as scales and phrasing. The processes were typical of a beginning band rehearsal: learning by rote, notation reading, and so forth. Skills were accumulative, sequential, and director-directed. Elizabeth made the exercises fun for the players. The second group (two alto saxophone players) was led by a graduate student assistant in the hallway outside the multipurpose room. They were working on the familiar tune *Mary Had a Little Lamb*. The assistant tried to facilitate an inclusive rehearsal culture by saying, "It's okay to make a mistake here." However, one saxophonist responded, "It's okay [to make a mistake] at home, but it feels different here." This showed that they were taking the rehearsal more seriously than practicing the instrument alone at home. A third group rehearsed in a separate area and consisted of two snare drummers led by another rehearsal assistant. They were working on three types of strokes: single, double, and buzz. Overall, the older adult learners were highly motivated and attentive. They observed, asked questions, and responded to questions with great enthusiasm.

The rehearsal of the advanced band began promptly after the beginner band finished. This group was larger and rehearsed in the same spacious room with a high ceiling, necessitating that the director use a microphone when speaking to the band. In all there were 40 players and two assistants present in addition to Elizabeth. The instrumentation included four flutes, nine soprano clarinets, two bass clarinets, eight alto saxophones (including one younger player), two horns, three trumpets, four trombones, one euphonium, one tuba, six percussionists, and two assistants (one helping on alto saxophone and the other helping with scores and parts). Of the older adult participants, 17 were female and 22 were male.

Elizabeth warmed up the band with a call-and-response activity in which she played different scales and arpeggios on her flute with the band responding by imitating each pattern. Players seemed to enjoy the challenge of this activity. She then began to rehearse the band's pieces, stopping the music immediately after an error was detected. Elizabeth's approach was fun, cheerful, and supportive as she gave directions and corrections, making the rehearsal enjoyable and relaxing for participants. Some examples of her comments were as follows:

- "Double check the key signature."
- "Some interesting notes in there." [referring to wrong notes]
- "Yeah, that's the right idea." [sort of there but not quite]
- "When you are the melody, bring it out. If you are not the melody, you support gently. . . . Thank you for supporting the whole notes gently."
- "Lay back, don't get too excited at the end. Enjoy it! [the music]." (Elizabeth)

The band's repertoire on the day of the visit (in September) included arrangements of *Santa Baby*, *All I Want for Christmas Is You*, and *Do You Hear What I Hear?* as well as original band compositions such as *Fantasy on a Burgundian Carol*, *Fantasy on a Fiddle Tune*, and the traditional Karl King march *Alamo*. Overall, the players appeared to be very attentive and knew when and what to play. They paid acute attention and were ready to follow Elizabeth's direction at all times. Seeing this high level of concentration and readiness in a large group of older adults was impressive.

4.4.1.3   Jazz Band (Mountain View Senior Center, Southwestern Region)
Also at Mountain View, the Young at Heart Jazz Band rehearsed in the multipurpose room. As with many of the other ensembles we observed, the dedication of members was evident in their early arrival to set up the band. This involved moving speakers, music and speaker stands, a sound system, musical instruments, and other equipment on carts. Once the equipment was in place, the five band members who helped with setup began warming up. Other members trickled in one by one. Henry, a White male clarinetist in the New Horizons band and saxophonist in the jazz band, had an interesting musical history. Henry was 91 and had been a career musician. He proudly displayed his unique saxophone made of plastic in the 1940s, when plastic first appeared. It actually sounded pretty good, but Henry intimated that it would break easily if dropped. Approximately 1,000 were manufactured, but only a few were left. Henry remarked that "you probably will see something like this in a museum." Apparently, Charlie Parker, the infamous bebop saxophonist, played the same model. No microphone was necessary for it to be heard in any group, even a rock group!

The jazz band included seven males and four females with the following instrumentation: one vocalist, one clarinet/alto saxophone double, one alto saxophone, two tenor saxophones, one baritone saxophone, one trumpet/

vocalist double, one trombone, one keyboard, one electric bass, and one drum set. Tony, the trumpet player and one of the vocalists, was also the group's leader. He held bachelor's and master's degrees in music education from a highly respected university and had taught music in public schools for 30 years (he was age 76 at the time). Tony's daughter was also in the band, and he referred to her as "the jam singer." Tony appeared to be well prepared for the rehearsal with a list of passages to be rehearsed, which displayed a professional level of sophistication.

The first chart was *Charade* (from the 1960s film of the same name), which was slow and soothing. On solos where players needed help, Tony provided support verbally or with his trumpet. He mentioned that they were preparing a program for a dance, reminding the players, "Got to slow down for the dancers." The next spot to be rehearsed was measure 44 in the early Chicago-style jazz tune *Do You Know What It Means to Miss New Orleans?* The rehearsal continued with Tony moving from piece to piece to rehearse specific passages. Throughout the rehearsal other center clients occasionally dropped in to listen. The rehearsal ended with *Summertime* (from the opera *Porgy and Bess*). Members displayed a high level of endurance, considering that the band had been rehearsing for approximately two hours at this point. Everyone was extremely attentive and totally dedicated to the rehearsal. The level of playing and expressive quality of the group was quite impressive. They also displayed a high level of *ensemble-ship*: listening to each other, hanging together as a group.

4.4.1.4 German and Polka Bands (The Center for Healthy Aging, Eastern Region)

Turning our attention back to the Center for Healthy Aging, two smaller combos – a German band and a polka band – also rehearsed in this senior center. The combos were similar in instrumentation; both had an accordion (same player in both bands), drum set, clarinet(s), and a baritone horn (euphonium). The German band additionally had a trumpet and a tuba, and the polka band also had an alto saxophone. Even though this center served a diverse population of older adults, members of both combos were White. The oldest player in the combos was Maurycy, the accordion player, who was 85 years old.

Musical selections were similar across both combos: polkas, waltzes, and "old-timey" tunes; however, the German band also played several tunes with German titles, such as *Die Lorelei* (The Lorelei, a song about a mermaid; played as a ländler, or slow waltz in 3/8 time), a polka titled *Trinken Immer Eine Tropchen* (*Always Drink a Drop*, sometimes translated as *Have Another Drink*), and the German drinking song *Ein Heller und Ein Batzen* (*A Penny and a Dime*), played in the style of a polka.

The leaders of both combos were volunteers who played in the groups and whose responsibilities included maintaining the music folders, starting and stopping each tune, and rehearsal setup and tear-down. Like the concert band in this center, rehearsals mainly consisted of running through tunes without stopping unless someone got lost or the piece fell apart. Tuning was approximate but no one seemed to care. Group members seemed to be very accepting of everyone's abilities.

One quality of these groups that was not to be missed and caused them to stand out from some of the other groups we observed was the incredible amount of fun they seemed to have in rehearsals. Every break between tunes was punctuated with kidding and raucous belly laughs! For example, Ulysses, the group leader, stopped to tell how he had missed the German word for head (*kopf*) in a crossword puzzle that morning and asked if somebody else now wanted to lead the German band. Everyone laughed. The saxophone player replied, "Just drink a little schnapps and it'll all come back!" Loud laughter ensued. Other examples of humorous comments (both verbal and musical) that elicited smiles and laughter were as follows:

- Trombone player whose slide was sticking: "Got to get a little slide oil – not working well." Trumpet player: "With a little STP in it!" Leader: "A little WD-40!"
- Trumpet player while cleaning his horn: "Brass players who don't clean their horns get sick!" Trombone player: "I'm afraid to clean my horn – don't know what might come out!"
- Baritone player sitting in front of the large plate-glass windows in the rehearsal room: "The sun feels so good on my back. I guess that means I'm a senior!" [He looked much younger than the other band members.]
- Trombone player who got lost in the trio section of a waltz: "I can't fake it like I used to." Tuba player: "How long ago was it that you could?"
- At the end of the rehearsal the German band leader said, "Thanks, that was a great rehearsal!" The baritone player then broke into *The Happy Wanderer* and others joined in for one chorus. The leader subsequently reminded them to keep their music in order and began to pick up the music. The trumpet player then broke into *I Can't Get Started*. There were grins all around.

Overall, group members seemed to be quite happy to be there and fun-loving in nature. They enjoyed having a place to play together and a group of which to be a part. This type of joyous and funny ambience would be hard to replicate for older adults who stayed at home alone.

4.4.1.5   Harmonica Club (Good Hope Senior Center, North Central Region)
The harmonica club that rehearsed at Good Hope Senior Center stood out as one of the more unusual musical groups we visited. The group rehearsed at the senior center and performed for donations at local and regional assisted living facilities, senior centers, for parties and other special events, and at a yearly harmonica festival held in the state where this center was located. The club was formed in 1976 and had approximately 30 members at the time of observation. There was one guitar in the group and several types and sizes of harmonicas. These included diatonic harmonicas; a chord harmonica built on the circle of fifths that was able to play major, dominant seventh, minor, and diminished chords (i.e., capability to play 48 different chords); and a chromatic harmonica with a button that raised pitches by a half step.

Ages of group members ranged from the 50s to the 90s; however, most members were in their 70s or 80s. All were White, even though the senior center was located in an area that was quite culturally diverse. One member was female; the rest were males.

Neil, the group leader, shared that the group played "old-timey tunes written prior to 1960." He described the group as an "ear group" but also remarked, "I can read the spots" (i.e., music notation). The group was open to anyone who wanted to join. As Neil described,

> Everyone is welcome, whatever [harmonica] you play. The members choose and create their own parts [by ear]. There is cooperationship [*sic*]. Members grow in their own directions within the group. (Neil, harmonica club leader)

Stan, the harmonica club's guitarist, described the group's weekly meetings as follows:

> It's a rehearsal jam. Eight to 10 people sit around a table at the senior center. We go around the group and everyone chooses a song, and we keep at it until it's good. A few players use sheet music when the song is difficult. Some are able to play in all keys on a C chromatic harmonica. Others have a lot of harmonicas – one for each key. (Stan)

Stan smiled and winked as he described the procedure for working someone into the group's performances. "First, they come [to the rehearsal] to play. When they are good enough, we invite them to come to a gig and play. If things go well [at the gig], we give them a microphone. Eventually, we plug it in [Stan laughed out loud]!"

The conversation then returned to Neil, who went on to explain that they never knew how many club members would show up at a gig, but Stan had to attend every gig because he was the only guitar player and provided the underlying harmony for the group. Neil owned the sound system, so he had to show up, too. Everyone had their own individual microphone. Neil, who played chord harmonica, had a chest harness complete with a boom and clip for his mic. This was because his chord harmonica was so large that it took both hands to play.

The observation of this group happened to take place on a "gig night," which both group members and the researcher (Lisa Lehmberg) found to be exciting! Six players (five harmonicas, one guitar) were in attendance. The event included a 30-minute rehearsal and sound check, followed by a 60-minute performance for independent, older adult residents of apartments within a local senior living community. The performance was held in a large, carpeted multipurpose room in the main building. Around 25 older adult females were in attendance. A majority were White, but some Black females were present as well. All appeared to be of middle-class socioeconomic status. Audience members seemed to greatly enjoy the performance, particularly the patriotic and state university tunes.

The group had a charming sound resembling carousel or hurdy-gurdy music. The guitarist played a bass line and chords simultaneously (including beautifully voiced, altered chords), which was quite impressive!

Most of the tunes the group performed on this evening were up-tempo. Twenty-three tunes were performed, including favorites such as *Beer Barrel Polka*, *Sentimental Journey*, and medleys of American folk and patriotic songs, to which audience members sang and clapped. Group members appeared to be very kind and welcoming – inclusive of both each other and the audience. Humor was evident in funny verses added to some of the tunes. An example was when the group invited audience requests and one attendee asked for the tune *Let Me Call You Sweetheart*. An ad hoc verse (not in the original) was added on at the end:

Don't you call me sweetheart, I don't love you anymore.
Since I saw you necking with the boy next door.
I will find another, whom I'll like quite well. [The word well was held
   out a long time with the group leader looking expectantly at the audience.]
Don't you call me sweetheart, you can go to hell!

Attendees and group members seemed to really enjoy this, and all joined together with gusto on the last phrase!

4.4.1.6   Guitar Classes 1 and 2 (Good Hope Senior Center, North Central Region)

Good Hope's guitar classes were on hiatus at the time of our visit; however, Nick, the guitar teacher and office manager, was available to share some information. He recalled that the original acoustic guitar class at the center began with two to four attendees and transformed into a much larger group with a jam session format. Since the inception of the first class, the center also added a second basic acoustic guitar class for adults with intellectual disabilities who lived in group home facilities and attended daily work skills programs.

The guitar classes at the center focused on forming chords. Nick utilized Chord Buddy devices (chordbuddy.com) for those who had trouble moving their hands. The Chord Buddy devices attached to the necks of guitars and helped form the chords so players could make music more quickly and easily. The downside of this was that due to the limitations of the devices, everything had to be played in the key to G. Thus, Nick's original Monday morning guitar class became known as "Guitar Jam in G."

Nick referred to the original guitar class for older adults as "almost like a fellowship group" in which attendees interacted, talked, and played songs. He reported that class members "love to perform for the center and *light up* when they do so." He believed that their performances were self-validating. Nick cited his reasons for teaching the classes as "mercenary at first." He needed money (this was before he accepted the position of center office manager) and it offered six hours of paid work per week, divided over two days. However, he shared that he now taught the classes primarily because of the camaraderie and relationships he had developed with the older adult participants. At the time of his interview, Nick was paid for his work as both the office manager and the guitar instructor.

4.4.1.7   Guitar Class 3 (The Senior Place, Southern Region)

This acoustic guitar class was held in a medium-sized room near the entrance of The Senior Place. Cultural diversity was clearly evident in this class. Sebastian, the 84-year-old teacher of the class and a native of Puerto Rico, spoke three languages: English, Spanish, and German (his wife was German). Sebastian shared that he sang and played several instruments (guitar, drums, maracas, and accordion) and had performed on television in Puerto Rico, and that he had worked as a policeman and as a printer in the United States. The two students in the class were Filipino females who spoke both English and Tagalog.

The focus of the class was singing and playing popular songs. Guitars were played with a mixture of strumming and picking. Students learned songs by ear and via the use of tab notation. Sebastian (the teacher) played by ear and did not read musical notation. Approximately 15 songs were covered during the 60-minute class. These were a mix of popular and ethnic styles, including *And I Love You So* (Elvis Presley), *Jamaica Farewell* (Harry Belafonte), *Sloop John B* (Beach Boys), *Bésame Mucho* (Consuelo Velásquez), and *I Walk the Line* (Johnny Cash). Sebastian led and the students followed. He gave occasional reminders and modeled how to play specific notes and chords. The class ended with everyone putting instruments and music away in a hurry to attend the eagerly anticipated center "teatime" (described earlier in the chapter) that featured a Latin combo with food, iced tea, dancing, and socialization.

4.4.1.8 Guitar Jam (Better Living Senior Center, Western Region)

The guitar jam met in a doorless room on the mezzanine level of the Better Living Senior Center. The group was culturally diverse, as was this senior center's clientele. Members included six males of White (3), Latino (1), Black (1), and Asian (1) ethnicity and one Asian female. One member played cello and acoustic guitar. Other instruments included an electric bass, an electric guitar, and four acoustic guitars. Most of the instruments looked well-used and rather old.

The group played mostly Beatles songs during their 90-minute rehearsal. The rehearsal was informal, with some group members coming and going during this time. Members utilized strumming and tab notation, with everyone singing along as they played. Songs that did not go as well as expected were repeated for improvement.

4.4.1.9 Ukulele Groups 1 and 2 (Sunnyside Senior Center, Northwest Region)

At the time of the visit, the ukulele groups at Sunnyside Senior Center had been in existence for five years and appeared to be hugely popular with group members, center clients, and center staff alike. We learned that the initial organizational meeting of the ukulele group had eight older adults in attendance including the two group leaders. There happened to be an article about the group in the city newspaper the next day, which resulted in 20 to 30 people attending the second group meeting. The group quickly got so large that it had to be split into two groups to fit into the center's available space. As of this writing, the groups had their own Facebook page and had posted several videos of their performances on YouTube.

Tracy, the outreach and development coordinator of the senior center, described the ukulele groups as having fluid entry points and being welcoming to newcomers. Brooke, the executive director, corroborated this, commenting on the benefits and dedication of the groups and why she was thankful that they were happening in this center:

> The ukulele club is an incredible program! There's a sense of community and it provides a creative outlet. The ukulele attendees show up even on terrible weather days. They bring a lot to the center – to those who don't make music as well. (Brooke)

Brooke also mentioned that as ukulele group members learned more about the center, they became more involved in other center activities. She proudly promoted the ukulele groups as showpieces whenever community members or officials visited, because the groups dispelled negative stereotypical images of older adults.

The two ukulele groups were co-directed by Les and Laurie, a husband-and-wife team. Les was a professional musician who had his own band. He led the groups through the weekly set of tunes, offering advice for forming chords, fingering, and strumming as needed. Laurie was less-experienced than Les as a musician but still helped to lead the group and took responsibility for the organization of the weekly group "jams." For example, she searched online for new charts (songs) for the group, made photocopies of these, and organized and brought to the jams a large plastic tote containing extra hard copies of music. She bought the paper herself and then used the center's copy machine at no cost. Les and Laurie also maintained an online, secure, file-storage account for the ukulele groups. Members supplied their emails and were granted access to pdf files of the groups' repertoire. The groups played for different community organizations and events such as nursing homes, senior centers, birthday parties, and a large, regional ukulele gathering. They donated any funds they received for performances to a matching grant program they had created that provided ukuleles for elementary school children.

The weekly jams had a fluid-entry-point, drop-in-and-out-at-free-will format, but most attendees were regulars. Each group met once weekly (on Tuesday or Thursday) on the small, crowded stage in Sunnyside Senior Center's multipurpose room. Groups were limited to 20 attendees per session because of city fire regulations. Laurie liked the small size of the groups, explaining, "That way, you can hear yourself play a little more." The low ceiling on the stage also added intimacy to the group jams.

Though this center was in a culturally diverse area of its surrounding city, the ukulele groups appeared to be largely homogeneous. The Tuesday jam had 15 attendees. Fourteen appeared to be White (including the leaders) and one appeared to be Asian, perhaps Vietnamese since there was a large Vietnamese population in the neighborhood surrounding the center. Most seemed to be in their 70s with a few appearing to be younger – possibly in their 60s. There were 11 attendees at the Thursday jam (not including the group leaders). Ten were female and one was male. Nine of the 10 females appeared to be White (as were the leaders) and one was Asian. The lone male attendee appeared to be White. The group also included two "out" lesbians.

Everyone in the groups played ukulele except for one member who played a banjolele. The leaders remarked that the Tuesday group also had a member who yodeled and played harmonica, spoons, and washboard, but that member was ill at the time and absent from the weekly jam.

Laurie and a few group members creatively used "found sounds" to add the timbre of percussion to the groups' music. For example, Laurie wrapped a dollar bill loosely around the strings and neck of her ukulele and held the ends together at the back of the neck as she played one song. When asked about this later, she replied that the dollar bill deadened the sound of the strings so that when she strummed her ukulele, it sounded more like a washboard (percussion instrument) and "added color." Some others got the same effect by muting all strings loosely with their fingers and strumming on all strings simultaneously. This reflected their use of an unconventional and creative strategy to achieve their musical goal.

Group members also added variety to their sound by alternating between ukuleles and kazoos on choruses and verses of the old standard, *Has Anybody Seen My Gal?* Some very funky-looking kazoo holders were evident in the group! They were bendable and coated with a rubbery material. Apparently Les had fashioned them out of gear ties purchased from a sporting goods store.

The rehearsal format and processes were similar and well-organized across groups. Most attendees had their own folding music stands and large individual notebooks with hard copies of lyrics and chord symbols for the groups' songs; no musical notation was evident. A few members had downloaded their chord charts to tablet devices and played from those. On our designated observation days, the jams began with announcements and introductions. Les then went into a riff and everyone joined in singing and playing the New Orleans Mardi Gras song *Iko Iko* in call-and-response fashion. The rehearsal process consisted mainly of running through many songs, but Les and Laurie stopped the groups to discuss playing techniques and instructed when things went wrong. This included reviewing chords and explaining and demonstrating finger positions, with time given for everyone to try them out. Repertoire consisted of older popular standards (e.g., *Ain't Love a Lot Like That?*), classic rock songs (e.g., *I Feel Fine*), island songs (e.g., *Honolulu Baby*), blues standards (e.g., *Hesitation Blues*), and novelty songs (e.g., *Chocolate Jesus*). In the last 10 minutes of the rehearsal, Les asked participants, "What do you want to do?" Group members then suggested old favorites or new songs to try.

The culture of the groups seemed welcoming, open, and flexible. To keep the weekly jams low-pressure, Les and Laurie made a point of *not* sending out weekly playlists ahead of time. This allowed participants to "go with the flow" and not be overly concerned with advance preparation. Group members participated on their own levels and appeared smiling and relaxed. Some sang with much feeling as they played; others played without singing. Most of the singing was in unison, but every now and then a participant might harmonize the melody. Strums tended to be simple and on the beat. Various techniques were evident in the strums: some strummed with the thumb only; some used the index finger only; and others used both the thumb and index finger. Additionally, some strummed right over the tone hole and others strummed further up the fingerboard. Though the group culture was supportive, members were strongly encouraged by the leaders to "own" their own participation. For example, they were required to go to the group's secure online storage account to access and download the music, print it or put it on a tablet device, bring their music and a folding stand to the jam session, and practice on their own.

Like the instrumental combos described earlier, an overarching quality of the ukulele groups' culture was the immense enjoyment that was evidenced in the jams. There was a great deal of kidding back and forth, and humor was incorporated into the songs they played. One example occurred in the classic rock song *Bread and Butter*, when Les did the characteristic falsetto on the lyrics, "I like bread and butter. I like toast and jam." Immediately afterward, he began coughing and then cleared his throat and quipped, "That's the only way I can get that stuff outta there!" At that point, another participant said with a big smile, "Another benefit of music!" Group members laughed together about that.

Other examples of humor across groups consisted of "characteristic" endings to some of the songs. For example, on the final beat of the songs

Hesitation Blues and *Ridin' Down the Canyon*, two or three female group members jumped straight up in the air from their seats, plopped back down hard on their behinds, and yelled, "Yeah!" on the last beat of the song. This might have been instigated by Laurie, who was observed doing a solo "seat plop" in a couple of other tunes.

While the jams were going on on the stage, other center attendees also congregated on the main floor of the multipurpose room to play cards, knit, and read. Several were listening and tapping the table where they were sitting in time to the beat of the music.

Overall, the two ukulele groups seemed to make important contributions to the center's identity. They enhanced not only the quality of life of group members, but through their music also indirectly the quality of life of other center clients and staff.

4.4.1.10   Ukulele Class (Better Living Senior Center, Western Region)

The Better Living Senior Center was located in a city with a large Asian population, and it was evident in our observations that some center activities were clearly preferred by Asians, such as mahjong, karaoke, learning Mandarin, line dance, and other types of dance. Likewise, there were also activities clearly preferred by Whites, such as bridge. Some activities, such as ukulele, tended to be preferred by a mix of center clients.

Similar to Sunnyside Senior Center, the Better Living Senior Center had a ukulele group that rehearsed weekly. However, this site also had a ukulele class that met immediately prior to the weekly group rehearsal and was geared toward ukulele group members who desired to play and learn more. On the day of our visit, this class started small with only a few attendees present; however, more and more people arrived and joined in as the ukulele group rehearsal time drew near. An hour before the rehearsal began, sporadic ukulele and singing sounds could be heard coming from the common room on the mezzanine level. Five ukulele players were already playing in the room and five more arrived in the next 20 minutes. Some were trying out songs from tabs, while they waited for bingo to finish in the nearby ballroom. By the time the rehearsal was 15 minutes away, the common room was totally full, with no empty chairs and hardly any space for more ukulele players. By the end of the class, thirteen ukulele players and one electric bass player were in attendance. The cultural makeup of the class was nine White attendees (five females and four males, including the White male facilitator) and five Asian attendees (three males and two females). They strummed and sang *I'd Like to Teach the World to Strum* (aka., *I'd Like to Teach the World to Sing*). The leader introduced a slack key tuning, in which he loosened some strings to tune them differently to make some chords easier to play. "I noted that the class generally played in tune and together. It sounded nice!" (Victor Fung, researcher notes). A few minutes before the ukulele group rehearsal began, all 14 players moved across the hall to the ballroom, which was transformed from a bingo setup to a circle of 25 chairs with ukulele players in a blink of an eye.

4.4.1.11   *Ukulele Group 3 (Better Living Senior Center, Western Region)*
After 15 minutes of setting up, the group was ready to start. The leader (a Filipino male) and the electric bass player (a White male) sat at the head of the circle. Aside from the leaders, the group comprised six Asian males (mostly Chinese, but including one Hawaiian), five Asian females (Chinese), three White males, and six White females.

Each player had three color-coded binders: blue for Hawaiian songs, red for oldies, and yellow for rock and roll songs. Favorite songs were marked with tabs. Some players used a music stand to hold their binders; others used another chair across from themselves to support their binders. The leader displayed a small whiteboard with tab notation for G, G6, and G7 chords. The group had two amplified instruments: the leader's ukulele and the electric bass.

The leader had been facilitating this group since 2007. He greeted everyone with an enthusiastic "*Aloha!*" and continued to speak and sing through a microphone for the remainder of the rehearsal. Rehearsal processes were organized and effective, with the leader calling the tunes and giving specific instructions for each song, such as "take the pinky away [while demonstrating this], now put the pinky back down. . . ." or "this place goes up to the 10th fret, and slide back. . . ." He also interjected humor as he taught. For example, in the tune "YMCA" he joked about MACY (as in the department store chain) being YMCA "spelled wrong." He clearly displayed solid techniques on his instrument. Because it was amplified, it also served to override many of the less competent sounds in the group.

Slack key tuning came up again with this larger group, with the leader explaining how it worked for F, G7, G, and C chords. He also suggested that players should get an extra instrument and leave that in slack tuning, so they would not have to tune back and forth between traditional and slack tunings. The group eventually returned to traditional tuning and more songs, but not in time for a couple of audience members. After the leader had been explaining the slack chords for a while, a White couple who had been sitting at the back of the room (i.e., just listening in at this rehearsal) walked out as if they were disappointed that they couldn't hear the group play very much. As they were walking out, the wife said, "How about *Goodnight, Irene?*" as if they would like to make a request for the group to play and sing that song. This was one of many incidences in which we found that the participation and impact of a musical group in a senior center went beyond the participating group members. Others who didn't participate in making music had expectations, too.

Most players were able to follow along with the rehearsal, singing and concentrating hard on strumming their own instrument. Some looked at the leader, paying close attention to his techniques (i.e., learning by watching). Players were also inclusive of others, helping each other if someone fell behind. This type of camaraderie was not uncommon in other musical groups we visited as well.

Near the end of the rehearsal, the leader passed the microphone in a clockwise direction so players could take turns in choosing and leading a song. The rehearsal ended with what appeared to be a customary closing ritual. The leader sang a sustained pitch, waiting for others to join in. Everyone then joined hands in a circle inside the circle of chairs and sang *Aloha 'Oe* in Hawaiian. Everyone in the group knew the song. They raised hands at the end and said "*Aloha!*" After a round of applause, everyone packed up and departed. This small ritual clearly showed the camaraderie within the group and a supportive context of the Hawaiian culture for the ukulele.

The instrumental activities we observed in the six senior centers showed a considerable amount of breadth and depth. The breadth was found in the variety of groups, from concert and jazz bands to harmonica to ukulele groups, and in the participants' level of expertise, from retired professional musicians to beginners. Also, the impact of these groups could go far beyond the members of the group, to other center clients and into the local community. If they shared their performances via the Internet, there was also a potential to influence a global community. The depth was mainly reflected in the deep meanings, socialization, and quality of life as gained by participating in these groups.

4.4.2   Singing Activities

Singing activities across the six centers we visited were in the form of three choirs or choruses and two karaoke groups. We were able to observe all of these except for the Good Hope Senior Center choir, which was on hiatus when we visited.

4.4.2.1 Choir/Chorus 1 (Good Hope Senior Center, North Central Region)

The center chorus met weekly during the fall, winter, and spring months but was on summer recess at the time of our visit. However, we were able to learn about the chorus via an interview with its director. Rebecca was retired from a career as a public school teacher and had been involved in music (e.g., piano lessons and participation in various choirs) throughout her life. She had been a member of the Good Hope Senior Center chorus for seven years and had served as its director for two years.

From Rebecca we learned that the chorus generally performed music from the 1930s, 1950s, and 1960s. The chorus year began in September with a "meet and greet." Members received their folders at that time and took them home. They returned one week later to begin rehearsals. Rebecca shared that there were many widows and widowers in the group and that in addition to musical direction she provided a substantial amount of social support for group members.

Chorus repertoire during the months prior to our visit included older popular standards such as *Side By Side*, *All I Have to Do Is Dream*, and *Always*, as well as Broadway musical songs such as *Climb Every Mountain* and *Getting to Know You*. Rebecca teared up and shook her head sadly as she mentioned that the chorus was also working on a song for detained immigrant children at the US border. Yearly performances included the senior center talent show (for which the chorus performed three songs), a Veteran's Day concert, and a Memorial Day concert. The latter two events also were accompanied by the recitation of poems and the sharing of chorus members' experiences as veterans or with veterans they knew. Rebecca went on to share that some chorus members had health problems. She recalled one year when none of the members could stand to sing – everyone sat in a chair to rehearse and perform. Rebecca believed that music helped to "get seniors out and doing something. It keeps their brain going. They function better and feel like they have a purpose and place to belong." She enthusiastically remarked, "I enjoy directing them – like to see their faces light up! I enjoy it."

Nicole, center manager, also commented on the importance of the choir in participants' lives:

> We almost lost the choir after the [former] director died. Choir folks don't come to the center for anything else. They live for the choir. They can do it no matter their age because they carry their instrument with them. So important for the participants. It builds connection and community. (Nicole)

She also emphasized the importance of the choir for center clients who were not music participants. Once again, it was not just the music-makers who benefited from the musical activities. "Music crosses all lines, borders, barriers. Even if they [center attendees] don't understand your language, they smile when someone sings."

4.4.2.2   Choir/Chorus 2 (Better Living Senior Center, Western Region)

This senior chorus was the center's largest class and the largest group we observed with 150 registrants. The size of the group necessitated that it rehearsed in the center's ballroom, the largest room in the center. The choir setup had been prepared the previous day and included eight chairs in each of 14 rows.

Like many of the other groups we observed, members tended to arrive very early. Forty-five minutes before the rehearsal began, there were already more than 10 people in the ballroom. They busied themselves with getting coffee, tea, and other refreshments ready, as well as laying out folders. Each folder contained the choir's songbook of 684 songs with lyrics and with no musical notation, chord symbols, or tabs. Visitors were handed a guest songbook, with the explanation that all the songs were numbered, and assurances such as, "You'll be fine. Just refer to the number that the song leader calls out." Early arriving chorus members also helped to set out seven sign-in sheets with 150 printed names and 10 spaces for write-in names of guests at the end. Each name had series of checkboxes after it and participants just checked off their names for the appropriate week as they arrived. It was hard to find an unchecked box. Participants continued to drift in and took their preferred seats as the rehearsal time drew nearer.

Everyone was friendly and welcoming. "I was inadvertently sitting in one woman's preferred seat as I took notes, and she very kindly let me know that it was her seat" (Victor Fung, researcher). Another woman shared that coffee and tea was available and mentioned that she had walked 38 blocks to get there! A man wearing a baseball cap volunteered, "Most of us know people in here, but we don't know each other's names."

Grace, the group's leader, had been a music education and performance major in college. She had hoped to teach music for her career but instead ended up working first as a communication and writing specialist in the corporate world and then later as an arts grant administrator in the state where the center was located. She had played piano since age 5 and also played clarinet and cello and sang in a church choir. She had been leading this group for four years, and during that time the membership had grown from 65 to 150. We also learned from her that the group had recently recorded a CD.

Fifteen minutes before the rehearsal began, most chairs were filled. Participants had to pre-register to join the group, which was limited to 150 members. On the day of our visit, a majority of participants were female and Asian, with a few Whites in the group. Conversations in Cantonese could be overheard now and then. From the senior center council vice president, we learned that the group's membership was approximately 80% Asian and 20% White. Around 50% were foreign-born, and approximately 33% had earned a college degree. The oldest member of the group was 98 years old.

At the scheduled starting time, a bell rang and everyone grew quiet. By this time only a few seats were left, and extra rows of chairs were being added at the back. Grace made announcements over a microphone at the front of the room and the group's accompanist was at the side ready to play an amplified piano. The first segment of the rehearsal lasted for approximately 30 minutes and included older popular standards such as *Try to Remember* and *I'd Like to Teach the World to Sing*, and Broadway songs such as *All I Ask of You* from *Phantom of the Opera* and *Do Re Mi* from *The Sound of Music*. The rehearsal consisted of more than just running through songs, with attention given to intonation and accuracy. Grace incorporated both music appreciation and theory into the rehearsal. For example, she talked about a fermata, dynamics, the backgrounds of different songs' composers, and other relevant information about the day's songs. The quality of singing was impressive for such a large group; however, intonation was less accurate when there were large leaps and accidentals in the melody. This segment of the rehearsal ended with a birthday song for three participants; however, it was not the customary "Happy Birthday." Instead, the lyrics were as follows:

> *Today is a birthday. I wonder for whom?*
> *I know it's for someone who's right in this room.*
> *So, look all around you for somebody who*
> *Is smiling and happy ... Happy birthday to you!*

Next came a 20-minute break during which participants lined up for refreshments and socialized. At the end of this time, another bell rang and the second half of rehearsal began. This segment was also approximately 30 minutes in length. Half of the group went outside the center with an assistant director to rehearse for an upcoming Sunday event.

Everyone else remained in the ballroom to sing a series of folk songs such as *Red River Valley*, *Clementine*, and *Shenandoah*. The rehearsal ended with *Happy Trails*, the traditional farewell song made famous by the renowned singer, actor, and television host Roy Rogers.

4.4.2.3 Choir/Chorus 3 (Mountain View Senior Center, Southwestern Region) Similar to most of the other senior center ensembles we visited, the members of the Mountain View Senior Center choir began arriving to rehearsal 30 minutes early and socialized in the rehearsal area until the rehearsal began. Participants on this day included 20 female singers and nine male singers. Everyone appeared to be White except for one Black singer who was 88 years old. We learned that the choir regularly reached out to the community via 20 to 25 performances each year, including July 4th and Christmas concerts. After July 4th, they were on hiatus for the remainder of the summer.

The director of the group was Bill, a White male who was retired from a career in information technology at a nearby university. Bill related that he came from a musical family and learned to play the trumpet and guitar at a young age. He had served as a volunteer director of various church and community choirs since his high school days. He shared that he enjoyed directing this choir, loved the people who sang in it, and saw the opportunity as "my way of giving back." Bill's mother-in-law served as the accompanist for the choir.

At the designated rehearsal start time, choir members stopped socializing and settled into chairs with their folders. The 90-minute rehearsal was typical of a choral rehearsal, with singers receiving instructions from Bill. First came warm-up exercises, followed by a run-through of the song *Getting to Know You* (from the musical *The King and I*) in unison. At that point, the choir began to rehearse older popular standards, such as *As Time Goes By* and *I Love You Truly*, in as many as four parts. The objective of the rehearsal was to choose songs for an upcoming performance, and the singers sang seriously, with focus. Bill concentrated on musical elements such as dynamics, repeat signs, and so forth, while marking songs as "yes," "no," or "maybe" for the upcoming performance. He promised to have a draft program for choir members' review and feedback the following week. Halfway through the rehearsal, the choir took a five-minute break.

After the brief break, choir members' enjoyment was revealed increasingly as the milieu became more relaxing, as evidenced in their interactions and reactions to song content. For example, they enjoyed making animal calls and playing woodblock "horse hooves" for the song *Happy Trails*.

They also joked about the lyrics to the Beatles' *When I'm Sixty-Four*, laughingly suggesting that more appropriate lyrics for them would be "When I'm Eighty-four." Bill affirmed that the choir had a strong social element and remarked that it "keeps people alive and brings them happiness." For him there was no question that this singing experience enriched their lives.

4.4.2.4 Karaoke Group 1 (Better Living Senior Center, Western Region)

Across the senior centers we studied, the karaoke groups stood out as attracting a high percentage of older adults of color. The Better Living Senior Center was located in a city with a sizeable Asian population, and this demographic was reflected in its karaoke group. Most members were Chinese, including ethnicities found in mainland China, Hong Kong, and Taiwan, also with a few participants of Chinese descent from Myanmar, Korea, and Indonesia. A few participants of Japanese ethnicity attended as well. The center's website described the group as "a social activity where people get together to sing songs, in both English and Cantonese." However, on the day we visited most songs were sung in Mandarin or Cantonese. Only occasionally was a song sung in English. The group appeared to be immensely popular, as was evidenced in the length of its meeting time on the Thursday: four hours and 15 minutes (from 11:45 a.m. to 4:00 p.m.)!

The leader of the karaoke group was Mandy, an Asian female who spoke Cantonese as a first language. She emigrated to the United States from Hong Kong in the 1960s and started coming to the Better Living Senior Center in 1998 when her husband retired at age 57. She had no musical background other than music classes in elementary school but loved to sing and had been leading this activity since 2006. At the time of our visit, Mandy was learning Mandarin so she could sing Mandarin songs better. She found the karaoke group rewarding because she could help others to be happy through singing. She noted that people enjoyed making friends by singing karaoke at the center and explained that although karaoke can be done at home, to do it at the senior center allowed attendees to learn songs others sang and be introduced to new songs; thus, enriching their personal karaoke repertoire. They could also improve their singing technique by listening to others sing, as well as their understanding of musical key centers and vocal ranges, so they would know how to adjust their own karaoke machine at home.

The karaoke room was small, comfortably accommodating around 30 participants. Two mahjong tables were set up in the common room outside of the karaoke room. The atmosphere was casual, with people going in and out of the room at their leisure to get food, drinks, or play mahjong. Some brought snacks with them. Most participants brought their own karaoke disc. Additionally, there were nearly a hundred karaoke discs available in the room for anyone to use. These discs were in older formats (e.g., VCD or video compact disc), and each contained about a dozen songs.

The order of singing was determined by a sign-up sheet, which was available approximately 15 minutes before the karaoke session began. Participants were only allowed to sign up to sing one song. If someone wished to sing a second song, they had to wait until the second round. Each song was typically five to six minutes in length. Mandy remarked that, in the past, some people chose to sing a Cantonese opera song, which typically lasted 10 to 20 minutes. A policy was eventually adopted that Cantonese opera songs must be cut to no more than eight minutes each; thus, allowing more time for others to sing.

Mandy intimated that cultural differences came into play when scheduling the karaoke activity. Apparently, the karaoke time had to be on Thursday afternoons to avoid conflicts with bridge players in the common room on Wednesday. There was only one double door between the two rooms, and bridge was engaged in mostly by White clients, who preferred to be quiet. Karaoke was too noisy for them. Mandy went on to say that mahjong and karaoke made a good combination, adding to a party-like environment, but might be too noisy for some.

On the day of the visit, karaoke began with the singing of "Happy Birthday" for participants whose birthdays were that week. One attendee even brought a cake for another's birthday. The group ambience was relaxed and social, with an atmosphere similar to that of a club or bar, with a lot of chatting, while the music started to play from the karaoke system. As the activity progressed, approximately half of the people in the room were paying attention to the singing. The other half were socializing or eating. Singing quality varied, but that didn't seem to matter to anyone. There were claps in between songs, but rarely enthusiastically because not many were paying attention to the singing. Two females were holding hands and dancing to a Mandarin song in the back of the room. Additionally, some attendees played mahjong in the common room while waiting for their turn to sing.

Mandy noted that although more than four hours for one activity seemed long, it was still not enough to satisfy everyone's desire to sing more. Additionally, even though each person was only allowed one turn to sing per round, some people complained that they had to wait too long before it was their turn to sing. Karaoke seemed to be a perfect fit for these older adults to fulfill a multitude of needs and to have meaningful experiences in their lives facilitated by the supportive context and the music that was intimately associated with the participants' culture, the way of socializing, and the related activities.

4.4.2.5 Karaoke Group 2 (The Senior Place, Southern Region)

Similar to the karaoke group previously described, the karaoke group at the Senior Place also attracted older adults of color. Participants in this group were of Latino, Filipino, or White ethnicity, reflecting the cultural diversity of the surrounding community. This group was also quite popular, as evidenced in the 2.5 hours it took to give everyone a turn to sing on the day of our observation.

Paul, the leader, was responsible for the setup of the activity and connected via a laptop to YouTube, to a Spanish-language karaoke website (karaokesound.com), and to two English-language karaoke websites (karafun.com and sunflykaraoke.com) while a sign-in sheet was circulating among participants. Chocolate and cookies were passed around too, which added to the relaxed, friendly, and welcoming ambience of the activity.

On the day of observation, the karaoke activity started with seven participants and grew to 19 participants over the next 90 minutes. There were many greetings with hugs and kisses as more participants arrived. The first song, *What I've Done*, was sung by Paul before the attendees began to take turns. There was a mix of pop, folk, and Latin standards, including, but not limited to the following: *Nosotros, Cielito Lindo, My Way, Danny Boy, The Way We Were, Historia de un Amor, Un Millón de Amigos,* and *Help Me Make It Through the Night*. Attendees clapped, smiled, and cheered after each song. Even though the physical space was limited, a few danced, particularly during instrumental interludes with driving rhythms. The observing researcher (Victor Fung) was invited to participate and encouraged to pick a song from a catalog of a few hundred songs. He chose *All I Have to Do Is Dream* by the Everly Brothers and remarked, "When it was my turn to sing, there was clapping, cheering, and some singing along. To my surprise, most of them knew the song well."

Midway through the karaoke session, everyone sang *Happy Birthday* to celebrate the birthday of a female attendee. At that point, a sign-up sheet for coffee was also passed around, so they would know how many cups of coffee to prepare. Shortly thereafter, a few attendees began drifting out. Again, there were plentiful hugs and kisses as those who were departing said goodbye. The group had dwindled down to 15 attendees by the time the activity ended. Overall, it was obvious that these older adults loved to sing, loved to be together, and hated to see the activity draw to a close.

Whether it was playing instruments or singing, participating older adults were eager and committed. They did it not only for the enjoyment of the music-making process and having music as part of their lives, but for the socialization and camaraderie within the group. The sharing of music within and outside the group seemed to have become a highlight of the week for many, with other activities seeming to be less important.

4.5 Insights: Music in Senior Centers

From these snapshots of music in senior centers and through analysis of the interview records and our observation and reflection notes, it was evident that the musical group activities, instrumental and singing, mirrored two of the themes that emerged from our broader look at the six senior centers at the end of the previous chapter: *active and welcoming*, and *variety and choice*. Specific to the musical group activities presented in this chapter, four additional themes emerged: *prevalence, musical development, enjoyment*, and *connection*. We discuss all six themes in the following pages.

4.5.1 Active and Welcoming

The previous chapter described the six senior centers as busy and friendly, and their music activities, particularly music-making activities, can undoubtedly be described in the same way. In our visits, we found that music activities across all centers were hands-on, active, and filled with eager participants. Relative to music-making, we also noted that participants felt quite comfortable both with each other and within their chosen activities. The ability to relax within their own participation in turn helped them to be welcoming, flexible, and open to helping others in need, whether that amounted to showing someone a new ukulele chord fingering, helping someone out of a wheelchair to dance to a favorite song, or making sure newcomers felt welcome and included in both the social and musical elements of these activities. As Mandy (karaoke leader, Better Living Senior Center) put it, "People here are happy, they socialize, enjoy, and are not so lonely. The center is their 'second family' [in Cantonese: *dai6 yi6 go3 ga1*, 第二個家]. People socialize in harmony through [musical] activities."

To the best of our knowledge, the theme of Active and Welcoming has not been reflected in previous scholarship on music in senior centers, but findings from multiple studies on older adult involvement in community music activities were related to maintaining a healthy, active lifestyle. For example, research emanating from various fields has shown that music participation improves older adults' physical functioning (e.g., Clift & Hancox, 2010; Coffman, 2009; Cohen et al., 2006; Engen, 2005; Hallam et al., 2012; Hays & Minchiello, 2005; Hillman, 2002; Jutras, 2011; Lally, 2009; Livesey et al., 2012; Michalos, 2005; Roulston, Jutras, & Kim, 2015) and that older adults perceive that their music participation revitalizes them and keeps them going (e.g., Creech et al., 2013; Dabback, 2008; Pothoulaki, MacDonald, & Flowers, 2012; Stige, 2012; Varvarigou et al., 2012). Additionally, multiple studies across various fields highlight benefits of music participation that compose elements of a welcoming atmosphere. These include (a) fluid entry points that allow older adults to join in at any time, regardless of previous musical experience (Fung & Lehmberg, 2016; Lehmberg, 2023), (b) willing acceptance into a group (Coffman, 1996; Dabback, 2008), and (c) the enjoyment of participation with others, which is discussed later in Section 4.5.6. It becomes clear that a welcoming environment to support an active lifestyle is evident throughout many activities in senior centers, and music activities play a prominent role.

4.5.2 *Variety and Choice*

Overall, we were impressed by the number of activities involving music in each center (passive and active listening, movement to music, and music-making). Though not all centers offered a great variety of music-making activities, we were surprised to see the multiplicity of activities offered *across* the six centers. These included seven instrumental ensembles with wind and rhythm instruments (concert bands, jazz band, polka band, German band, harmonica club), eight ensembles or classes involving plucked and strummed stringed instruments (three guitar classes, one guitar jam, one ukulele class, three ukulele groups), and five vocal and choral groups (three choirs or choruses and two karaoke groups). This variety of activities confirmed findings from our previous research that there was no "one-size-fits-all" regarding music-making activities for older adults and that a variety of choices of musical opportunities is needed to support a better quality of life (Fung & Lehmberg, 2016; Lehmberg, 2023). The variety and choice in these activities are reflective of the unique characteristics of the population residing in the local area, including their preference, socioeconomic status, culture, and values that guide their choices.

We noticed some differences in center attendees' choices of music-making activities that we thought could be attributed in part to culture-related musical preferences or current or past socioeconomic status. Instrumental music-making activities involving wind instruments were attended by mostly White, middle-class older adults. Very few older adults of color or lower socioeconomic status (White or of color) participated in these activities. These ensembles' repertoire generally fell within traditional US concert band, big band, or polka band jazz traditions, which might have been less relevant to some older adults of immigrant or non-White cultures. Additionally, older adult members of most of these ensembles (except for one beginner band) were not novices on their instruments; some had played their instrument continuously since childhood and others had stopped for a time and then picked up their instrument again later in their life. It could be that for socioeconomic reasons, some older adults of color did not have access to a wind instrument, either later or earlier in life. Thus, they chose to participate in center musical activities that did not require the rental or purchase of an expensive instrument. We also noticed that older adults of color tended to participate more often in music-making activities that had fluid entry points, in other words, activities that allowed them to enter at any time with no previous experience required.

Other cultural factors also appeared to relate to older adults' choice of music-making activities. We noted that the Asians and Hispanics in the centers we visited tended to prefer louder, more informal music-making activities such as karaoke much more than did White older adults. In addition, some music participants appeared to prefer songs in their native languages, as is supported in the research of Yeung, Baker, & Shoemark (2014). We also noticed a mix of participants with different cultural backgrounds in other choral activities and in ukulele and guitar activities. These factors warrant further investigation.

4.5.3 Prevalence

Merriam-Webster (n.d.) defines *prevalent* as "generally or widely accepted, practiced, or favored." The interviews with senior center staff and center clients (particularly those involved in music-making activities) as well as our own observations clearly showed that four types of music activities were without a doubt *widely accepted*, *practiced*, and *favored* within the six centers. These included (a) passive listening (such as stretching exercises with soft music playing in the background), (b) active listening (such as concerts by local musicians and center music groups), (c) purposeful or deliberate movement to music (such as Zumba, line dance, and social dances), and (d) music-making (as exemplified in the instrumental and vocal groups discussed in this chapter). Tracy, Sunnyside Senior Center outreach and development coordinator, described her center as a "music-loving center. Even the most curmudgeonly people relate to music!" Wanda, coordinator of Sunnyside Senior Center, shared that musical activities had the highest attendance of activities at her center. Nicole, Good Hope Senior Center manager, labeled her center's music activities as "very important." Furthermore, we would be remiss if we did not mention once again the importance and prevalence of center music activities in the life of the Asian woman who walked 38 blocks to attend her senior center's chorus rehearsal (Better Living Senior Center). Clearly, musical activities constituted an important element of each center. Evidently, prevalence is also supported by the availability of various choices as described in Section 4.5.2.

4.5.4 *Musical Development*

All older adults we observed involving themselves in center music-making activities appeared on one level or another to want to get better at making music via those activities. This desire for musical development manifested itself in different ways, from learning how to make a sound correctly on an instrument, to learning new fingerings or strumming techniques, to learning new repertoire, to learning to function and collaborate as a member of a musical group. Musical development also took place within a range of music teaching and learning settings, such as from director-directed learning within concert bands to the self-directed learning that occurred when a harmonica group member figured out their own part by ear, without the use of musical notation. It is worth noting that this musical development took place in low-pressure environments. Mistakes were okay and it was fine to participate on one's own level.

Continuous musical development is a strong desire of many older adults who choose to participate in music. This finding has surfaced repeatedly in previous research as a benefit of music-making in older adulthood, evidenced in multiple studies overlapping the fields of music, music education, music therapy, and psychology (e.g., Balsnes, 2017; Coffman, 1996; Coffman & Adamek, 1999, 2001; Dingle et al., 2012; Hays, 2005; Joseph

& Human, 2020; Joseph & Southcott, 2018; Jutras, 2006; Krause et al., 2018; Lehmberg, 2023; Woody et al., 2019). Perhaps music participation is a highly preferred avenue for older adults to acquire improvement in their broader life experiences, that is a better quality of life.

4.5.5 Enjoyment

It goes without saying that enjoyment was threaded throughout the passive and active listening, moving to music, and music-making activities in the six senior citizen centers. The older adults loved being part of a musical group or other activity involving music! In the next chapter, we explore this further through their words; however, we can share at this point that their enjoyment was both broad and deep. Broadly, older adults derived joy from connecting with others, participating in music together, and being active. Deeply, they derived joy from musical expression and development of their skills and identity as musicians and members of a vibrant senior community. This broad and deep enjoyment generates multidimensional layers (i.e., social, musical, physical, and psychological) in their meanings of music participation.

The theme of enjoyment has been threaded through previous research as well and has been identified as one of the most basic and prevalent benefits of older adult music participation. Studies from the 1990s to the present have reported that older adults participate in music simply because they greatly enjoy it (e.g., Coffman, 1996, 2009; Coffman & Adamek, 2001; Fung & Lehmberg, 2016; Hays & Minchiello, 2005; Jutras, 2006; Lehmberg, 2023; Southcott, 2009; Taylor & Hallam, 2008; Roulston et al., 2015).

4.5.6 Connection

The theme of connection was strongly evident across all senior centers' music-making activities. Older adults participated in these activities to not only make music and express themselves musically, but also connect with other human beings with similar interests. As described earlier, enjoyment was evidenced in the hugs and kisses shared at the beginnings and ends of musical activities, in the humorous comments they enjoyed together, and in the ways they looked out for each other and helped each other. These connections seemed to lift their spirits, boost their energy, feed their psyches, and help them feel like they belonged. Connection seemed to be a substantial and vital element that enhanced their quality of life, whether it was with others in the present or with their past as they engaged in songs from earlier years.

As with the theme of enjoyment, the theme of connection has strongly emerged in previous research across various fields of study as an important social and psychological benefit of music participation of older adults (e.g., Clift & Hancox, 2010; Creech et al., 2013; Coffman & Adamek, 2001; Cohen, 2006; Gembris, 2012; Hays & Minchiello, 2005; Jutras, 2011; Lally, 2009; Southcott, 2009; Stige, 2012). Connecting with others can help older adults to develop a sense of belonging and community at a time of life when self-identity may be in flux due to retirement and other life changes (Fung & Lehmberg, 2016).

4.6 Insights from Diverse Settings

Earlier research findings resonate strongly with this chapter's emergent themes of connection, enjoyment, musical development, and variety and choice (Fung & Lehmberg, 2016). Furthermore, the research described in this chapter, conducted in previously unstudied musical settings within six senior centers, uncovers the new themes of (a) active and welcoming and (b) prevalence. Insights gained from these diverse settings could have tremendous implications for the administration and implementation of musical offerings at these centers if they are to fulfill the needs of diverse populations. Clearly, these needs go far beyond music, reaching deep into the social, psychological, physical, and spiritual beings of the participants.

4.7 Further Thoughts

Moving from broad views of senior centers to narrow foci on specific musical activities in this chapter, we have thus far taken a close look at six senior centers across the United States and the musical activities within them. Although the older adults who used the government-funded senior centers we visited were culturally, ethnically, and socioeconomically diverse, themes presented earlier are in line with the contributors of music participation to lifelong engagement and quality of life we discovered previously in a predominantly White middle-class retirement community (Fung & Lehmberg, 2016): Connections (social and temporal), Entry Points (enter and re-enter at any time), Ownership (autonomous learning), Meaningful Participation (commitment, socialization, and supportive context), and Variety (musical styles and activities). In the next chapter, we home in further to learn more about the role of music in senior centers and in older adults' lives through their own words. We also set the stage for a synthesis of findings related to music participation in senior centers and quality of life to be presented in Chapter 6. This should further illuminate the consistent connection between older adult music participation and quality of life across diverse cultural, ethnic, and socioeconomic groups.

CHAPTER 5

Older Adults' Perspectives on Music

In this chapter we home in further to examine how music played a part in the lives of older adult clients of the six senior centers we visited. Interviewees' colorful words and stories combine with our recollections of our visits to weave a figurative tapestry of senior center clients' musical histories and music participation, both within and outside senior centers. We also make a brief foray into the musical backgrounds of the center activity leaders we met. All of this information sets the stage for an exploration of these adults' motivations for engaging in music and the barriers some encountered along the way. The chapter ends with a brief synthesis of the role of music participation in interviewees' quality of life.

Across the six senior centers, we interviewed a total of 75 individuals who assumed different roles in the centers and together represented multiple perspectives. The group of interviewees included senior center clients who participated in musical activities within or outside the senior center, center managers and staff, leaders of center music-making activities or activities involving purposeful movement to music, a manager and a staff member who also led music-making activities, a music-making activity leader who also participated as a member of another center musical group, and senior center clients who identified as music nonparticipants. It is notable that all but one self-identified nonparticipant actually met our criteria for music participation as presented in Chapter 1. Figure 5.1 presents, at a glance, the number of interviewees in each category, and also shows the overlaps that occurred when interviewees fit into more than one category.

As is evident in the sets of interview questions found in Appendix B, the senior center clients we interviewed were asked about their music participation and the role of music in their lives. Activity leaders were queried about their musical backgrounds, current musical activities, reasons for choosing to serve as activity leaders, and their views on the role of music in older adults' lives. In contrast, senior center managers and staff were asked mainly about center operations, services, funding, activities, and client

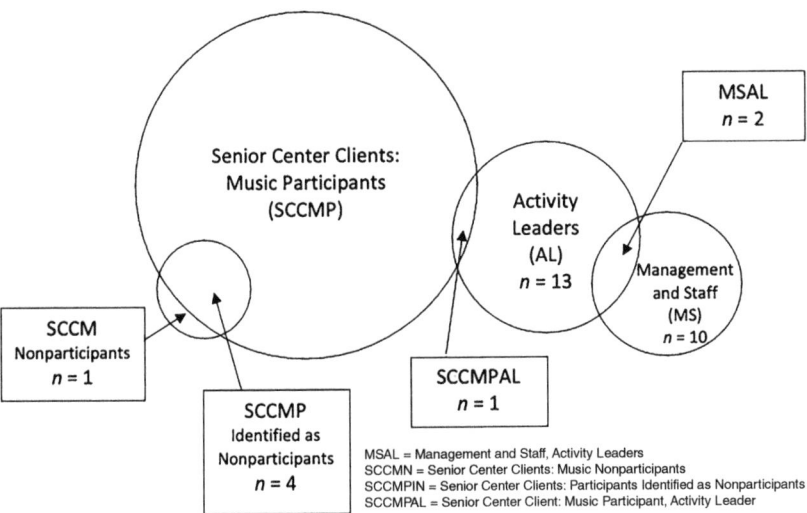

Figure 5.1   Interviewee numbers by category, with category overlaps

demographics, but some also weighed in with their views on the importance of music for older adults. We move next to the musical histories of senior center client interviewees, including both music participants and clients who self-identified as nonparticipants.

5.1   Musical Opportunities

Though our earlier research showed that most older adult music participants had chosen to involve themselves in musical activities prior to reaching older adulthood (Fung & Lehmberg, 2016), we were still surprised at the breadth of musical histories of this group of senior center clients. Almost all (including those who claimed to be music nonparticipants) had participated in music in some ways in their earlier years. We counted over 50 different forms of music participation (see Figure 5.2) that fit into our definition of music participation presented in Chapter 1, which included "music making and creating, music listening, and moving to music."

5.1.1   Music-Making Earlier in Life

We did not set out to share our definition of *music participation* with interviewees and discovered that most equated music participation with *music-making*. Thus, it was not surprising that music-making was by far

Figure 5.2 Forms of music participation: Senior center clients

the most commonly reported form of music participation. Figure 5.2 shows a word art hierarchy of forms of music participation across this group of senior center clients. The larger the font size, the greater the number of interviewees who reported participating in that respective form of music-making. Most prominently displayed are private lessons outside school, school band, community choir, family music-making, and self-directed music-making, followed by secondary school band, community band, professional musician, school choir, church choir, and rock band.

5.1.1.1 *Preferred Ensembles*

As depicted in Figure 5.2, past involvement in school, church, and community choirs was quite prevalent across this group of interviewees. One choir afficionado who stood out because of his age (101 years old) and endearing personality was Mr. Noah, a Black man who was a member of the Good Hope Senior Center choir. At the time, Mr. Noah reported that he had sung in a church choir for 50 years. He believed that singing in church helped him to receive the blessing of a long life, and intimated, "Singing has always been a part of my life. It's a gift of God. You see, I'm 100 years old. Make a joyful noise unto the Lord." Other examples of interviewees who chose to participate in school, church, and community choirs were Viviana, a Latina client of the Senior Place who had sung in a high school choir in her native Ecuador; Mallory, a White female client of Sunnyside Senior Center who majored in music and was proud to have participated in a semi-professional adult choir in the Northeast; and Jacob, a White male client of Better Living Senior Center and holocaust survivor who shared that he had been singing all his life and had conducted a church choir in earlier adulthood. A final example was Lily, an Asian female attendee of Better Living Senior Center, who summed up her participation in various choirs and variety shows with the comment, "All my life has been singing."

Also very common was participation in various types of school, community, and private bands of varying types and styles (such as blues, concert, country, jazz, marching, polka, rock, etc.). Henry, a White male member of the Mountain View Senior Center concert and jazz bands, conjured up memories of Meredith Wilson's musical, *The Music Man*, as he described how a traveling musical instrument salesman came to his town to sell instruments, telling residents that the town needed a band. The town council approved of this idea and indeed decided to start a band. The salesman then sold four instruments to Henry's father: a trombone for his sister, a trumpet for his brother, a baritone horn for another brother, and a clarinet for Henry. His musical memories included marching with his clarinet for 5 miles in a Mardi Gras parade and playing it in his junior high and high school bands. At age 14, he started his own dance band specializing in Mexican music, demonstrating the eclecticism of his growing interest in music. In adulthood, he became a professional musician in a large city in the Southwestern US, performing regularly in show bands, symphony orchestras, and a rock band.

In the Eastern region of the United States, Maurycy, an 86-year-old White male, shared his own history of lifelong "gigging" in polka bands. Though he had enjoyed a 64-year career as a pharmacist, over time he became better known in his geographical area as a professional musician. He shared that during World War II, he took private accordion lessons for two years. Most of the musicians at the time had been drafted, so he played a lot of gigs as a 12-year-old, performing regularly in a polka band with a 90-year-old violinist and a drummer. Maurycy continued his polka band participation throughout his life, becoming increasingly involved as his children grew up. One of his proudest moments was in 1975 when his polka band performed in the main tent at the Eastern States Exposition, one of the largest regional fairs in the United States. Other examples of interviewees who chose to participate in school, community, and private bands were Travis (Sunnyside Senior Center client), who had played piano in blues, country, and rock bands; and Diane and Ken (both clients of Good Hope Senior Center), who had played clarinet and drums, respectively, in their schools' bands.

5.1.1.2 *Instrument Accessibility and Preference*

Though the older adult interviewees had a broad range of musical experiences, the voice, the piano, and the guitar were clearly more commonly used across the groups. Accessibility and socioeconomic status likely had contributed to the voice being the most popular choice. Everyone has a voice, and it doesn't require money to access it. For example, Evelyn (White female client of Sunnyside Senior Center) explained that when she was young, her family was poor. Purchasing an instrument would have been quite a luxury. Family values might have also played a role in the choice to participate in music via singing. An example of this was Stan (White male client of Good Hope Senior Center), whose family had a quartet and sang in four-part harmony. They entertained at family reunions, sang regularly in church, and performed and recorded professionally. Another evidence of singing as attributed to cultural values was found in the karaoke group in Better Living Senior Center, which served a large number of Asian clients. As karaoke was invented in the 1970s in Japan and had popularized quickly throughout many parts of Asia, karaoke singing is integral to many Asian immigrants' musical culture. This could explain why more than four hours of karaoke singing was still not enough to satisfy the participants in the senior center.

Similarly, the choices of piano and guitar might have been related to family and cultural values. Some interviewees who chose to play these instruments made music initially with their families. Stan, whose singing involvement was already mentioned and who also served as the guitarist in the harmonica group in the same senior center, proudly shared that he was "born with music." His dad played "anything with strings" and his mom played guitar and banjo. Stan got his first guitar at age 10. Other interviewees were able to begin music participation on family owned instruments. Neil, one of the organizers of the harmonica group and a White male, described how his family had a harmonica at home and he taught himself to play it. Later in life, his dad bought all of his grandchildren harmonicas for Christmas one year, and Neil's son subsequently became proficient at playing harmonica. Leah's (White female Sunnyside Senior Center client) family had a piano in the house when she was growing up and she was able to pick out tunes by ear and taught herself to play simple sheet music. Figure 5.3 presents in word art the instruments (including voice) utilized by senior center clients in their music-making activities. Again, font size indicates a hierarchy of instruments utilized, from less often (smaller font) to more often (larger font) across the group. The voice stood out as the most oft-used instrument, followed by the piano and the

Figure 5.3 Instruments utilized in music-making by senior center clients

guitar, then the clarinet, the ukulele, the violin, the alto saxophone, the organ, the trombone, the trumpet, and so forth. A few folk instruments were on the list also (e.g., accordion, banjo, and harmonica).

Related to instrument accessibility and preference were musical genres associated with older adult participants' cultural values. An example was their desire to sing the more lengthy selection of Cantonese opera songs in the karaoke group (Better Living Senior Center). A policy was needed to impose an eight-minute limit when choosing these songs to sing in the group. Still, some participants were choosing these songs for their love of the genre, which is reflective of their cultural values rooted in their native land. Note that the more sophisticated karaoke singers would recognize and attempt to reproduce the different vocal production techniques and timbres when singing Cantonese opera songs compared to other popular song styles.

5.1.1.3 Musical Histories of Activity Leaders

We were able to interview 15 activity leaders across the six senior centers. Thirteen led musical groups and one led a stretching exercise class in which attendees moved deliberately and purposefully to music. Another did not lead a musical group but led sing-alongs on center bus trips. Like the senior center clients, a majority of the information they shared concerned music-making. Their musical histories were quite colorful and varied, with examples ranging from Laurie (White female), who had limited music participation prior to serving as co-leader of the Sunnyside Senior Center ukulele group; to Grace (White female), who led the Better Living Senior

Center choir and volunteered as a musician at a pediatric hospital; to Linda (White female), who led exercise classes in her community and at the Mountain View Senior Center; to Les (White male, ukulele group co-leader, Sunnyside Senior Center), a self-taught guitarist who played professionally with rock bands and Elvis impersonators; to Tony (White male, jazz band leader, Mountain View Senior Center), Xander (White male, concert band leader, Center for Healthy Aging), and Elizabeth (White female, concert band leader, Mountain View Senior Center), who enjoyed careers as school music educators. Brief descriptions of their past music participation, as well as their music participation at the time of their interviews, are presented in Appendix C. A common thread across the group of activity leaders was that all had participated in music (via making music or moving to music) at some point prior to leading activities at their respective senior center. Most singing activity leaders have singing in their life's history; a few also have instrumental playing experience in their background. For instrumental group leaders, they almost uniformly have instrumental participation in their history. As a whole, the breadth of activities of musical activity leaders was noteworthy.

5.1.1.4 *Other Forms of Past Music Participation*

We found it interesting that when discussing their musical histories, fewer senior center clients or activity leaders mentioned the other forms of music participation we put forth in Chapter 1: moving deliberately and purposefully to music, listening to music, and creating music. Figure 5.4's pie chart shows the distribution of the forms of music participation, as well as music nonparticipation, across the group of senior center clients and activity leaders. Aside from music-making, most-often mentioned was music listening (20 interviewees), in the form of attending musical events or listening to music alone or with others in interviewees' free time. This was followed in frequency by moving to music (13 interviewees), via dance and exercise classes or ballroom dance events. We found it interesting that of the 13 who mentioned moving to music, 11 were female. Edward (White male, Good Hope Senior Center choir member), a still-active ballroom dance aficionado, and James (Asian male, Better Living Senior Center choir, karaoke, and line-dancing participant) were the only males to mention moving to music. It was surprising to us that creating music was only mentioned once across the entire group of 59 senior center clients and activity directors. Neil, the "unofficial" director of the harmonica group, described how the harmonica group was an "ear group" with members creating their own musical parts for each tune. The scarcity of

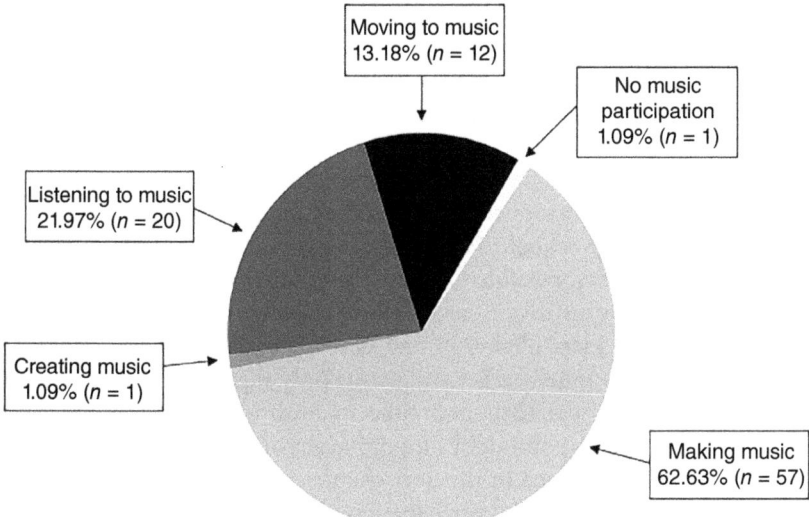

Figure 5.4 Music participation and nonparticipation across senior center clients and activity leaders

participation in musical activities other than making music, such as composition or improvisation, warrants further attention, and is addressed in Chapter 6.

5.1.2 Current Forms of Music Participation

In our study, we also asked senior center clients and activity leaders about their current music participation, including music participation within and outside of senior centers. Again, we found the range of activities across these groups to be extensive.

5.1.2.1 Within Senior Centers

Collectively, the senior centers we visited offered multiple types of opportunities for interviewees' music participation. As described in Chapter 4, a majority of center music-making opportunities involved singing (choirs, karaoke) or playing in various types of wind bands (concert, jazz, polka, German). Many of these were similar to music-making and performing opportunities interviewees had taken advantage of earlier in life. Some of the centers also offered music-making and performing opportunities that were different from those that interviewees had experienced previously, such as ukulele groups, guitar classes and groups, and a harmonica club. At the time of the interviews, most of the older adult center clients who were participating in a music-making activity that was new to them were involved in guitar, ukulele, or harmonica activities. Some had little musical experience prior to that time. For example, Tara (White female) had been playing in a ukulele group for older adults for nine years, but did not participate in music before that time, except for playing piano in fourth grade in elementary school. This suggests that these particular activities had fluid entry points, possible for someone to join in at any time, without previous experience in that form of music-making. Additionally, though musical activity leaders obviously had developed their musical expertise earlier in life (some much earlier and others only slightly earlier), for some (such as Laurie) it was their first time to lead a musical activity. The impacts of fluid entry points and supportive environments warrant further attention and are explored in the next chapter.

Opportunities for music participation that did not involve music-making were plentiful across the six senior centers as well, including opportunities for engaged music listening. Most centers regularly brought in community musicians to perform concerts and play for dances for clients. Center musical groups (including some dance groups) performed as well. In addition, multiple types of activities that involved purposeful movement to music were available, such as Zumba, line dancing, ballroom dancing, aerobics, and so forth. Fluid entry points were evident in these activities as well – any center client could join in at any time, regardless of previous experience.

5.1.2.2 Outside Senior Centers

Several center clients and activity leaders kept their schedules quite full of church and community music-making activities in addition to their center musical activities. Many of these involved multiage musical groups and audiences, and the older adult interviewees (including activity leaders who were older adults) were able to sustain quality contributions despite advancing age. Some examples of their participation were as follows:

- Jacob (White male, Better Living Senior Center) served as a cantor in a synagogue and remarked that he was "still reaching high C."
- Stan (White male, Good Hope Senior Center harmonica club guitarist) played guitar professionally for 20–25 hours per month and sang and recorded with a gospel group.

- Neil (White male, Good Hope Senior Center harmonica group leader) performed at an annual harmonica festival, which he also helped to run.
- Rebecca (Black female, Good Hope Senior Center choir leader) sang in her church choir.
- Ulysses (White male, German band leader at the Center for Healthy Aging) performed in five community musical groups outside the center.
- Xander (White male, concert band leader at the Center for Healthy Aging) played trombone professionally with big bands and sang in a church choir and a Renaissance *a cappella* group.
- Maurycy (White male, accordionist in the Polka and German Bands at the Center for Healthy Aging) performed solo on his accordion at a local German restaurant and played many styles of music.
- Diane (White female, ukulele group member, Sunnyside Senior Center) sang in an interfaith gospel choir.
- Kay (White female ukulele group member, Sunnyside Senior Center) performed in classical ukulele groups.
- CJ (White female ukulele group member, Sunnyside Senior Center) sang with the area lesbian choir and had done so for 35 years.

Other center clients engaged in music-making at home, alone or with family. Some worked to maintain or improve their musical skills. For example, Mr. Noah watched a "learn to play piano" television show to improve his skills. At the time of his interview, he still played "when no one is home. I keep doing things so my brain will keep working." Leonard (Asian male choir participant, Better Living Senior Center) liked to sight-read music at home and was also learning to play by ear. Kay (Asian female, the Senior Place) shared that she enjoyed singing karaoke and playing guitar at home. Likewise, James (Asian male karaoke, choir, and line-dance participant, Better Living Senior Center) also liked to sing karaoke at home, either alone or with friends, and remarked that he sang a few popular songs every day.

Several center clients kept a busy schedule of listening to music via attendance of musical events. For example, Carol (self-identified music nonparticipant, Sunnyside Senior Center) enjoyed attending big band and piano concerts. Ella (Black female karaoke participant, Mountain View Senior Center) also attended concerts and was especially interested in opera and symphony orchestra performances. Ella held a season pass to a performance venue in a nearby metropolitan area and enjoyed attending performances of a drumming group from a nearby university.

Others preferred to listen to music in private. For example, Ashwin (Asian male karaoke participant, the Senior Place) enjoyed listening to classical music and songs from his Indian cultural heritage. James preferred to listen to big band tunes such as *Stardust*, which he referred to as "long hair" music. He regularly scoured local garage sales for used LPs and CDs. Evelyn enjoyed listening to music on her car radio, and Carol enjoyed listening to guitar and piano music.

It appeared that the senior center clients we interviewed had no trouble finding outlets and opportunities for music participation. However, for some, music participation was not without difficulties.

5.2 Challenges Related to Music Participation

Despite the overwhelming interest in and demand for music participation, some older adults faced challenges related to participation in music activities in senior centers. These challenges concerned health, a negative attitude, the need for patience, and more (e.g., finance, logistics, and family).

5.2.1 Health-Related Challenges

Across the group of center clients and activity leaders, health-related issues posed the biggest challenges related to music participation. However, most participants were able to supersede the barriers they encountered and discover solutions that enabled them to keep participating. Some examples illustrating this are as follows:

- Neil (White male, Good Hope Senior Center harmonica group leader) had peripheral neuropathy, which caused the muscle between the thumb and index finger in one of his hands to atrophy. He used a rubber band to assist the muscle when playing his woodwind instruments and attached it to a key on the instrument.
- Udele (White female concert band member, the Center for Healthy Aging) used a wheelchair sometimes and could no longer play her flute well because of her arthritis. She shared that Xander had said, "You come. Even if you don't play a note." That made her feel encouraged and included and she persisted in her participation.

- Maurycy (White male, accordionist in the Polka and German Bands at the Center for Healthy Aging) acquired an accordion that ran on a battery, so he no longer had to squeeze the bellows in and out.
- Les (White male, co-leader of the Sunnyside Senior Center ukulele groups) turned to ukulele when it became too difficult for him to play his guitar due to Ménière's disease and was able to continue his music participation.
- Charles (White male guitar class participant, Good Hope Senior Center) did not use Chord Buddy but shared his opinion that the device allowed people with arthritis to play 90% of the songs that were popular at the time.
- James (Asian male, chorus member at the Better Living Senior Center) tried to learn the guitar but was unsuccessful because his fingers hurt, so he turned to other forms of music participation that were a better fit for him physically (singing, line dancing).

Unfortunately, a few interviewees' music participation diminished or ceased because of health-related problems. For example, as a young adult, Udele went to college to study music, but had to drop out because the school wasn't accessible to students with physical disabilities and she used a wheelchair. Henry recounted that he had to give up the oboe, because he was losing his sense of touch in his fingertips. Lastly, Irene (Asian female karaoke participant, Better Living Senior Center) had stopped participating in dance classes at her senior center because of concerns about air quality. Believing that the classes were too crowded, she reported, "When you breathe, the air is filthy."

5.2.2 Negativity

Another category of challenges surrounded negativity, in the form of attitudes and comments of others. Regrettably, some were hurtful enough that they put a halt to others' music participation. Leah stopped participating in music in the fifth grade because a music teacher said she could not carry a tune. Charles was in the chorus for his senior high school play until the director told him he could not sing and moved him to the job of stagehand. Though he did not stop performing professionally, Henry was affected by negative perceptions of nonmusicians. He posited that the general public regarded musicians as lower-class citizens and recounted that when he worked as a musician in a country club in the Southern US, he and other musicians were not allowed to use the front entrance but had to enter the club via the back entrance, where the trash and dumpsters were located. Occasional attitude-related challenges occurred within senior center musical activities as well. Mandy described how sometimes clients would complain that they had to line up to sing, that someone was cutting the line, and other misunderstandings. On the positive side, Mandy also pointed out that these were mainly isolated incidences from a few individuals.

5.2.3 Patience

Still another challenge related to stick-to-itiveness and having enough patience and resilience to see music participation through to a positive result. One example came from Theo (White male), who reported that Neil influenced him to join the harmonica group that rehearsed at Good Hope Senior Center. At that time, Theo had no prior musical experience. He started playing diatonic harmonica and it took him two months to learn the first song "one note at a time, by ear." He still struggles with musical notation but said he "can read music laboriously." He was happy he stuck with it, as music eventually became the most important activity in his life. In contrast, Eva lost patience and quit piano lessons as a child because she felt she was progressing too slowly. Moreover, a constant frustration for Sebastian was the lack of finger dexterity of his guitar students, slowing down their progress. He lamented, "I have got through hell with them ... little by little teaching them ... You have to dedicate time, and time, and time."

5.2.4 Other Challenges

Less frequently mentioned across the group of senior center clients, but still significant, were challenges of finances, logistics, and family. Concerning finances, for example, Rebecca had to work at her community music school's front desk to pay for her piano lessons, and she later had to drop out of her high school choir to take a job and save money for college. Related to logistics, for example, Anna (White female) showed her dedication to sing at the Better Living Senior Center by walking 38 blocks to attend rehearsals. Likewise, Mei attended activities in the same senior center by walking for 15 minutes to take a bus, with a total travel time of approximately one hour. Regarding family, Denise (White female, Sunnyside Senior Center) stopped participating in music after her parents forced her to take piano lessons in childhood and she hated it. At the time of the interview, she had only recently begun to participate again via her center's ukulele groups but was very happy to get back into music. Finally, Betty Ann (White female ukulele group member, Sunnyside Senior Center) shared how she continued to participate in an orchestra during adulthood but had to take a hiatus in completing her Bachelor of Music degree until her children grew older. She remarked that it was tough to go to school and be married with a young family.

Despite these examples, it is heartening to know that most senior center clients were able to find ways to continue their music participation, even in the face of different types of challenges. These examples also brought up a critical question. We wondered why they persevered in music participation and what it brought to their lives.

5.3 Why Participate?

As has been shown over and over in research, older adults participate in music because they benefit from it in multiple and substantial ways (Fung & Lehmberg, 2016; Krause et al., 2018), and the data from our senior center visits strongly support this finding. Here, we present a broad view of the reasons senior center clients chose to participate in music, accentuated with their words and those of their activity leaders. At this point we also bring in the perspectives of the senior center managers and staff, who were able to observe the music participation of older adults within the senior centers from a distance and over time. The most strongly emergent themes are *pleasure, health, connection, giving to others, self-worth, safe space,* and *spiritual uplift*.

5.3.1 Pleasure

As might be expected, senior center music participants were unanimous in the belief that music participation was enjoyable, it brought them pleasure, and it made them happy. As stated simply by Cal, "Those who participate enjoy the music. Audiences enjoy it, too. I just love music!" Similar comments were echoed by senior center clients in every center we visited, as evidenced in these sample comments:

- "Music is the most joyful thing I do." (Denise [White female, ukulele group member, Sunnyside Senior Center])
- "It makes you happy." (Brenda [Asian female choir member, Better Living Senior Center], James [Asian male, chorus member at the Better

Living Senior Center], Leah [White female music listener who self-identified as a music nonparticipant, Sunnyside Senior Center], and Mallory [White female, ukulele group member, Sunnyside Senior Center])
- "I feel happier when singing." (James)
- "Fun." (Irene [Asian female karaoke participant, Better Living Senior Center], Ken [White male ukulele group member, Sunnyside Senior Center], Stan [White male, Good Hope Senior Center harmonica club guitarist], and Ulysses [White male, German Band leader and member of the Polka Band at the Center for Healthy Aging])
- "I love it!" (Eva [White female ukulele group member, Sunnyside Senior Center])

Activity leaders were in agreement that center clients experienced great pleasure from music participation. Neil remarked that "Performing is fun for the [harmonica] group." Bill stated that the choir he directed "keeps people alive and brings happiness." Laurie (ukulele group co-director) described music participation as "a respite of joy – highly, extremely, enjoyably important for those who participate." Rebecca pointed out that her choir members' joy was contagious to her, stating "I enjoy directing them – [I] like to see their faces light up!"

Senior center managers also chimed in to confirm the high level of enjoyment their clients derived from music participation. Eileen (manager, the Center for Healthy Aging) was confident that her center clients loved their musical activities. Maria (manager, the Senior Place) exclaimed, "Music is amazing! Music is huge! [Center clients] love to move [and] listen, it's a huge part of the center." Nicole (manager, Good Hope Senior Center) summed it up with these statements: "Music brings joy to everyone. . . . Music is universal. Music crosses all lines, borders, barriers. Even if [center attendees] don't understand your language, they smile when someone sings."

5.3.2 Health

Senior center clients, activity directors, and managers alike attested to the multiple health-related benefits that could be accessed via music participation. For many, music was therapeutic. Specific physical benefits experienced by interviewees included exercise for the body (Brenda, Viviana), increased mobility (Jack [White male manager of Mountain View Senior Center]), accelerated healing (Nicole), improved lung capacity (Mandy, Wanda [Latina, activities coordinator, Sunnyside Senior Center]), reduced pain (Grace, Mandy, Susan [White female member of the Better Living Senior Center choir]), stimulation for the body (Brenda), improved blood pressure (Evelyn), increased energy (Brenda), increased relaxation (Brenda, James), and feeling younger (Brenda). Psychological benefits included increased production of endorphins (Evelyn) and dopamine (James), improved mood (Evelyn, Irene, Jack, James, Mandy, Nicole), increased sense of accomplishment (Sondra [White female member of Sunnyside Senior Center ukulele group]), alleviated depression (Ken), reduced stress and worries (Ashwin, Brenda, Denise, Sondra, Viviana), eased loneliness (Ashwin, Mandy), eased sorrow (Ashwin), increased resilience (Betty Ann), and transcendence of life's problems (Ashwin, Carol, Charles, Sondra, Susan).

The benefit of music participation mentioned most often was music's positive effects on the brain, which is documented in research across various fields (Fung & Lehmberg, 2016). Twelve interviewees commented that music participation enhanced cognition and brain functioning (BG [White female ukulele group member, Sunnyside Senior Center], Carol, CJ, Grace, Kay, Laurie, Les, Mr. Noah, Nicole, Rebecca, Tara, Wanda). As CJ commented, "Music lifts my spirit and challenges the brain." Tara mentioned brain studies that found that music activated all areas of the brain and believed that music helped her brain stay active. Les also remarked that music used all parts of the brain and referenced the documentary *Alive Inside*, which told the story of a patient with advanced Alzheimer's disease who still responded to music. Les added that some participants came to his ukulele group to "stay crisp." Speaking from personal experience of having a mother with Alzheimer's disease, Grace recounted that in the last year of her mother's life, she could not speak but could still sing. She also had a family member with dementia who could play Chopin on the piano but could not remember her name. She concluded, "Music is secure and protected from traumas in the brain or to cognitive abilities." As Evelyn summed it up, "Music is powerful."

5.3.3 Connection

The senior center clients viewed music participation as a wonderful means of meeting new people, making friends, developing a sense of camaraderie with like-minded people, and connecting with the surrounding community. As Kay pointed out, "Musical groups are a magnet for people." Several interviewees emphasized the importance of music participation as a means of socialization. Joe (White male, Better Living Senior Center) believed that socialization was a critical element that drew participants to his center's choir. He emphasized that the customary break in the middle of the rehearsal was very important, because that was when people socialized with each other. He added that for some, the choir's rehearsals might be the only time they could connect. He went on to describe his choir's atmosphere as open and low-pressure, where participants had the freedom to sing or not sing. In a similar vein, Tara posited that socialization within music-making groups was even *more* important than development of musical skills, remarking, "If you want to get better, take [private] lessons." In addition, activity leaders looked forward to the socialization that was inherent in the groups, lessons, and classes they led. After Sebastian's wife passed away, he "felt alone" and considered the center to be "a life saver." He stated, "I enjoy this place a lot and I enjoy teaching [the guitar]." Center managers also attested to the value of socialization via music participation. For example, Mandy referred to her center as a "second family" where clients "socialize in harmony" through activities involving music.

Socialization within center musical activities naturally led to *camaraderie* among music participants. Relative to that, Ulysses described his musical involvement as layered, with camaraderie leading to a broader sense of community:

> One layer is the music itself and my own musical competence or lack thereof. A second layer is the camaraderie I enjoy with members of the group. A third layer is the spirit of the group itself and sense of brotherhood. (Ulysses)

Nick referred to his guitar class at Good Hope Senior Center as "almost like a fellowship group" in which attendees interacted, talked, and played songs. Nicole also commented that music participation there "builds connection and community." And Brooke (manager, Sunnyside Senior Center) similarly stated, "There's a sense of community and it provides a creative outlet."

Music participation in the senior centers also provided an avenue for connection with community members. Bill told how his choir at Mountain View Senior Center reached out in the community through their performances, and that this outreach was very meaningful to them. Community engagement sometimes manifested in humorous ways as well. Cal described how he used to sing with bands in the senior center and would bring fresh zucchini from his garden to his performances. Anyone who recognized a tune got a zucchini. "The ladies fought over them!"

A few interviewees mentioned that music participation helped them connect with their past. For Stan, music was "therapeutic, reminiscent; songs bring back memories." Sara and Alice (choir members, Better Living Senior Center) liked to sing songs that were popular when they were growing up and brought back memories of that time. For Amy (choir member, Better Living Senior Center), singing brought back memories that were both good and bad. The good memories were reminders of good times with her husband after they got married. The bad memories were associated with missing her husband, who had passed away.

5.3.4 Giving to Others

Closely related to, and perhaps evolving from, connection is the desire to *give* to others, including the desire to *give back* to convey thankfulness for received benefits or good fortune. According to Bill, the Mountain View Senior Center choir found it meaningful and enriching to reach out to the community via their performances, and he volunteered his services as director as a means of giving back to the community. Grace also felt that she gave back to the community through her work as director of the Better Living Senior Center choir. Mallory enjoyed volunteering in the community via her ukulele group, which donated ukuleles to local elementary schools in addition to performing in the community. Henry not only gave back to the community through performances with Mountain View Senior Center musical groups, but also, as an instrument repair specialist, made a custom flute device for a 13-year-old girl who wanted to play the flute but was without fingers on her left hand. He was very proud of the outcome and shared that James Galway (internationally known flutist) wanted to meet him because of that. These desires and actions to give back align with previous findings that senior center participants are both beneficiaries and contributors of the center (Pardasani, 2018; Weil, 2014) and extend into the community.

5.3.5 Self-Worth

Music participation helped the senior center clients to feel valued and needed, which increased their self-esteem at a time in life when it could be in flux due to retirement, relocation, or change in socioeconomic status (Fung & Lehmberg, 2016). Rebecca believed that music helped to get center choir participants "out and doing something. ... They function better and feel like they have a purpose and place to belong." Sondra felt that in addition to enjoying music for its own sake, it held other values related to self-esteem. She intimated that, "At the end of life, and at the end of a day, it makes you feel like you've done something. It's something to look forward to – you've *done* something [to better yourself and contribute to society]."

Self-worth also increased as music participants improved their musical skills. Mandy described how karaoke participants improved their own singing by listening to others sing. They improved their understanding of pitch and key, which helped them know how to adjust their own karaoke machine at home. Within the context of her ukulele group, Dorothy liked the challenge of learning new words and strums. A member of the same group, Mallory, was working on difficult chords and stretching her skill by taking a jazz ukulele class. Also on the topic of music skill improvement, Neil remarked that harmonica group members "grow in their own directions within the group."

5.3.6 *Safe Space*

The fluid entry points of many of the senior center musical activities helped members consider these groups as safe spaces for music participation – spaces in which they felt welcome and valued. According to Stan, the harmonica group was inclusive of members' musical preferences and supported individual choice. The group met weekly and utilized a "rehearsal/ jam" format. Generally, eight to 10 people sat around a long table at the senior center. They went around the table and each attendee had a turn to choose a song, and they "keep at it until it's good." These opportunities for individual choice helped group members to feel welcomed and valued and contributed to a positive, inclusive rehearsal climate.

Similarly, Mallory, Diane, Denise, Tara, and Evelyn described the Sunnyside ukulele group as inclusive and welcoming. Tara referred to group members as "lifelong learners who may be accomplished in other career fields" and as friendly people who welcomed everyone regardless of previous musical experience. Mallory described the group as "accepting, with no pressure," and Kay called it "a safe place to participate in music." As Evelyn remarked, "You get to this age and you don't care about a lot of things," meaning that it is okay to participate but not play perfectly. She added that the group provided a new entry point into music for many.

5.3.7 Spiritual Uplift

Several interviewees believed that music participation nourished the human spirit, though they differed in their beliefs about how this manifested. As Maria put it, music "entices your soul." Xander described it as "a spiritual thing." Grace believed that music was spiritually uplifting because it met so many different human needs, such as connection with others, purpose in life, improved health, and pleasure. Betty Ann believed that music-making was a way to connect spiritually with departed loved ones. She advised, "Play your best song. Loved ones [who have passed away] will hear." Carol believed that music held great benefits for participants, one of which was "spiritual benefits, but not religious."

In contrast, even though she did not participate in music in public, Leah commented that, "For those who participate, music can be a way of expressing religion." Henry was in agreement, commenting that, "Music is a gift from God." With tears in his eyes, Mr. Noah intimated, "Holy spirit comes over me when I sing." Viviana summed it up with the comment, "Music is the most wonderful thing done to humans." Clearly, music touched these interviewees in deep and spiritual ways.

5.4 Quality of Life

Considering the benefits of music participation more broadly, it is easy to discern that music participation was a positive contributor to the center clients' overall quality of life, a finding which is congruent with previous research. Specific connections to extant literature are discussed in Chapter 6; however, it is important to share interviewees' comments relative to quality of life here.

All interviewees felt that music enhanced the quality of life of those who participate in it, but different people experienced this enhancement in different ways and to different depths. Some saw music simply as an enrichment of their quality of life. Ken (a former public-school educator) remarked that, "It's a way to fill my cup. While teaching, my tank was empty. There was no way to recharge. Music is fun." Music helped get his mind off things and helped him to "be in the moment." He felt that it was good to lose himself in something in the moment, to remove himself from problems. Henry also believed that music enriched his life and remarked, "Love it, wouldn't have any other life."

For others, music played a more substantial role in their quality of life, in that it was one of the most important elements of their lives. Tony shared that the three most important things in his life were music, other family members, and his Christian faith. Music would always be a part of his life. Music was also one of the most important parts of Eva's life, along with art, birding, hiking, and biking. Ulysses emphasized that music was the most important activity he did all week.

However, for some, music had an even deeper meaning, to the extent of being a reason for living. Kay described her quality of life as "a 10-plus on a scale of 10, mainly because of the ukulele. It keeps you going." Nicole recounted how, at the senior center she managed, "We almost lost the choir after the director died. Choir folks don't come to the center for anything else. They live for the choir." Nick agreed that "It gives them a reason to be." Linda (exercise leader) took this further and remarked, "I would not get out of bed if not for this class, and I would have been buried a long time ago." In kind, Harry (client of the Senior Place), emphatically stated, "If someone were to turn off music, I would die." Likewise, Jacob volunteered, "Singing makes me alive until now." And finally, Betty Ann's statement, though simple and concise, clearly said it all regarding these interviewees: "Music is *critical* to quality of life."

The following chapter is a synthesis of the information presented in Part II (Chapters 3–5). We reaffirm our previous research findings and those of others that music participation is critical to the quality of life of older adults involved in music-making.

CHAPTER 6

Toward Enhanced Quality of Life through Musical Activities in Senior Centers

We learned much from our visits to six different senior centers in the Continental US, and thoroughly enjoyed our experiences in each locale. Some of what we encountered supported the earlier research findings of ourselves and others, which deepened the current body of knowledge on older adult music participation. However, we are excited that new findings relative to music within senior centers emerged that could help our understanding of, and contribute to, a better quality of life.

In this final chapter of Part II, we take a broad view of the sights, sounds, and stories we shared in Chapters 3–5, point out findings that support earlier research, and introduce and discuss new findings that emerged from this research journey. Our conclusions are organized in three large sections that mirror the foci of the previous three chapters: the six senior centers, music in the centers, and perspectives on older adult center clients' music participation. We end the chapter with thoughts and ideas relative to the role of music in senior centers and in older adults' lives.

6.1 The Senior Centers

The senior centers we visited were welcoming, informal, bustling, vibrant spaces that served as activity and resource hubs for local older adults. Their come-as-you-are inclusiveness helped attendees of different socioeconomic strata and backgrounds to feel welcome and comfortable. The busyness of each center, with multiple comings and goings of clients, with activities and services taking place simultaneously, almost left us breathless! Moreover, each center's positive ambience encouraged socialization and attracted older adults who wanted to connect with other people and make friends. The latter quality supported earlier research findings of Aday and colleagues (2006), who found that senior center environments encouraged the development of friendships, and also the research of Krout (1983), who discovered that older adults involved themselves in senior center activities because they wanted to be with other people.

6.1.1 Center Clientele

Congruent with earlier research (e.g., Aday, 2003; Cannon, 2015), we learned that the six senior centers we visited mainly served clienteles of low- to middle-income older adults. The cultural diversity of the surrounding neighborhoods was often represented in center clientele, and management and staff continually strove to attract greater numbers of ethnically diverse neighborhood clients. This was sometimes a challenge because some ethnic groups, such as the Latino population surrounding Good Hope Senior Center, tended to socialize within close-knit family groups and were not as interested in associating with outsiders.

We also found it interesting to learn that two other demographics of eligible older adults chose *not* to involve themselves in their local senior center. Tracy, the outreach and development coordinator at Sunnyside Senior Center, remarked that *affluent older adults* tended not to attend her center's activities because they preferred to involve themselves in activities that were "more upscale." It is advisable to design activities that would attract affluent older adults to senior centers and those that might integrate participants of all socioeconomic backgrounds.

Staff from several centers also mentioned difficulties in attracting *baby boomers*, or older adults born between 1946 and 1964 (*Merriam-Webster*, n.d.). Tracy believed that attracting baby boomers was one of the *biggest* issues her center faced because they constituted the next older generation, and their participation would be critical to the senior center's sustainability. At the same time, she was encouraged that baby boomer attendance had increased for free or inexpensive events utilizing a DJ and popular music from boomers' teen and adult years. This related to our earlier research finding that older adults enjoyed listening to and participating in musical selections and styles they had enjoyed earlier in life (Fung & Lehmberg, 2016).

For both of these demographics (affluent older adults and baby boomers), we wondered if the term *senior center* could have had negative, ageist connotations in the centers' surrounding communities and could have been a bigger deterrent than the lack of preferred activities. Perhaps this could be a reason for recent trends in the United States of redesigning and re-marketing senior centers as multiage community, wellness, or lifelong learning centers (Pardasani & Thompson, 2012) that provide a wide array of activities and services (Dal Santo, 2009) in response to community needs, instead of catering solely to older adults (Lawler, 2011).

6.1.2 Center Accessibility

It goes without saying that accessibility is basic to the functioning, sustainability, and success of any senior center. Without it, senior centers would cease to be "community focal points" (Pardasani, 2010, p. 49) and would miss the mark to serve the populations of older adults who need them most. The senior centers we visited featured multiple types of accessibility. They were *physically accessible* to older adults via walking, driving a car, or riding in center-sponsored mini-buses or public transportation. They were *socioeconomically accessible* in that center memberships were free or at nominal cost. For example, the most expensive membership of the centers we visited, available at Better Living Senior Center, cost only $20 per calendar year. Similar to other senior centers (Havir, 1991; Krout, 1985), a variety of *recreation activities were readily accessible.* Clients could participate in most of these gratis; however, some required a small fee to cover materials or instructor fees when an outside expert had to be hired to lead an activity. *Health and wellness services were also accessible* via free or low-cost programs subsidized by community organizations or local and state governments. Easy access to these centers' facilities, services, and activities helped their clients to remain independent, which has been shown to be critical to a good quality of life (Burckhardt & Anderson, 2003; Flanagan, 1978, 1982).

6.1.3 Health, Wellness, and Basic Needs

As introduced in Chapter 2, Pardasani (2018) emphasized that senior centers play "a vital role in maintaining the health ... of older adults" (p. 314). A multiplicity of activities, programs, and services covering a wide range of health-related needs were available in each of the centers we visited. These included, but were not limited to, activities and classes that supported physical health (such as exercise and dance classes), individual strength-training sessions, health screenings, and specialty clinics (such as foot clinics). Most centers also ensured that nourishment was accessible to their clients, via free or low-cost, nutritious meal programs, healthy snacks available at various times during the day, and community partnerships that regularly provided bread and fresh produce for center clients to take home. To further mental health, the centers hosted various groups to provide support for specific conditions or situations, such as support groups for individuals with Alzheimer's disease and their caregivers, or for older adults who were raising their grandchildren alone. The centers also provided activities to encourage mindfulness and spirituality, such as meditation groups and yoga.

It was clearly evident that the main mission of the centers we visited was to support the health, wellness, and independence of older adult clientele by helping them to meet their basic needs. Since the enactment of the Older Americans Act in 1965 (Pardasani, 2010; Wick, 2012), most US senior centers have adopted the same mission. We were interested to learn from center managers that activities shown in empirical research to benefit older adults frequently garnered government funding, which allowed centers to offer health- and wellness-related activities when they might not have funding for other types of activities, including musical activities.

6.1.4 Resources

Each center we visited was severely challenged due to insufficient resources. Deficiencies across centers included inadequate funding, not enough physical space, and not enough human resources to staff centers and provide needed services and activities. As described in Chapter 3, Brook (executive director, Sunnyside Senior Center) shared that one of her biggest management challenges was a lack of resources and that government funding had diminished over the last several years, causing her center to offer fewer activities and services or else find additional sources of funding to support them. Both Brook and Nicole (manager, Good Hope Senior Center) expressed dissatisfaction about the limited space in their centers' facilities. In our visits, we noticed that every inch of center space was utilized for something. For example, in some centers we conducted our interviews in small, crowded rooms that were utilized for both client services and storage. There was barely room for a desk and a path to get to it. Additionally, Wanda (coordinator, Sunnyside Senior Center) and Francine (assistant manager, the Center for Healthy Aging) both felt that a major challenge in their centers was a lack of human resources that was exacerbated by a lack of funding. Relative to musical activities, we noted that at least two centers had lost their choirs due to a lack of volunteers to lead them. Research has shown the lack of resources to be a major barrier in the implementation of programs within senior centers that enhance the quality of life of participants (Bobitt & Schwingel, 2017).

Considering the resource-related challenges faced in the six centers we visited, it was nothing less than outstanding that staff and administrators were able to maintain accessibility and a critical focus on health and wellness. We were also amazed at the busyness of the six centers and how friendly and welcoming everyone appeared to be in the face of these challenges. Perhaps the realization that they were enhancing the quality of life of others drove and sustained staff and administrators and kept their hopes alive that these challenges would someday be alleviated somewhat or completely.

6.2 Music in the Centers

When we initially searched for senior centers to explore, we looked for ones that offered opportunities for music participation in the forms of active listening, deliberate and purposeful movement to music, creative musical activities, and music-making activities. We learned that many US senior centers offered *active music-listening* experiences via performances at various points during a month or year by local musicians, as well as regular activities that involved *movement to music*, such as exercise and dance classes. However, we soon discovered that it was rarer to find *music-making* activities in senior centers and quite unusual for a single center to offer a *variety* of music-making activities. Furthermore, opportunities for creative music participation that included *improvisation* or *composition* were practically nonexistent. Perhaps this was due in part to a lack of government funding to support musical activities in senior centers; however, this is a new finding that warrants further study. The senior centers we eventually chose to visit stood out because they offered multiple music-making activities as well as activities that involved listening or moving to music. To the best of our knowledge, this book is the first to report on such activities across a group of senior centers.

During our center visits, we observed multiple and varied musical activities in which center clients were playing, actively listening, and purposefully moving to many different genres and styles of music. We also noticed that music was frequently playing in the background (allowing for passive listening) during unscheduled time and during nonmusical activities such as meals, card games, meditation and movement classes that did not involve purposeful movement to music, and so forth. The omnipresence of music in these centers seemed to convey an underlying belief that music was appreciated and important in creating a positive center ambience and climate. Whether or not they were aware of it, most center clients encountered music in some form or another throughout their senior center experience!

6.2.1 Accessibility of Music-Making Activities

Through our observations of music-making groups, we tried to uncover the essence of what made them work so well for the older adult clients of the six centers. Aside from the benefits participants experienced through music participation (most of which were identified in earlier research and are discussed briefly in the next section), was there a particular combination or intermingling of characteristics that made these groups a good fit for their members? Via qualitative data analysis followed by much reflection and dialogue, we were able to identify several qualities that appeared to be critical across center music-making activities. We found it interesting and a new finding that *all* revolved around the concept of *accessibility*.

Accessibility to the things one needs or cherishes in life is desired by humans of all ages but can become particularly important in older adulthood. At a time in life where mobility, identity, and financial security may be changing, it is critical for older adults to have easy access to opportunities, services, activities, and other essentials that enhance their quality of life (Fung & Lehmberg, 2016). We discovered that center music-making activities comprised several qualities that combined to form an easily accessed conduit to music participation.

6.2.1.1 Physical Access

It is a given that in order to participate in in-person, senior center music-making activities, older adults must be able to travel to a center to join in. As was mentioned earlier, the six centers were easily accessible by individual, center-sponsored, or public transportation. Centers and local governments took care to provide necessities such as accessible parking and indoor facilities. Another important and new consideration, however, was the physical accessibility of the music-making activities themselves. Musical activities across the centers were quite flexible and inclusive of those who needed accommodations. For example, the concert band rehearsal room at the Center for Healthy Aging was accessible by wheelchair, which allowed Udele to participate on days when physical pain limited her mobility. Another example was that choir members at Good

Hope Senior Center were encouraged to sit to rehearse and perform if standing was difficult. According to Nicole, there was a year when the entire choir sat in chairs to perform. Likewise, members of the Good Hope Center guitar class utilized the Chord Buddy mechanism to form chords when their fingers were too stiff or arthritic to do so. The effort these groups made to include and accommodate those who wished to participate was commendable.

6.2.1.2   Financial Access

Closely related to physical accessibility was the financial accessibility of music-making. Instrumentalist participants needed to have the financial capability to access the instruments they needed to participate in their chosen musical group. Some used instruments they had owned and played since childhood or adolescence (e.g., concert and jazz band participants); others (such as ukulele group, harmonica club, or beginning band members) purchased new instruments to learn as beginners. Singing group members, of course, had the most accessible instruments (their voices) and carried them with them wherever they went. The most important consideration was for instruments to be accessible at low cost or no cost, so older adults who needed to watch their finances could choose to participate in musical groups.

As mentioned earlier in this chapter, research has shown that older adults tended to participate in the same types of musical activities as those in which they involved themselves earlier in life (Drummond, 2018; Fung & Lehmberg, 2016; Pitts, 2012). Some authors posited that this may have had to do with personal identity (Drummond, 2018) or family influence and culture (Pitts, 2012); however, we put forth the idea of financial circumstances possibly playing a role. Rather than purchasing a new instrument, it may have been less expensive to choose to sing or to dust off a stored instrument that was played earlier in life.

6.2.1.3   Access and Entry Points

It was critical to many interviewees that musical activities had fluid entry points, meaning that someone could join in and be welcomed at any time, without prior musical experience. Fluid entry points were evidenced across center music-making activities, for example, within karaoke groups, choirs, guitar classes, ukulele and harmonica groups, and in a beginning band. Participants seemed to open their hearts and minds to new members and were willing to do whatever they could to help them succeed and feel like they belonged. All appeared to be accepting of different ability levels and committed to helping each other to have a positive experience. This facilitated a collaborative, inclusive, welcoming group culture that led to participants' perseverance in their musical group or groups over time.

We also noted that entry points were inherently *not* as fluid in the more advanced wind-instrument groups we observed, which made sense because these participants had been playing their instruments for years. There was an expectation that new members would possess the skill level to play the group's musical repertoire. That said, group leaders were more than willing to give extra help to participants who wanted it. Overall, members of these groups were very supportive of each other's efforts to achieve high-quality performances.

Our earlier research also emphasized the importance of fluid entry points in older adult music-making (Fung & Lehmberg, 2016; Lehmberg, 2023). Fluid entry points allowed participants the freedom to belong to a musical group, to develop an identity as a music maker, and to choose music-making as a way to spend leisure time (Lehmberg, 2023). Though advanced-level music-making opportunities are and should be available to older adults who desire them, it is critically important to include all older adults who wish to make music through the provision of music-making opportunities at all levels or with fluid entry points.

6.3   *Accessibility of All Musical Activities*

We have to this point enjoyed sharing our findings related to the accessibility of center *music-making* activities; however, we would be remiss if we failed to point out that accessibility was an important thread running through *all* senior center musical activities. Center staff, activity leaders, and attendees were aware of and inclusive of older adults' physical capabilities, as was evidenced in the availability of chair exercise classes (with music) for those with mobility issues, chair dances within special dance events, and the Senior Place example of several attendees helping another attendee in a wheelchair to rise and dance to her favorite song. Clients' financial strata were also taken into account. Concerts and other musical opportunities were generally offered at low or no cost to center attendees. Overall, entry points for many music-making activities, and most music-listening and movement activities were fluid; new participants were welcomed at any time without previous experience required. Clearly, an overarching goal of the musical activities at these centers was to be inclusive of all older adult attendees.

6.4 Center Clients' Music Participation

Center clients who participated in music within and outside of senior centers overwhelmingly enjoyed their experiences and felt that they benefited deeply, broadly, and in multiple ways from their music participation. In Chapter 5, we shared their stories to embellish and discuss seven themes that emerged across centers and surrounded the benefits clients received from music participation: (1) pleasure, (2) health and well-being, (3) connection, (4) give to others, (5) self-worth, (6) safe spaces, and (7) spiritual uplift. All of these have been previously identified in research from the field of music; however, the theme of *safe space* has been explored less frequently and mainly in scholarly articles focusing on school-aged youth (e.g., Hendricks et al., 2014; Lewis, 2021). More study is warranted to examine facets of safe space relative to older adult music participation. Table 6.1 illustrates the connections of our emergent themes with research conducted after 2015. Some of these can also be found in our recent book chapter (Lehmberg & Fung, 2023) in *The Oxford Handbook of Care in Music Education*.

In addition to the research included here, other researchers in different fields have identified multiple physical, psychological, and social benefits experienced by older adults via music participation. Our previous book, *Music for Life: Music Participation and Quality of Life of Senior Citizens* (2016), presents an extensive list of these through 2016. An exhaustive list of over 500 perceived benefits across age groups can also be found in an article by Krause and colleagues (2018). We posit that the benefits of music participation are perhaps the most important findings to emerge from research to date on older adult music participation.

6.4.1 Qualities of Desired Musical Activities

Via a thorough examination of center clients' music participation and the multiple benefits they received from it, we were able to identify several qualities that were inherent in participants' most-desired musical activities. Figure 6.1 shows these at a glance. On the most basic level, the activities were *accessible* (physically, financially, etc.), *active*, and *enjoyable* for many reasons. Clients described the groups they participated in as having warm, *supportive cultures*. Many also featured fluid entry points and were *inclusive* of older adults of different skill levels and with different prior musical experiences. There was room for clients to participate on their own level, with support for their efforts. The activities also provided opportunity for

Table 6.1. *Benefits of older adult music participation: Connections between current study and previous research*

Current study finding	Appearance in previous research
Pleasure. Older adults derived pleasure from music participation.	Barbeau & Cossette, 2019; Barbeau & Mantie, 2019; Lee et al., 2016; Roulston et al., 2015
Health and Well-being. Music participation enhanced the health and well-being of older adults. It kept them going.	Barbeau & Cossette, 2019; Bugos & Kochar, 2017; Creech et al., 2020; Hudak et al., 2019; Joseph, 2022; Joseph & Human, 2020; Joseph & Southcott, 2018; Krause et al., 2018; Lee et al., 2016
Connection. Music participation provided a means for older adults to connect with their inner selves, with others, and with their musical and life histories.	Barbeau & Cossette, 2019; Creech et al., 2020; Fung & Lehmberg, 2016; Joseph, 2022; Joseph & Human, 2020; Joseph & Southcott, 2018; Lee et al., 2016
Give to others. Older adults were able to give to others via their music participation.	Joseph, 2022; Joseph & Human, 2020; Southcott & Li, 2018; Joseph & Southcott, 2018
Self-worth. Music participation increased older adults' feelings of self-worth, including feeling valued, needed, and like they belonged. Self-worth also increased as music participants improved their musical skills.	Balsnes, 2017; Joseph, 2022; Joseph & Human, 2020; Krause et al., 2018; Southcott & Li, 2018; Woody et al., 2019
Safe space. Fluid entry points allowed access to safe spaces for music participation, within which older adults felt welcomed and valued.	Lehmberg, 2023
Spiritual uplift. Music participation was spiritually uplifting.	Fung & Lehmberg, 2016; Krause et al., 2018; Lee et al., 2016; Southcott & Li, 2018

connection with like-minded others and with participants' own musical histories. Musically, the activities provided opportunities to *build musical knowledge and skills*, which fostered *ownership* of learning with opportunities for participants to *give to their community* through their music. In sum, these desired activities were achievable by participants and provided spaces in which they could grow as musicians and through connections with others, belong and feel appreciated and needed, enjoy their lives, and

Toward Enhanced Quality of Life Through Musical Activities 131

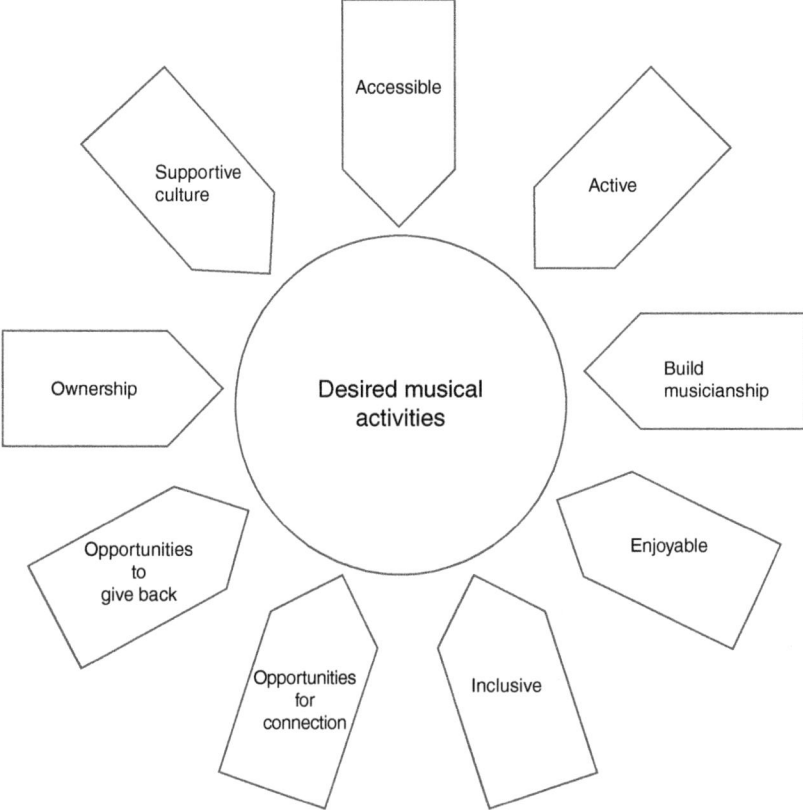

Figure 6.1   Qualities of desired musical activities

enhance the quality of life of others. It is little wonder that we heard participants remark that, "Music keeps me going."

6.5   Role of Music in Senior Centers

It was quite obvious that music played an important and multifaceted role in the senior centers we visited. It attracted older adults to the centers, and some who came to enjoy musical activities also involved themselves in other center activities over time. Center music-making groups, such as the ukulele groups at Sunnyside Senior Center, functioned as center showpieces, attracting community attention and involvement and sometimes leading to increased funding in the forms of monetary and in-kind donations and partnerships. Activities that involved movement to music exemplified the centers' focus on health and wellness, bringing government funding and drawing older adults who were concerned about their physical fitness and psychological well-being and who also enjoyed moving to music. Center-sponsored concerts by local musicians, DJ events, and cultural celebrations involving music brought in large numbers of older adults who enjoyed active listening. These large audiences served to publicize the centers' offerings, promote their reputations, and increase outreach in their surrounding communities.

The variety of musical activities offered in the senior centers we visited also contributed to the positive center climates we sensed and observed. The frequency of these activities and the obvious enjoyment of participants and listeners fostered happy, inclusive ambiences, further developing the centers' reputations as welcoming and enjoyable spaces within which to spend quality leisure time.

6.6 Role of Music in Older Adults' Lives

In Chapters 3–5, we offered a close-up look at music in six senior centers across the United States, through the memorable sights, sounds, and stories we encountered on our visits. From the large amount of data we collected, we were able to determine that accessibility in its various forms was basic and yet key to older adult music participation within these centers. It was also exceedingly obvious (and supported in earlier research) that older adult center clients experienced multiple benefits from music participation, regardless of whether the form of music participation was listening, moving to music, or making music. From the older adult center clients' descriptions of their musical activities, we were able to identify nine common qualities across their desired musical activities, which we presented in Figure 6.1. We now zoom out to present a bigger picture of how the music participation of senior center clients affected their quality of life.

6.6.1 Identity

For senior center clients who involved themselves in musical groups, music-making was a path by which they developed and strengthened their identities in older adulthood, which has been shown to be a time of uncertainty due to changing roles and situations (Fung & Lehmberg,

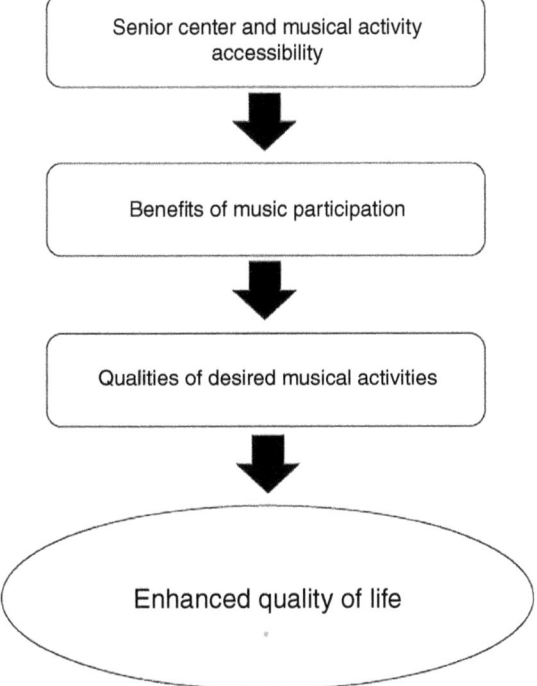

Figure 6.2   Toward enhanced quality of life

2016). No matter whether these older adults had prior musical experience, they identified at the time as musicians and members of their musical group or groups and felt valued and needed.

Clients who participated in activities involving exercising or dancing to music also identified as valued members of their groups. Likewise, those who attended dance or musical performance events at their center identified as members of like-minded groups of people who enjoyed such gatherings and appreciated specific genres of music with which they identified. Regardless of their mode of musical involvement, all senior center music participants could be identified as lifelong learners, appreciators, and consumers (or sometimes makers) of music. The identity they established through music participation at their senior center gave them a sense of purpose in life, enhanced their quality of life, and kept them going.

Table 6.2. *Quality of life model and related findings on senior center clients' music participation*

Quality of life model	Related findings in the current study on senior center clients' music participation
Quality of life scale (Burckhardt & Anderson, 2003)	
1. Material and physical well-being	Benefits experienced through music participation enhanced physical well-being.
2. Health	Benefits experienced through music participation led to improved physical and psychological health.
3. Relationships with parents, siblings, and other relatives	No direct relationship observed.
4. Having and raising children	No direct relationship observed.
5. Relationship with spouse or significant other	Some center clients and activity leaders found music participation with a spouse or significant other to be an enjoyable activity.
6. Relationships with friends	Senior center clients were able to connect with others via music participation and develop and strengthen new friendships.
7. Helping and encouraging others	Participants described their musical activities as having a culture of supporting others.
8. Participating in organizations and public affairs	Participation in musical activities in the form of music-making, moving to music, or performing in public constituted participation in public, community organizations.
9. Intellectual development	Participants enjoyed developing their musical knowledge and skills within their musical activities.
10. Understanding of self	Music participation aided in the development of personal identity at a time of life when identity might be in flux.
11. Occupational role	Participation in musical activities allowed retirees to assume the role of musician. Their roles as group members gave them a purpose in life.
12. Creativity/personal expression	Musical activities allowed participants to express themselves creatively.
13. Socializing	Musical activities provided the opportunity for socialization and connection with others.
14. Passive and observational recreation	Passive music listening was a form of recreation for participants.
15. Active and participatory recreation	Active music listening, movement to music, and music-making constituted participatory recreation for participants.

Table 6.2. (cont.)

Quality of life model	Related findings in the current study on senior center clients' music participation
16. Independence, doing for yourself	To participate in musical activities, center clients had to be independent and able to do for themselves.
Extensions (Fung & Lehmberg, 2016)	
17. Free choices	Participants chose to attend their senior center and to participate in their preferred musical activities at their chosen level of involvement.
18. Supportive context	Senior centers supported the goals of individual clients and of the musical activities, such as being flexible while using the structure and format inherent in the involved musical culture (e.g., director-led structured rehearsal for a concert band or a party-like flexibility for a karaoke group; and a choir may sit rather than stand in performance).

6.6.2 Flanagan's Model and Extensions

Our data suggest a path for senior center clients to move toward an enhanced quality of life through musical activities. It begins with musical activities accessible to older adults, which leads to center clients reaping the benefits of music participation. Observing these benefits could help center staff and clients to identify the qualities of desired musical activities, enabling an enhanced quality of life. A visual representation of this path is presented in Figure 6.2. Returning to Flanagan's (1978, 1982) quality of life model as revised by Burckhardt and Anderson (2003), we note that the music participation of senior center clients supported 14 of 16 items in their measurement scale. Table 6.2 shows the 16 scale items, with a brief explanation of how senior center clients' music participation related to 14 of the items. These findings demonstrated that the benefits went far beyond recreation (item numbers 14 and 15). The same table also includes two extensions based on our prior study (Fung & Lehmberg, 2016): availability of *free choices* from a wide variety of activities and *supportive contexts* (e.g., highly structured or open and informal) conducive to achieving set goals. Various forms of well-being and development were attached directly to the senior center clients who participated in musical activities.

Through one of the first studies examining musical experiences within US senior centers and the music participation of senior center clients, our data revealed without a doubt that senior center clients' musical experiences provided rich, deep, and multifaceted support to enhance their quality of life. We have also shown the importance of offering a wide range of musical activities within senior centers, as a way to make music accessible to older adults who desire to participate. Though our findings greatly expand the body of knowledge on music in senior centers, our research serves only as the "tip of the iceberg" as much more is yet to be learned. That said, it is satisfying to confirm that music was a special phenomenon in the six senior centers we visited, and that for those clients who participated in music, a better quality of life was ensured.

PART III

Entering a New Normal

CHAPTER 7

Musical Opportunities in US Senior Centers Pre- and Mid-Pandemic

The world took an unexpected turn at the onset of year 2020, when a contagious virus spread quickly to different parts of the world. It arrived in the United States in March 2020 as the nation and the world were learning more about it. Any form of human interaction became a risk of being infected. Most organizations and activities, from classes in schools to dinning in restaurants or flying on an airplane, faced this risk and changes were made to avoid it. Senior centers were no exception. While many decision makers reacted with abrupt changes such as temporary shutdowns, others were in an observation mode or scrambled to find alternatives such as utilizing the existing online technologies to avoid direct human contact. We were fortunate to have collected the data presented in the previous chapters with insights gained in the musical offerings in senior centers prior to March 2020, but we were concerned about how senior centers and their clients could adjust to the sudden changes without losing the vibrancy in senior center communities. We turned our focus to senior center management.

7.1 Studying Senior Center Managers

The purpose of this chapter is to present our findings on the status of musical offerings in a sample of US senior centers in the mid-pandemic (October 2021) compared to the pre-pandemic period (pre-March 2020). We also investigated center managers' intentions for music activities going forward. We acknowledge the different nomenclatures for center managers (e.g., program director, program supervisor, executive director, etc.); we use the most common one, "manager," for simplicity. The managers included in this report had been working in their corresponding center from 2 to 22 years (average = 9.3 years). In this investigation, we targeted the same six cities in which the six senior centers described in previous chapters were situated, including small, medium, and large cities across the six US regions (Northwest, Western, North Central, Southwestern, Eastern, and Southern). Rather than focusing on only one senior center per city, we broadened our scope to include all senior centers in the counties in which the six cities were located.

7.2 Surveying the Senior Centers

We developed a survey based on the literature, on our pre-pandemic findings on activities in senior centers presented earlier in this book, and on the goal of our study (see Appendix E). Musical activities were considered in three categories: music-making activities (singing, playing of instruments, musical improvisation, or musical composition), exercise with music in the background (including dance), and attending live music performance events. The survey included questions regarding various aspects of the senior centers, their clients, and their activities at the time of the survey (mid-pandemic in October 2021) and prior to March 2020 (pre-pandemic). In the three types of musical activities, we asked whether they were available for beginners, experienced attendees, or both; whether a participation fee was required; and whether the activity leader was paid. We also asked how the pandemic has affected the musical activities at the center and the managers' intention for change going forward.

An electronic survey link was sent to 88 managers of publicly funded senior centers in the counties in which the six cities were located across the six US regions. We received 37 responses (42.0%), and only 23 were complete (62.2%), yielding a final response rate of 26.1%. The less-than-ideal response rate could be due to the absence of musical activities or the temporary closure of some centers at the time of the survey. This speculation was supported by the response of a nonparticipating center manager who stated that they did not offer any type of music programming and that they did not congregate either in person or online for activities for nearly two years due to the pandemic. To maximize data legitimacy for the purpose of this survey, subsequent analyses were based on completed surveys only, assuming an unknown number of senior centers were closed or did not have musical activity at the time of the survey as well as the typical nonresponse to surveys. Distribution of these senior centers across the six regions are presented in Table 7.1.

The majority of center managers who completed the survey worked for stand-alone senior centers (87.0%); the rest were from multiage centers. They collectively served ethnically diverse populations with 56.5% of the managers reportedly serving older adults of Asian, Black, Hispanic and

Table 7.1. *Distribution of senior center managers who completed the survey*

	City size		
Region	Small	Mid-sized	Large
Western			6
Southern		2	
Eastern	5		
North Central			4
Northwest		4	
Southwestern	2		
Subtotal	7	6	10

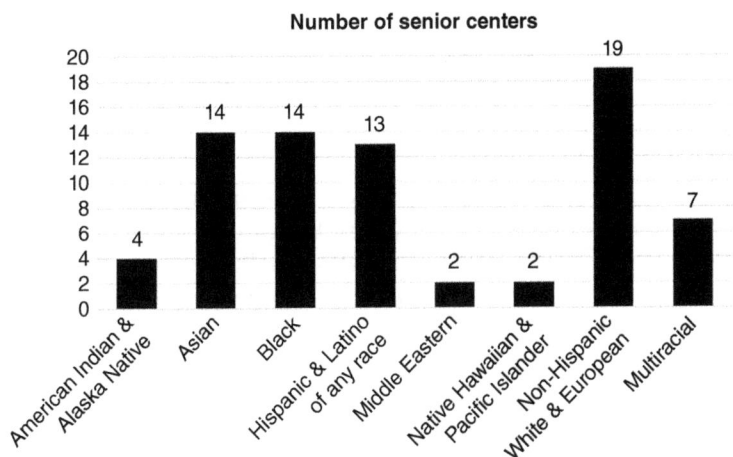

Figure 7.1 Number of senior center managers reporting their clients' ethnicities

Latino, and non-Hispanic White and European origins. Four centers had Asian clients at 35%, 50%, 51%, and 95%; two centers had Black clients at 65% and 90%; and one center had 30% Hispanic and Latino clients. Furthermore, 11 centers had 35% to 98% clients of non-Hispanic White and European origin. Figure 7.1 represents the number of senior center managers reporting the representation of their clients' ethnicities. A small number of managers identified a representation of American Indian and Alaska Native (4), Middle-Eastern (2), Native Hawaiian and Pacific Islander (2), and multiracial (7).

Regarding the state of the senior centers' operation, most centers received funding from local city governments (87.0%) and donations

Table 7.2. *Activity formats at the time of the survey, October 2021*

Activity format	Number of senior centers	Percentage
Open for in-person on-site activities (e.g., classes, rehearsals or jams, concerts, wellness exercise, games, celebrations, social gatherings, special interest groups, etc.)	20	87.0%
Open for in-person on-site services (e.g., meals, tax help, legal or health consultation, support group, etc.)	15	65.2%
Currently scheduling and operating off-site in-person outdoor activities (e.g., trips, outdoor wellness activities, etc.)	9	39.1%
Currently scheduling off-site services (e.g., meals on wheels, social worker visits, etc.)	11	47.8%
Currently scheduling and operating online activities (e.g., classes, music meet-ups, games, celebrations, social gatherings, special interest groups, etc.)	15	34.8%

(69.6%). Less than half of the centers were supported by the federal (43.5%), state (43.5%), or county (30.4%) governments. A few (8.7%–26.1%) received support from foundations, religious organizations, fees, and other sources. Most senior centers involved in this study were open for in-person on-site activities such as classes and wellness exercise (87.0%) and services such as meals and tax help (65.2%). Less than half of the centers also had off-site services such as meals on wheels (47.8%), off-site outdoor activities such as field trips (39.1%), or online activities such as classes and celebrations (34.8%). Table 7.2 provides more details about these activities. Furthermore, most of the center managers (87.0%) indicated that adults in their 70s composed the largest age group among their clients (see Figure 7.2 for more information on age-group distribution of the center clients), who were required to be a minimum age of 50 years or older depending on the center's policy. Only one center welcomed those at age 49 or younger. The oldest clients collectively in these centers were between 90 and 105 years old (mean = 99, median = 100). Since these senior centers were from small, mid-sized, and large cities, there was a wide range in the number of clients they served, from 21 to 40,000 per week and from 75 to 90,930 per year prior to March 2020, and from 6 to 1,500 per week and from 21 to 40,000 per year in October 2021. This dramatic decrease in the number of clients served was probably attributed significantly to the broader social well-being changes.

Musical Opportunities during Pre- and Mid-Pandemic 143

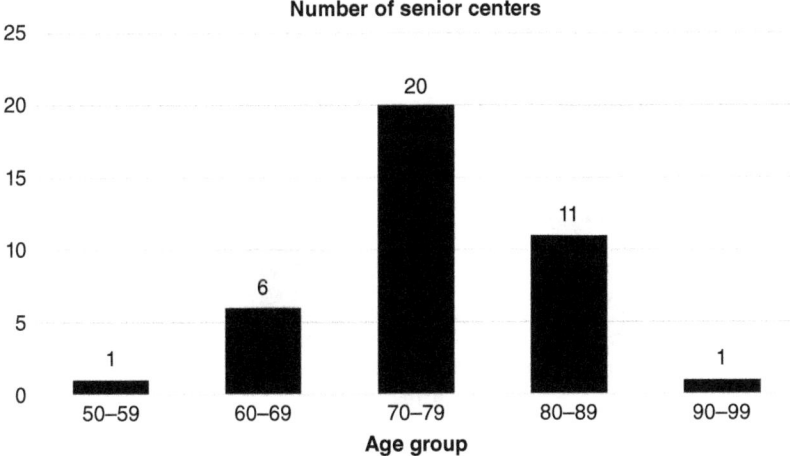

Figure 7.2 Approximate age group of most center attendees (each center manager could choose up to two age groups)

7.3 Musical Activities in Pre- and Mid-Pandemic Periods

The majority of senior centers (87.0%) offered music-making activities prior to March 2020, but just over half (56.5%) offered them at the time of survey (i.e., mid-pandemic). A similar trend was found in the live music performance events (73.9% pre- and 30.4% mid-pandemic). These findings posed a stark contrast to the dance- or exercise-focused activities with music; all senior centers, except one, offered them in both the pre- and mid-pandemic periods. Figures 7.3–7.5 shows a visual comparison of the number of senior centers offering the three types of musical activities in the pre- and mid-pandemic periods.

Differences were also reflected in the fee requirement to participate, and the fee paid to the activity leaders. Clients were not required to pay a fee for 70.1% of the music-making activities and 70.6% of the live music performance events, but only 52.3% of the exercise activities did not require a fee. More interestingly, a little over half of the leaders for music-making activities (52.4%) and live music performance events (55.0%) were paid, while the majority (80.0%) of the exercise activity leaders were paid. These findings reflect the cost, demand, and level of professional training of the activity leaders in the three types of musical activities. Note that nearly all music-making activities were designed for beginners and experienced attendees, and all exercise activities with music

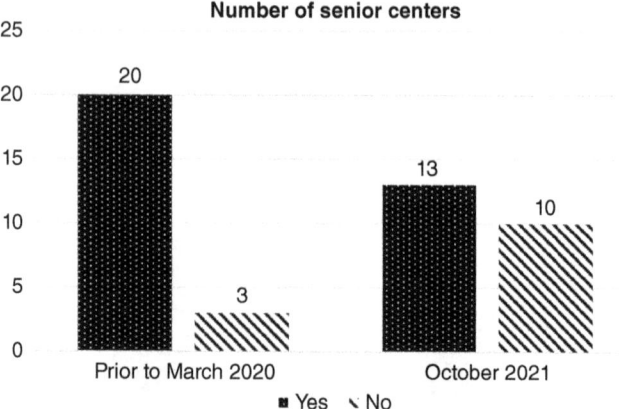

Figure 7.3 Number of senior centers offering three types of musical activities in pre- and mid-pandemic periods: Music-making activities (singing, playing of instruments, musical improvisation, or musical composition)

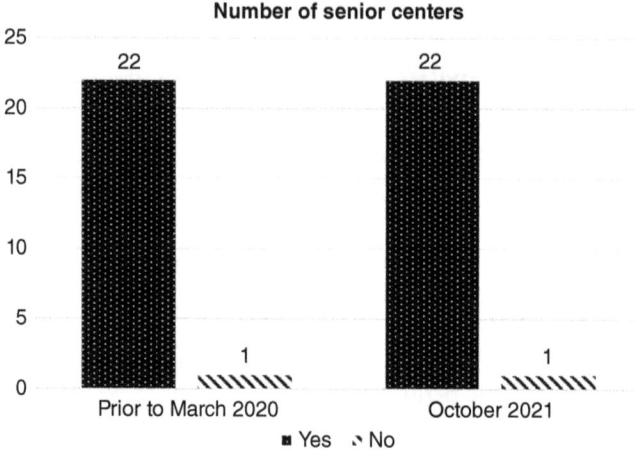

Figure 7.4 Number of senior centers offering three types of musical activities in pre- and mid-pandemic periods: Dance- or exercise-focused activities in which attendees move to music or exercise-focused activities with music in the background
Note. The number 22 should have been 137 due to a center manager entering "116 Fitness Classes" as one activity in the "Dance and Exercise with Music" category (see Appendix D).

and all live music performances welcomed beginners and experienced attendees. Table 7.3 is a summary of the number of musical activities expressed in terms of availability for beginners or experienced attendees, fee requirement, and paid activity leader.

Table 7.3. *Number of musical activities in relation to availability for beginners or experienced attendees, fee requirement, and paid activity leader*

Musical activities	For beginners*		For experienced attendees*		Materials or other required fee		Activity leader paid	
	Yes	No	Yes	No	Yes	No	Yes	No
Music-making: Singing, playing of instruments, musical improvisation, or musical composition	35	4	41	0	11	26	22	20
Dance- or exercise-focused with music in the background	57**	0	57**	0	21	23	44	11
Live musical performances	20	0	20	0	5	12	11	9

*Almost all musical activities for beginners and experienced attendees were the same activities.

**The 57 activities could have been 172, because a center manager in a large city in the Northwest entered "116 Fitness Classes" as one activity in the "Dance and Exercise with Music" category (see Appendix D).

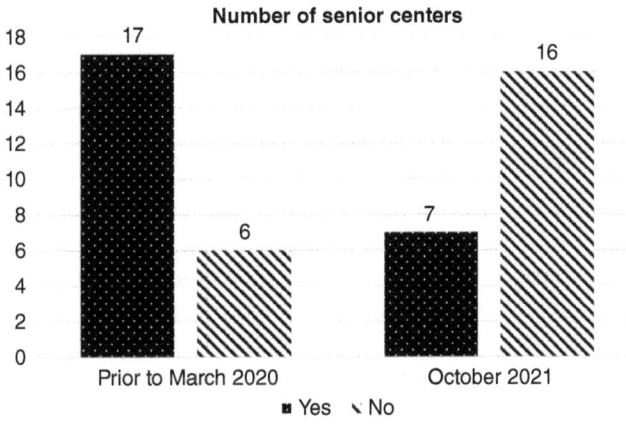

Figure 7.5 Number of senior centers offering three types of musical activities in pre- and mid-pandemic periods: Live musical performance events

Table 7.4. *Center managers' responses to the effect of the pandemic on musical activities*

	Music-making: Singing, playing of instruments, musical improvisation, or musical composition	Dance- or exercise-focused with music in the background	Live musical performances	Total
Cancelled completely	12	11	9	32
Cancelled for a time, then reinstated in person but less frequent	13	9	4	26
Cancelled for a time, then reinstated online but less frequent	1	1	1	3
Cancelled for a time, then reinstated in person resuming pre-pandemic schedule	7	10	2	19
Cancelled for a time, then reinstated online resuming pre-pandemic schedule	3	2	0	5
Not cancelled; moved online but less frequent	0	2	0	2
Not cancelled; moved online continuing pre-pandemic schedule	0	5	2	7
Not cancelled; continued to meet in person but less frequent	0	0	0	0
Not cancelled; continued to meet in person on pre-pandemic schedule	1	0	0	1
Total	37	40	18	95

The impacts of the pandemic on the offering of musical activities became obvious in the responses of center managers as of October 2021. These impacts ranged from making no change and continuing to meet in person on pre-pandemic schedule in one musical activity (youth piano recital for older adults during lunchtime in a mid-sized city in the North Central region) to completely cancelling 32 musical activities. For most musical activities, the alternatives involved cancelling for a time, then reinstating in some form, such as meeting less frequently or online. Initial cancellation seemed to be inevitable for the majority of musical activities (see Table 7.4). Only ten out of the 95 reported musical activities were not cancelled. Nine of the continuing musical activities were moved online. However, the 95 reported activities should have been 210 or more, because the manager of a senior center in a large city in the Northwestern region entered "116 Fitness Classes" as one activity in the "Dance and Exercise with Music" category and explained that these classes included "balance, cardio, strength training, etc." (see Appendix D in the Dance and Exercise with Music section). It is possible that other managers might have abbreviated their listings rather than responding with a comprehensive list.

7.3.1 Beyond Mid-Pandemic

Regarding center managers' intention going forward, 14 center managers (60.9%) planned to resume all musical activities to a pre-pandemic, in-person schedule after the pandemic is under control. However, there was still a high degree of uncertainty as reflected in how the center managers might modify the format of the activities with mixtures of in-person, remote, and hybrid formats, and between resuming and reducing the activity frequency. Figure 7.6 shows this coexistence of the hope to resume to pre-pandemic level and the uncertainty of future directions in this group of center managers. The four managers who selected "Other" as their plan reflected that (a) there was potential to explore "new programs" (a center in a large city in the Northwest), (b) they "have already moved forward,"

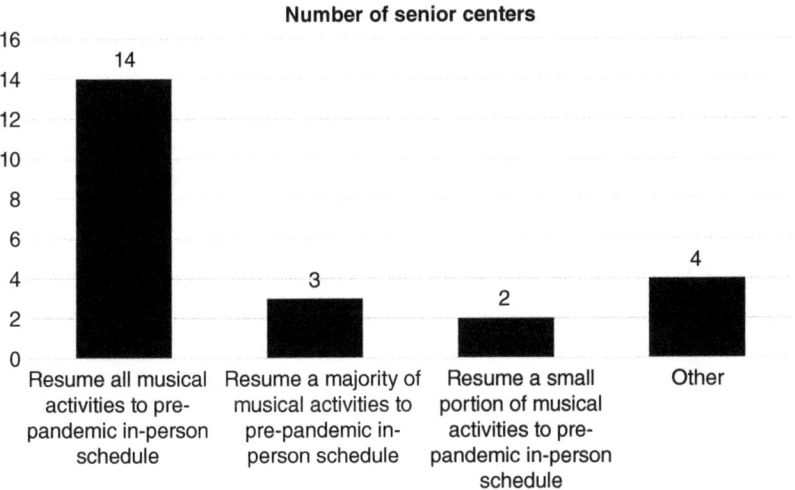

Figure 7.6 Senior center managers' plans for musical activities after the pandemic is under control

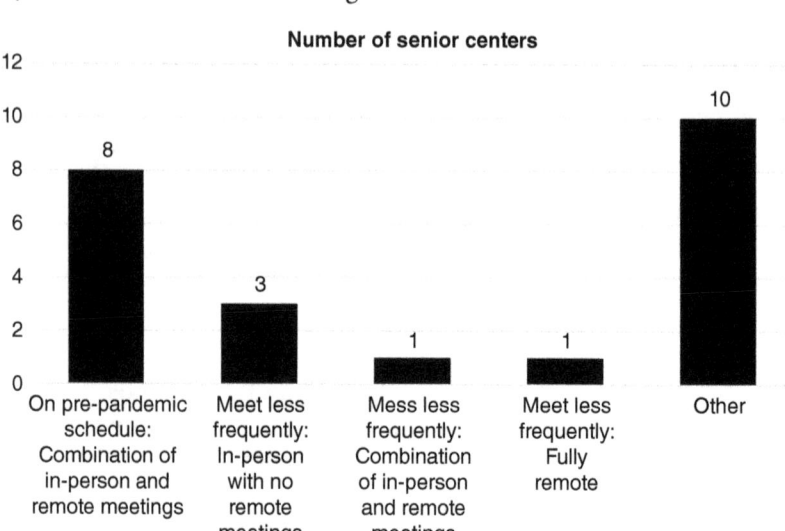

Figure 7.7 Ways musical activities might be modified after the pandemic is under control

implying resumed at the pre-pandemic level (a center in a small city in the Eastern region), and (c) they were in a state of wait-and-see depending on the "comfort level" of all involved, the choice of the activity leaders, and the nature of the activity such as live music entertainment versus instructional classes (two centers in small cities, one in the South and the other in the East). When asked specifically how their musical activities would be modified, the overall sense was that there should be no modification or a combination of in-person and remote formats. Figure 7.7 demonstrates this ambience with their specific choices. Eight center managers (34.8%) chose to return to the pre-pandemic schedule with a combination of in-person and remote formats and ten (43.5%) chose "Other," among whom six clearly indicated no change while returning to pre-pandemic in-person format. One stated that most activities had already returned to the pre-pandemic in-person schedule, one suggested using a hybrid format, one wrote "unknown," and one did not write any comment.

7.4 Implications

The findings from our survey study on musical offerings in senior centers, coupled with what we learned from our senior center visits, led to several insights related to health and well-being, community-based lifelong learning, and musical activity leaders. Our broad look at center musical offerings also provided us with a sense of what activities and formats may be here to stay and where there might be potential for change or expansion. From the insights we gained, we present several implications for center managers and activity coordinators, musical activity leaders, music teacher educators (school or community), and senior center clients.

7.4.1 Music in Relation to Health and Well-being

Our earlier work (Fung & Lehmberg, 2016) and that of others (e.g., Krause et al., 2018) illuminated multiple physical, psychological, and social benefits older adults receive from music participation. Regardless, during the mid-pandemic period, musical activities consisting of exercise to music or with music in the background continued in the same number of senior centers, while music-making activities and music-listening opportunities (such as live concerts) were offered in a much smaller number of centers. It appeared that musical activities that enhanced the physical health of older adult center clients were somehow prioritized over those that brought psychological and social benefits via aesthetic experiences, musical self-expression, and connection and collaboration with others. We had learned earlier from our senior center visits that the same was true relative to funding. Activities shown in empirical research to benefit older adults' health and wellness (such as exercise to music) tended to be government-funded, while music-making and listening activities were not. Centers might have needed to conserve funding mid-pandemic and put activities that were not government-funded on hiatus, or possibly music participation in the forms of music-making and listening were not as highly regarded as exercising to music, which is more directly linked to physical benefits. It is also possible that management and clients simply wanted to decrease physical contact within centers mid-pandemic and opted for offering smaller exercise groups rather than larger music-making groups or audiences attending live performances. Additional research is needed to shed light on these speculations.

7.4.2 Music and Lifelong Learning in the Community

From the number and different types of musical activities (making music, moving to music, and attending live music performance) offered pre-pandemic in the senior centers whose managers responded to our survey, we discerned that opportunities for lifelong learning in music were valued across the centers and constituted a significant part of their programming. Considering the decrease of music-making and music-listening activities in senior centers mid-pandemic amid a widespread practice of social distancing, we wondered how it might be possible to continue such activities in some form for center clients who were self-isolating. This could involve taking advantage of broad technology access to reach self-isolating clients and potentially going even further to extend musical offerings to would-be center clients who were homebound and unable to access their local center in person. As the pandemic subsides or becomes endemic, we encourage senior center executive boards, managers, and staff to not only carefully and healthfully reinstate the musical activities they offered pre-pandemic, but also explore ways to offer opportunities for lifelong learning in music to the local self-isolating or homebound older adult constituency. Perhaps online options for synchronous music-making activities could be explored further, including access to video-conferencing platforms with low levels of latency. This would allow center clients to make music together online but at a physical distance, yet in real time without much sound distortion. It could also be worthy to explore live music-listening or participatory opportunities for homebound, self-isolated, or nongregarious local older adults via phone, Internet, or in person in their homes.

7.4.3 Musical Activity Leaders

We noted that very few musical activities reported by senior center managers appeared to involve creativity in the form of music composition or improvisation. Our visits to senior centers showed this to be true as well. Supportively, research from the field of music education has shown that school music educators are generally not comfortable teaching music composition or improvisation and lack training in these activities (e.g., Hickey & Schmidt, 2019). At the same time, literature in adult education (e.g., Knowles, 1980) and gerontology (e.g., Cohen, 2000, 2005) has long suggested that older adults have accumulated a wealth of life experiences that can serve as a basis for learning and artistic creations including music. Cohen's (2005) research shows that frequent participation in "dance" and in "playing a musical instrument" are among five most effective leisure activities that can reduce "the risk of dementia and cognitive decline" (p. 25). The other three are "playing board games," "doing crossword puzzles," and "reading." We encourage senior center music activity leaders to take advantage of older adults' life experiences and offer more opportunities for center clients to create music, such as writing their own songs that express a segment of their significant life experiences and perform them for others, which may involve singing and playing music instruments in a group setting. Among suggestions that facilitate older adults' creative process in senior centers, Beisgen and Kraitchman (2003) encouraged cultivating a spirit of play and experimentation, using positive and constructive feedback, rewarding achievements, and providing a safe space for risk-taking and opportunities for group interaction and creative work display. They also suggested that creating music and other arts not only offers opportunities for "self-expression and achievement" and "lifelong learning and service to others," it "provides a sense of self-worth" and "can be used as vehicles to explore what it means to grow old." Furthermore, it can help "relieve isolation through opportunities for engagement with others" (pp. 106–107).

These ideas are in accord with Cohen's (2005) *liberation* phase in the second half of life (from age mid-50s to mid-70s) when "plans and actions are shaped by a new sense of personal freedom to speak one's mind and act according to one's needs" and "new neuron formation in the information processing part of the brain is associated with a desire for novelty" (p. 52). Along with the next phase, *summing up* (from late 60s into the 90s), when "people are motivated to share their wisdom" and have a neurological contribution to the "capacity for autobiographical expression" (p. 52), the age range between mid-50s and the 90s seems to have a perfect social, psychological, and neurological setup for creative work based on their rich life experiences and wisdoms. In music, creative work may be shared with others through performance, which can be viewed as a way to give back to society. This is vital to senior centers as this age range matches perfectly with the vast majority of center clients (see Figure 7.2).

In addition, we suggest that senior center managers reach out to their local communities to find qualified individuals to lead these types of musical activities in their center. Organizations that prepare music educators and musical activity leaders (university degree programs, community music programs) could provide individuals enrolled in their programs with experiential explorations of pedagogical strategies for leading creative musical activities in senior centers.

A closely related issue concerns the preparation and selection of individuals to lead dance and exercise activities with music in senior centers. In our visits to senior centers, we noticed that those who led exercise activities to music out of necessity appeared to have knowledge, training, or experience regarding the physical capabilities of older adults. Likewise, we noticed that the leaders of some music-making activities had degrees in music and were or had been career music educators. However, we also noticed most musical activity leaders who, while seemingly experienced, enthusiastic, and able to connect easily with others, did not appear to have much formal training in the musical activities they led or in their pedagogical approaches, other than self-guided learning or informal experiences. These activity leaders were nonetheless successful, which led us to expand our earlier thoughts on fluid entry points. If fluid entry points are essential for older adults without previous musical experiences to join center music-making activities, then the concept of fluid entry points might apply to musical activity leaders as well. It might be worthy to explore whether individuals with excellent leadership qualities and related personal musical experience can effectively lead a musical activity in a senior center. Additional suggestions are that (1) programs that prepare potential musical activity leaders in senior centers (music educator preparation programs, community music programs) could consider placing more focus on creative activities and the preparation of future leaders of these and (2) senior center management may wish to further standardize screening and vetting processes for musical activity leadership positions so that all musical activity leaders are highly qualified through training or experience. We recommend that *all* musical activity leaders be paid for their services, to encourage the most-highly-qualified individuals to apply for these positions.

7.4.4 *What Is Here to Stay*

Throughout the pandemic there have been questions as to what can be learned from mid-pandemic senior center musical activities and can be applied to improve these opportunities moving forward. We believe that the options of online synchronous and hybrid instructional formats are here to stay, because they are convenient and easily accessible for most, and can thus provide means to include more older adults than in pre-pandemic times. We also believe that government funding for musical activities shown in empirical research to benefit older adults' health and well-being is here to stay, and hope that more empirical research can document social and psychological benefits of older adult music participation in senior centers to garner additional funding. It is evident that musical activities are here to stay in senior centers and will continue to constitute important and substantial portions of senior center programming. And finally, we believe that older adult music participation in all of its forms is here to stay because of the multiple benefits that have already been, and are yet to be, evidenced.

7.4.5   What Is Going to Change

As indicated at the beginning of this book, the aging population is increasing. Different generations with a range of backgrounds and experiences are entering the second half of life. This is coupled with the increasing diversity in the US population. We anticipate that the growth and diversification of older adults are continuing to lead to more changes in the operation and offerings of senior centers. Along with the growing body of research in various fields, we expect that changes in musical offerings in US senior centers are going to be influenced by:

- An ever-increasing access to the Internet by all generations
- The changing roles and expectations of senior center activities
- The evolving cultural and musical landscapes locally and globally
- The evolving funding and administrative models of senior centers

7.4.6   Potential for Expansion

The pandemic has caused most of us to think about the strategies that helped us to survive as music participants, educators, or consumers, and of those strategies, which should be kept as we move forward. In sum, we suggest that musical connections should continue beyond the local in-person community via the Internet (e.g., via real-time streamed performances, music-making meet-ups, and social gatherings). Particularly for music-making, a need must be met for wider access to applications and platforms that reduce or eliminate latency, so real-time music-making is possible. We also advocate for more choices of creative musical activities in senior centers. These could be explored through partnerships between senior centers and community music organizations and universities, or via sponsored, stand-alone professional development events for music educators and community musicians. Music activity leaders in senior centers could improve their quality of service by becoming more knowledgeable in gerontological health and well-being. Moreover, we advocate for new ways to provide musical opportunities to homebound, self-isolated, or nongregarious older adults via phone, Internet, or in person in their homes with live music performances. Finally, we encourage older adults to join in musical activities regardless of whether they have previous musical experience, to express themselves creatively, and experience the multiple benefits music participation has to offer.

CHAPTER 8

Lifelong Music Participation and New Considerations

Music in senior centers in the United States is clearly an understudied area. The juncture between music and senior centers has opened up new social, physical, psychological, and artistic spaces for older adults, who need to express, share, learn, and create for self and others, to maintain their well-being, and to push their quality of life to the highest. Music is mighty yet malleable and ubiquitous, offering infinite avenues for exploration and engagement, from enjoyment to life-changing experiences. Senior centers are hidden gems integral to local communities, offering an open and vibrant ambience while serving clients of all backgrounds so lives are connected interpersonally and intergenerationally. With the help of available technologies, the connections may be extended far beyond the senior centers. In this chapter, we take discoveries from all previous chapters and venture into new considerations when the global pandemic is seemingly becoming endemic. We organize these new considerations by constituencies most directly involved in musical activities in senior centers; at the same time, we encourage all other constituencies to be aware of these considerations and do their part to enhance older adults' quality of life. These considerations are addressed to older adults, their service providers, and researchers.

8.1 For Older Adults

We began this book with the premise that music participation included all forms of music-making, listening, and creating, as well as moving to music in such ways as dancing and exercising. However, we have learned that older adults, and most other senior center personnel, tended to equate music-making with music participation, which is narrower than our intention. Consequently, self-identified nonmusic participants almost uniformly fall into our frame of music participants. Those who do not make music in senior centers listen to music purposefully or in the background. When moving to music is included, it becomes even clearer that basically everyone is a music participant. In addition, we realize that composing music is largely absent in older adults' mindset on musical activities, which should not necessarily be the case because there is tremendous prospect for older adults to explore their creative potentials (Cohen, 2000, 2005, 2006).

In regards to music in senior centers, our findings suggest that older adults' quality of life is influenced by the availability and delivery of musical activities at the center and the decisions and actions of which older adults are capable. Older adults may consider all activities, musical and otherwise, offered through the senior center as a palette of choices. Simply learning what activities are available would be the first step toward engagement in an activity. They may do so by personally exploring various activities within the center or through people they know and via other media. Family members, friends, or anyone they live with or close by can be of great assistance. Most senior centers contain an embedded hub for a great variety of resources, activities, services, and networks aimed at serving older adults in the neighborhood. It would be beneficial for everyone, especially older adults, to be aware of the functions of these centers.

Since the vast majority of musical activities offered through senior centers are open to beginners and experienced participants and have fluid entry points, older adults should take advantage of this setting, to try and explore, then decide on an individualized level of involvement suited to achieving their own goal, from observing and learning to getting involved in organizing and leading. Whereas most center clients participate in between observing and leading, there is ample space for activity participation in the middle range of this continuum for older adults to pursue a better quality of life. The flexibility in entry point and level of participation allows clients to make connections as desired. Here, connections can be made to the music, other clients, the client's previous life experience, or the nature of the activity (music-making, moving to music, or attending live music performance).

Creative music-making can be seen as a way to make connections within the self. Connections are made when music is used to express an emotion, communicate a thought, or tell a story. Although primarily all musical activities in our current study were based on precomposed music, newly composed music can be equally or more effective, too. Unfortunately, we saw only minimal evidence of creative music-making in our data. The example we found was in the harmonica group in Good

Hope Senior Center, in which members created their parts for each tune by listening to how notes could fit together, similar to improvisation. We see much potential for older adults to engage in and benefit from creative musical activities in senior centers. We recommend that older adults consider engaging in improvising, composing, or using a user-friendly composition or music production app (e.g., GarageBand) that is easily accessible and requires minimal musical training. Song-writing activities could have an added advantage, because participants may work individually or collaboratively in writing lyrics, composing the main melody, arranging accompaniment parts, working on a rhythm section, playing a musical part in performance, or using a combination of these. Any creative musical activities would allow participants to use their wisdoms and rich life experiences that can be transformed into communicative pieces of music to be shared with anyone and to give to the community.

Exercising the brain through music-making activities is a prominent benefit reported by many senior center clients. This is worth noting, because cognitive decline has been a major concern for older adults. Twelve of the senior center clients we interviewed commented on an enhanced cognitive and brain function as a result of their music participation. Older adults may consider choosing a musical practice for the sake of their well-being rather than musical achievement, because for older adults, well-being is at a higher priority than the making of quality musical sound. Evelyn from the ukulele group in Sunnyside Senior Center intimated that participating in the group is much more important than playing the music perfectly. We observed that this sentiment is shared by many center client music participants. Therefore, we suggest that older adults should be worry-free and be focused on their well-being even if they experience the challenge of not producing a perfect musical sound.

Older adults may start on a musical activity in a senior center as having "something to do" as seen in the literature and in some center clients in our data. However, if possible, we recommend committing to an activity for a longer period, so benefits and learning can be maximized. For example, the social network in a musical group takes time to establish. Friendship, trust, and camaraderie take time to develop. Physical pain reduction, if any, may be short-lived if music participations are incidental and sporadic. Focus of attention, eye–hand coordination, and psychomotor skills are built into many music-making activities, yet they all take time to practice and develop.

8.2 For Older Adult Service Providers

Since senior centers are constructed for the people and by the people, all center personnel should consult and collaborate with the local population of older adults. In this section, we address new considerations for center managers, activity leaders, educators, and policy makers from the standpoint of their challenges identified from the prior chapters in this book.

8.2.1 Center Managers

In our visits to senior centers, the managers shared that they had problems in locating quality activity leaders who could commit for the long term. We realize the difficulty surrounding this and offer the suggestion of reaching out to local colleges and universities, community music schools, state music education organizations, churches, and local school and community music educators to identify high-quality, potential music activity leaders. We also suggest exploring new avenues for funding these activities, such as local or state arts organization grants, so leaders could be paid for their service and the rate of turnover might be reduced. Thus, the quality of the musical activities in the center could be improved as music activity leaders might have more experience and be better qualified.

Another problem shared by center managers was attracting members of younger cohorts of older adults, specifically baby boomers. Perhaps efforts could be directed toward reducing the stigma of senior centers as "places for old people" and instead more vigorously marketing them as vibrant, enjoyable places to spend leisure time. We suggest that center-sponsored concerts could feature musical groups who play styles and selections from the 1960s to the 1990s, which would be familiar to most baby boomers. Additionally, consideration could be given to offering more participatory music-making activities with fluid entry points, such as circle singing, drum circles, or rock bands, none of which were evident in our data.

A third challenge mentioned by senior center managers was attracting affluent older adults who are looking for leisure activities that are more "upscale" than those offered in senior centers. We suggest reaching out to this constituency to ask about (a) the reasons why they choose not to participate in senior centers and (b) what types of musical activities might attract them. It could also be worth finding out the types of community service activities in which they choose to involve themselves, and exploring ways that some of those might be held in senior center settings, possibly for the benefit of the respective center.

We posit that the emerging trend of multigenerational community centers with a focus on wellness might prove a positive path toward attracting both younger and more affluent cohorts of older adults. This could help to destigmatize the "senior center" and make way for an inclusive and collaborative ambience toward supporting the wellness, well-being, and quality of life of all generations.

8.2.2 Activity Leaders

It is important to emphasize our appreciation for senior center musical activity leaders who are paid little or not at all, and yet continue to enhance the quality of life of senior center clients through their dedication and service. We suggest that they continue to learn as much as possible about the characteristics and capabilities of older adults via professional development activities, to develop and maintain effective teaching practices that are current and innovative. This way, customized strategies for making music, moving to music, or listening to music may be created to meet the needs of specific older adults.

We also suggest exploring the possibility of grant funding via local or state arts organizations to help provide instruments, sound equipment, instructor salaries, and funding for guest artists to support musical activities. Whereas leading a musical activity in a senior center may be viewed as a way to give back to the community, more resources should be utilized to serve a wider population and to keep improving the quality of the activity experience of older adults.

8.2.3 Educators

For adult educators in general, we point out the critical importance of cognizance of the human need for flexibility, choice, fun, and creativity within teaching and learning experiences. We suggest providing flexible opportunities for older adults to join in an activity at any time and construct their own learning at their own pace, with ample opportunities for choice and encouragement for fun and creative self-expression.

Jorgensen (2021) stated that, "the values that guide music education and the objectives and methods consistent with them should be tailored to people at each phase of life" (p. 67). For music educators and music teacher educators who wish to be or to prepare effective, engaging, facilitative instructors of older adults, we advocate for increased emphasis on community music education through professional development opportunities and coursework in undergraduate and graduate music education degree programs, including preparation for leading creative and participatory musical activities with fluid entry points. One avenue for this might be community engagement partnerships, internships, and other projects with local music organizations, including amateur and professional community music groups and community music schools, as well as colleges and universities. If more educators are better prepared to work with older adults in senior center settings, not only will the quality of center activities be improved, but also the older adults' quality of life will be enhanced.

8.2.4 Policy Makers

Perhaps policy makers such as elected officials, government social service and community employees, and volunteer community service organization and senior center executive board members are in the best position to advocate for empirical research that clearly shows the benefits of music participation for older adults. We suggest prioritizing efforts to identify and seek out funding for such research, which would certainly add to the body of knowledge surrounding adult music participation and lead to additional quality music participation opportunities for older adults in senior centers.

We also call for a commitment to offer musical opportunities (and multiple musical opportunities where possible) in *every* US senior center, so that senior center clients everywhere may be privy to the enhanced quality of life that music participation provides. National organizations on aging could assist by placing new emphasis on the arts (including musical opportunities) by creating and making publicly available at no cost a database that senior centers could draw from, to identify available and interested musical activity leaders across the United States.

Due to the widespread stigmatized image of senior centers across the United States, policy makers should draw upon resources for a nationwide reform and a marketing campaign. We suggest that the reform should make senior centers more integrated with different public sectors, such as libraries, gyms, farmers' markets, grocery stores, medical clinics, public parks, offices of financial consultants and lawyers, and so forth. This integration will likely engage all generations in the community. Then a large-scale rebranding and marketing campaign is needed. This way, older adults' quality of life is not an isolated pursuit but enhanced through linkages to everyone's quality of life.

8.3 For Researchers

As revealed in Chapter 2, an extensive body of research exists in studying various aspects of senior centers and their clients. In contrast, studies of musical activities in senior centers are sporadic at best. Given the diverse nature of musical activities and the complex and multifaceted nature of senior centers, there is a need for growth in research on music in senior centers. Specifically, music researchers may latch onto the framework already developed in senior center research, such as the use of specific participation variables (number of activities participated in, frequency of participation, and duration of participation) rather than a straightforward participant-versus-nonparticipant divide. These details are critical and informative in the development of musical offerings in senior centers.

Our study shows declines in music-making and live music performance events in senior centers mid-pandemic (October 2021) compared to pre-pandemic (prior to March 2020). We wonder if these reductions were associated with practices of social distancing, lack of funding and resources, priority given to health-related activities (including dancing and exercising), or a combination. A study that teases out these possibilities could be informative to policy makers and center managers going forward.

Studies on music, senior centers, and quality of life can represent three separate research fields. Trends in studying senior centers or quality of life *per se* require interdisciplinarity, typically across the fields of psychology and sociology, among others. Research in senior centers also commonly connects to literature in aging studies, gerontology, and social work; research on quality of life often relates to literature in medical and health sciences, education, and business. The focus of musical activities in senior centers that aim at enhancing older adults' quality of life brings in a new perspective that drives toward a bigger need for more research that can be conducted by researchers from any of the relevant fields. We suggest that forthcoming research on the topic should continue to be interdisciplinary; cross-disciplinary collaborations are encouraged.

From a theoretical perspective, the prominent desire for musical activities in senior centers may be explained by the concept of gerotranscendence (Tornstam, 1994, 2011) and the theory of socioemotional selectivity (Carstensen, 1991; Carstensen et al., 1999; Fung et al., 1999). They have a high degree of resemblance in that, for older adults, there is a realignment of priorities, shifting from materialistic and surface-level pursuits to more selective, deep, and meaningful social contacts in order to maximize positive and lasting outcomes. Interestingly, it reminds us of the nature of humans taking actions to promote prosperity and to avoid adversity (Fung, 2018), although no life stage is attached. More theoretical and empirical work is needed to confirm the extent to which (a) these concepts and theory share common explanations and (b) senior center clients' choice for musical activities and their engagement at a high level of commitment is explained by such concepts and theory.

After the current mid-pandemic state and heading toward a new normal at senior centers, research is needed to explore opportunities to use technology (e.g., the Internet and various electronic devices) to engage older adults who might not yet have engaged musically. Along this line of inquiry, we should attend to the level of acceptance in using social-distancing behaviors (e.g., hand sanitizing) and their tolerance (e.g., understanding the need for mask-wearing) in a variety of music activities. We notice that such behaviors and tolerance were practiced for those with respiratory discomforts in some nations (e.g., Japan) long before the global pandemic began in 2020.

Finally, we chose the United States as our site in these studies, but we do not doubt that potential similarities exist elsewhere. The differences could only be in the structure, format, and styles that cater to the specific local setting. We eagerly await more studies in other nations to confirm the benefits of musical activities for everyone, particularly for older adults. Until then, we hope to see continuous growth and prosperity in musical activities in senior centers everywhere.

APPENDIX A

Detailed Description of the Study
Purpose, Design, and Methods

The purpose of the six case studies presented in Chapters 3–6 was to investigate (a) the role of music participation in the quality of life of older adults who utilize government-funded senior centers in culturally and socioeconomically diverse communities and (b) the role of music itself within these centers. As in our previous research (Fung & Lehmberg, 2016), we based our conception of quality of life on Flanagan's (1978, 1982) model, later revised by Burckhardt and Anderson (2003), which included the domains of material and physical well-being; relationships with others; social, community, and civic activities; personal development and fulfillment; recreation; and independence. Based on our data (Fung & Lehmberg, 2016), we suggested that two additional domains of availability of free choices and supportive context should be added to this model, so our model of quality of life for this study includes these domains as well. For the purposes of this study, we defined *musical activities* as activities in which one makes or creates music, moves to music, or listens to music.

A.1 Qualitative Design

To address the purpose of our study, we used a qualitative, naturalistic inquiry research design to acquire a rich data that would lead to a deep understanding of the topic. According to Guba (1978), *naturalistic inquiry* utilizes a discovery-based approach and minimizes researcher manipulation of the research context. Patton (2015) further describes naturalistic inquiry research as taking place in real-world settings with the goal of documenting what takes place and understanding the day-to-day realities of research study participants. There are no prior constraints placed on the research. On the contrary, researchers are open to whatever findings emerge and to a flexible research design that can change as the fieldwork unfolds. "Observations take place in real-world setting and people are interviewed with open-ended questions in places and under conditions that are comfortable for and familiar to them" (p. 48). Advantages of naturalistic inquiry are that it allows for the complexity of changing, real-world phenomena and provides a path toward understanding of participants' experiences.

Our research took place in the real-world settings of senior centers. Data were collected via unobtrusive observations, semi-structured and open interviews, and online searches for publicly available artifacts. Throughout our observations, we took care to let the phenomena of interest (senior centers, older adults, senior center activities) unfold naturally and not manipulate them in any way.

A.2 Method

We wished to collect data that were representative of different regions of the United States, yet were limited by time and funding. These constraints dictated that our research be conducted within the Continental United States. Since we are members of the music professoriate, we conveniently applied the divisions used by the National Association for Music Education: Eastern, North Central, Northwest, Southern, Southwestern, and Western (see Figure 3.1 for a diagram of these regions). We decided to visit one senior center within each of these regions. To enhance our ability to make valid comparisons across senior center sites and to increase our chances of encountering diverse senior center users, we limited data collection sites to government-funded senior centers that served culturally and socioeconomically diverse populations of older adults. We also sought sites that together represented a balance of small, mid-sized, and large cities. We searched online to identify one government-funded senior center that met our criteria per region, and then contacted the center administrator via email to arrange for a visit. The group of sites included two small, two mid-sized, and two large cities.

We sought multiple sources of evidence to obtain a data set that was as rich and deep as possible. Each researcher was assigned three senior center sites to visit and made multiple visits to each center, most of which were day-long. Data were collected via unobtrusive observations, semi-structured and open interviews, publicly available records such as senior center demographics, and publicly available artifacts such as printed flyers, newsletters, and website pages.

We interviewed 74 individuals, including senior center administrators and staff; center clients who, at the time of data collection, were participants in center musical groups (music participants); center clients who, at the time of data collection, were not participating in any musical groups (nonparticipants); music activity directors and leaders; and an exercise activity director (the activity utilized music). We also observed many more center clients and staff during our visits.

Participants were adults of different ethnicities (Asian, Black, Latino, White, or mixed race). All were healthy enough to attend their senior center independently. Ages of participants ranged from the 30s (some senior center staff) to 101 (senior center music participant).

All interviews were conducted in person at the senior center sites. Managers and staff were interviewed via semi-structured interviews, and music participants and nonparticipants were interviewed via open interviews that were either scheduled ahead of time or unscheduled and informally conducted in the halls and other open areas of the senior centers. Different sets of interview questions were utilized with center managers and staff, center clients, and music activity leaders. See Appendix B for sets of interview questions we utilized. To avoid causing our study participants to feel uneasy, we chose not to record interviews. Instead, each researcher took copious notes during interviews and reflection notes soon after.

Data comprised interview notes, observation notes from center visits, researcher reflection notes, and publicly available artifacts such as flyers, newsletters, center demographic printouts, website information, and YouTube videos of musical groups. All data were entered into the Dedoose qualitative and mixed-method data analysis platform and were coded. Because both researchers were coding, we conducted several checks for coder consensus to ensure consistency across the coding process. Data were then analyzed to determine emergent themes.

APPENDIX B

Interview Guides

B.1 Semi-structured Interview Guide for Senior Center Management

1. Senior center information:
   - What are the days/hours of operation of the center?
   - Approximately how many older adults are served each week by the center?
   - Are all older adults who utilize this center served within the center? Or does the center also do outreach programs that serve older adults in their homes (such as Meals on Wheels, etc.)?
   - Does the center provide transportation to and from the center for older adults?
   - How many staff are employed, and what are their responsibilities?
   - What types of activities are offered here? Can you provide me with a weekly/monthly schedule of activities?
   - Of those who lead/facilitate activities at this senior center, how many are hired and how many are volunteers?
   - Are there community members who volunteer their time at the center, but do not lead activities?
     - If so, how many?
2. Older adult population served:
   - What can you tell me about the older adults who utilize this center (e.g., their ages, ethnicities, languages spoken, highest educational level achieved, socioeconomic status, mental/physical health, mobility, etc.)?
   - Can you share any demographic statistics on the older adult population served by this center?
3. Musical activities:
   - What musical activities do you offer at the center?
     - How often are these activities offered?

- What is the attendance like at these musical activities?
- Are there musical performances in the center that are attended by older adults but in which they do not participate (other than as an audience member)?
  - If so, who are the performers and what types of music do they perform?
  - Are the performers hired or are they volunteers?
- Are there musical activities in which older adults participate actively?
  - If so, how are older adults participating in these musical activities (e.g., sing, play, listen, move/dance, or compose)?
  - Who leads these activities (if not answered already)?
- Are the leaders hired or are they volunteers?
- How important are these musical activities to the older adults?
- What benefits do you notice that older adults receive from attending or participating in these musical activities?
- Do the older adults who utilize this center have other venues for musical activities (e.g., home or church) of which you are aware?

4. Management challenges:
   - What are some challenges you face in the operation of the center?
5. Funding:
   - How is this senior center funded?
   - Is the funding for musical activities part of the funding from the legislature?
     - If so, what specific government programs fund musical activities here?
   - What other funding sources are there to support musical activities at the center?
   - Compared to other activities in the center, do you feel that musical activities are sufficiently funded?
6. Priorities:
   - About what percentage of all activities in the center would you consider to be musical activities?
   - Do other activities have about the same attendance rate as musical activities?
7. Influence of public policies:
   - To what extent is the operation of the center influenced by public policy, for example policies related to government funding?

B.2 Unstructured Interview Guide for Senior Center Clients

Free open conversation with participating older adults regarding:

- their current and past music participation
- the role of music in their lives
- their desired activities
- their quality of life
- the most important people in their lives
- what they do in their spare time
- their level of satisfaction regarding where they live and how they live
- the extent to which they are working or volunteering
- how they feel about their life in general

B.3 Unstructured Interview Guide for Musical Activity Leaders (If Available)

Free open conversation with leaders of musical activities regarding:

- their background and training in music
- the role of music in older adult participants' lives and their quality of life
- whether they are involved in leading or participating in any other activities in the senior center
- reasons for them to serve the senior center in such capacity as leading a musical activity

APPENDIX C

Activity Leaders
Names, Ethnicities, Activities Led, and Musical Histories

Name and ethnicity	Activity led	Musical history
Bill (White male)	Choir leader: Mountain View Senior Center	Bill's parents were both musical. His mother had a master's degree in piano performance and composition. Bill learned the trumpet and the guitar and sang in a youth choir when he was young. When he was in high school, he directed a musical and a boys choir at church. Through the years, he directed about 3,000 choir students. He was a retired university professor of information technology. At the time of his interview, he directed the Mountain View Senior Center choir as a volunteer, saying "It's my way of giving back!" The choir did 20–25 performances per year, including July 4 and Christmas.
Elizabeth (White female)	New Horizons band leader: Mountain View Senior Center	Elizabeth had been a middle school band director for six years early in her career. At the time of the interview, she was a music education professor at a nearby university and had been there for 20 years. She started the bands at this senior center and had been leading them for 19 years, as a way to keep her musicianship going.
Grace (White female)	Choir leader: Better Living Senior Center	Grace had played the piano since age 5. She played clarinet in her school band and cello in her school orchestra. She sang in her high school choir, in church choirs, and in an *a cappella* choir, and served as pianist for various choirs. Grace went on to major in music performance and music education at a local university. She wanted to teach but ended up working in the field

Appendices

(cont.)

Name and ethnicity	Activity led	Musical history
		of writing and communication within a corporation. She later worked on funding and grants for her state's arts council, serving as arts grants administrator. She also volunteered as a musician at a pediatric hospital, and taught voice and piano lessons occasionally. At the time of her interview, she had been leading the center choir for three to four years. She became involved in the choir through a center client whom she met in a ceramics class sponsored by another organization. That person heard Grace singing to herself while making ceramics and invited her to "come to the center and sing with us." She did and gradually became more involved. At that time a volunteer couple was leading the activity. Grace occasionally served as the substitute piano accompanist, then the substitute song leader. When the couple was not able to continue, she stepped in to take over. The group grew from 65 to 150 and had produced a CD.
Laurie (White female)	Ukulele co-leader: Sunnyside Senior Center	Laurie was married to Les, and together they led the ukulele groups at Sunnyside Senior Center. Before playing ukulele, Laurie had no formal background in music. She never had private lessons but did participate in a grade school chorus. She met a friend who was similar in that she didn't have any musical background but her husband was a musician. Laurie went to Hawaii to visit his friend and saw her playing ukulele and thought she could do it too. She started to play without her husband Les knowing. Soon, Laurie was playing in a ukulele group in a nearby town and decided to start a group at the senior center. Les agreed to join her in leading the group.
Les (White male)	Ukulele co-leader: Sunnyside Senior Center	Les came from a musical family. His birth father played upright bass and worked his way through college as a jazz musician. Later, Les had a stepfather who played harmonica and clarinet, and a stepbrother who played professionally in a rock band. Les played horn for a while in high school;

(*cont.*)

Name and ethnicity	Activity led	Musical history
		however, he had problems with truancy and dropped out of school. In the 1960s, he moved into a commune and found an abandoned red, white, and blue guitar with five strings in the house. Les went outside to the woods and practiced. Later he took a few lessons but was mainly self-taught. He ended up playing professionally in rock bands and for Elvis impersonators and toured internationally. Unfortunately, he contracted Ménière's disease and lost his hearing and his balance. He tried to get engaged with the guitar again but was not as successful as he wished to be. He finally began healing and saw an ad for a well-known Japanese women's duo who sang American pop songs and played ukuleles. He started playing ukulele then because it seemed to him to be "an instrument of low expectations." After attending his first ukulele festival, he decided to join Laurie in leading the center ukulele groups.
Linda (White female)	Stretching exercise leader: Mountain View Senior Center	Linda became an exercise leader due to the influence of Jack LaLanne (1914–2011), the first to bring exercise to television in the 1950s. She saw his show in the late 1960s and was hooked. She was also inspired by Jacki Sorensen's aerobic dance routines to music. Because her husband was with the government, they were transferred quite a bit, and she lived in many different places. Everywhere she went, she led classes on a voluntary basis in places like the YMCA. After moving to the area surrounding Mountain View Senior Center 23 years ago, Linda volunteered to lead exercise classes at the center as a sub. She then became the regular exercise leader.
Mandy (Asian female)	Karaoke leader: Better Living Senior Center	Mandy had no musical background other than music classes in elementary school. She started this karaoke activity in this center in 2006, in response to a request by her friends. Her friends noticed that she liked to sing-along as she participated in other activities, so they asked her to

(cont.)

Name and ethnicity	Activity led	Musical history
		establish the karaoke group. In her spare time, she loved to listen to music and sing along, and participated in line dancing several times per week.
Neil (White male)	"Unofficial" harmonica group leader: Good Hope Senior Center	Neil began clarinet in fifth grade and played all through his elementary and secondary schooling years. He had no formal musical training other than what was provided in school. Neil played saxophone in high school and played in a rock and roll band. He also played baritone saxophone in a county concert band. Later, Neil played in his state university's activities band. At the time of the interview, he had recently purchased a bassoon and was teaching himself to play it. Neil taught himself to play harmonica and was a member of a professional harmonica quartet. At the time of his interview, Neil played harmonica regularly in senior centers and at a well-known annual harmonica festival that he also helped to run.
Nick (White male)	Guitar class leader: Good Hope Senior Center	Earlier in life, Nick participated in school choirs and glee clubs. He started performing professionally at age 17. At the time of the interview, he was working full-time as a professional entertainer and part time at the center as the office manager and guitar class instructor. He performed for corporate events, nursing homes, and senior centers, and also did production (sound/electrical) for a local adult contemporary radio station.
Nicole (Black female)	Sing-along leader: Good Hope Senior Center	Nicole was the manager of the Good Hope Senior Center and identified as a music nonparticipant; however, she regularly led sing-alongs on the bus on center-sponsored day trips to local venues (outdoor markets, arts events, etc.).
Rebecca (Black female)	Choir leader: Good Hope Senior Center	From ages 8–12, Rebecca was enrolled in a community piano school, where she took piano lessons and music theory classes. She got a job at the school's front desk to pay for her piano lessons. In sixth grade, Rebecca joined her middle school's choir

(cont.)

Name and ethnicity	Activity led	Musical history
		and continued to participate in choir into high school. She had to quit the chorus in her last year of high school so she could work a job to pay for her last year of high school and save money for college. Rebecca enjoyed a long career as an elementary school educator and collaborated regularly with the school's music specialist to bring music into her curricula. Upon retirement, she joined her education association's retired teachers chorus. In 2012, she joined the center's choir and eventually became its director. At the time of her interview, she directed the center chorus for two years.
Sebastian (Latino male)	Guitar teacher: The Senior Place	Sebastian was a self-taught musician from Puerto Rico who remarked that "I just play what I learn." He played guitar and maracas in a six-piece combo that supported a Cuban singer, and he performed on television. He also performed professionally as a drummer and singer and held a career job as a court interpreter. At the time of the interview, he had been playing the guitar for about 60 years, remarking that "It takes years to learn and practice." He bought his first guitar in 1967 and had five guitars at the time of his interview. He was also teaching a few private students to make money to pay for his tea and pizza.
Tony (White male)	Jazz band leader: Mountain View Senior Center	Tony started playing trumpet, guitar, and piano in fifth grade, and participated in instrumental music throughout high school and college. He received his bachelor's and master's degrees in music education from a large, highly respected university in the Southwestern US. He taught high school band, junior high, and elementary music for 30 years, and in retirement he moved to the area surrounding Mountain View Senior Center. At the time of his interview, in addition to leading the center jazz band Tony played in two large jazz organizations, a jam quartet, a large

(cont.)

Name and ethnicity	Activity led	Musical history
		country band, a Dixieland band, and a vintage jazz group. He said that the vintage jazz group was unusual in that participants *discussed* music and musicians for an hour and then jammed for another hour.
Ulysses (White male)	German band leader: The Center for Healthy Aging	Ulysses shared that he had been involved in music his whole life. There was strong family support for music in that his father played trumpet and encouraged Ulysses to play trombone. At the time of his interview, Ulysses was a member of seven musical groups. He served as leader of the German band that met at the center and played in the concert band and polka band there. He was also a member of a church choir, a community band in a nearby city, and a community chorus in a different city. This chorus functioned as a mixed chorus in the fall and a men's glee club in the spring. During summers, he participated in a male chorus that performed concerts in the Northeastern US. His most challenging group was an area Renaissance *a cappella* group.
Xander (White male)	Concert band leader: The Center for Healthy Aging	A lifelong musician, Xander earned bachelor's and master's degrees in music and spent 35 years as a career music educator (mostly band) in middle and elementary schools in the Northeastern US. He was also a professional trombonist and performed with big bands. In addition, he played percussion and had sung professionally with an internationally known men's *a cappella* group. At the time of the interview and in addition to conducting the center concert band, Xander sang in a church choir and in an area Renaissance *a cappella* group.

APPENDIX D

List of Musical Activities from Senior Center Managers' Responses to the Survey
Music-Making, Dance and Exercise with Music, and Live Music Performance

	Music-making			
Senior center (US region/ city size)	Offer music-making activities Prior to March 2020	In October 2021	Name of the activity	Explanation of the activity
Eastern/small	Yes	Yes	[a] John and Simon Duo	Birthday party
			[b] Fitness Program	All levels
			[a] Vocalist Entertainer	Holiday concerts
			[a] Good Samaritan Opera House	Trip
			[a] Newsome Playhouse	Trip
Eastern/small	Yes	No	Senior Concert Band	Performance group
			German Band	Performance group
			Senior Sing	Group sing
Eastern/small	No	No		
Eastern/small	Yes	No	Chorus	
Eastern/small	Yes	Yes	Blue Bell Singers	
Southwestern/ small	Yes	Yes	Mission	They sing songs
			Choir	They practice and prepare for performances. Someone plays piano
Southwestern/ small	Yes	Yes	Chorus	Currently meeting to practice weekly, performances out in the community are limited due to COVID-19

174

Appendices

(cont.)

	Music-making			
Senior center (US region/ city size)	Offer music-making activities		Name of the activity	Explanation of the activity
	Prior to March 2020	In October 2021		
			New Horizons Band	Run by local university, director is paid through university, not our organization
			Young at Heart Band	Local jazz band, utilizes space for practice, members enjoy listening
			Hand Drumming	Volunteer leads djembe hand drumming classes
			Guitar Lessons	Guitar lessons and ukulele lessons
Southern/mid-sized	Yes	Yes	Choir	Group singing
			Dance	Group dance
Southern/mid-sized	Yes	No	Choir	Religious group singing hymns
			Drum Circle	Instrument group led by local nonprofit
Western/large	Yes	No	Singing	Group
			Ukulele	Group
			Guitar Jam Session	Group
Western/large	Yes	Yes	Music Appreciation	Professional musician, historian plays videos, occasionally plays live music and the group listens and discusses
			Sing-along	Professional musician offers a sing-along group opportunity weekly
			Older Adult Choir	Professionals lead older adult participants in group setting

(cont.)

Senior center (US region/ city size)	Offer music-making activities Prior to March 2020	In October 2021	Name of the activity	Explanation of the activity
Western/large	Yes	Yes	Creative vibes	
Western/large	Yes	Yes	Samhang Pinoy	Filipino group singing traditional Filipino songs
			Las Guitarras	Folk songs in Spanish accompanied by guitar
Western/large	Yes	Yes		
Western/large	Yes	Yes	Pan Project Drumming Conga	Steel drumming Conga Choir
North Central/ large	Yes	No	Chorus	
North Central / large	Yes	Yes	Singing	Choir
North Central / large	Yes	Yes	[a] Piano Recital	Youth performance for older adults during lunchtime
			[a] Special Events	Musical performance during monthly special event
North Central / large	No	No		
Northwest / mid-sized	Yes	No	Choir	Singing
			[b] Weekly Dances	Live music
Northwest / mid-sized	Yes	No	Jam session	Play jazz
Northwest / mid-sized	Yes	Yes	Slow Jam	Jam sessions
			Music Lessons	Vocal
Northwest / mid-sized	No	No		

[a] These activities might belong to the "live music performance" category, but we keep them in the "music-making" category to reflect the center managers' responses.
[b] These activities might belong to the "dance and exercise activities with music" category, but we keep them in the "music-making" category to reflect the center managers' responses.

Senior center (US region/ city size)	Offer dance and exercise activities with music		Name of the activity	Explanation of the activity
	Prior to March 2020	In October 2021		
Eastern/small	Yes	Yes	Fit for Life	Exercise
			Chair Yoga	Exercise
			Gentle Exercise	Exercise
			Circuit Workout	Exercise
Eastern/small	Yes	Yes	Healthy Joints	Arthritis exercise
			Line Dancing	Line dancing
			Shake Your Soul	Improvised movement class
			Zumba	Zumba
Eastern/small	Yes	Yes	Line Dance	Line dance, some classes are run by volunteers, others are fee-paying, led by a paid instructor
			Social Ballroom Dances	A group of individuals who get together to dance various styles of ballroom once a month
			Ballroom Dance Lessons	Formal lessons
			Zumba Class	Zumba exercise program
			Zumba Class 2	Same as above, different instructor – attempted to return but then cancelled
Eastern/small	Yes	Yes	Boomer Bootcamp	
			Yoga	
			Tai Chi	
			Line Dancing	
			Belly Dancing	
Eastern/small	Yes	Yes	Cardio Fitness	Cardio fitness
Southwestern/ small	No	Yes	Line Dancing	Seniors learn how to line dance
Southwestern/ small	Yes	Yes	Middle Eastern Dance	Belly dancing lessons and two annual performances

Dance and exercise with music

Appendices

(cont.)

Senior center (US region/ city size)	Offer dance and exercise activities with music		Name of the activity	Explanation of the activity
	Prior to March 2020	In October 2021		
			Tap Dance	Beginner and intermediate tap dance lessons
			Line Dance	Beginner and intermediate line dance lessons
			Social Dance	Salsa, foxtrot, two-step, swing, rhumba, etc.
Southern/ medium	Yes	Yes	Ballroom	
			Line Dance	
Southern / medium	Yes	Yes	Line Dancing	Line dancing led by volunteer
			Chair Dancing	Chair dancing led by staff and videos
Western/large	Yes	Yes	Line Dancing	No partner
			Ballroom	Partner needed
			Round Dancing	Partner needed
			Chinese Line Dance	No partner
			Hula	No partner
Western/large	Yes	Yes	Always Active	Low stress group exercise routine
			Zumba	Highly active exercise routine
Western/large	Yes	Yes	Dance for life	Zoom class
Western/large	Yes	Yes	Tai Chi	Tai chi outside, weather permitting
Western/large	Yes	Yes		
Western/large	Yes	Yes	Line Dance	
			Aerobics	
			Chair Exercise	
			Yoga	
North Central/ large	Yes	Yes	Line Dance	
			Silver Sneakers	
			Arthritis Exercise	
			Yoga	
			Total Fitness	
			Zumba Gold	
			Silver Tappers	Tap dance

Dance and exercise with music

Senior center (US region/ city size)	Offer dance and exercise activities with music		Name of the activity	Explanation of the activity
	Prior to March 2020	In October 2021		
North Central/ large	Yes	Yes	Line Dance	
			Zumba	
North Central/ large	Yes	Yes	Ballroom Dance	
			Line Dance	
			Silver Sneakers	
			BOOM	
			Zumba Gold	
			Salsa	
North Central/ large	Yes	Yes	Yoga	
			Belly Dancing	
Northwest/ mid-sized	Yes	Yes	116 Fitness Classes	Balance, cardio, strength training, etc.
Northwest/ mid-sized	Yes	No	Open Dance	Weekly ballroom dancing with live band
			Zumba Gold	Zumba
Northwest/ mid-sized	Yes	Yes	Line Dance	Dance
Northwest/ mid-sized	Yes	Yes	Stretch	Exercise

Live music performance events

Senior center (US region/ city size)	Offer live music performance events		Name of the activity	Explanation of the activity
	Prior to March 2020	In October 2021		
Eastern/small	Yes	No		
Eastern/small	Yes	Yes	Musical Entertainment	Golden Senior Club
Eastern/small	Yes	Yes	Entertainment	Multiple entertainers – during pandemic we

	Live music performance events			
Senior center (US region/ city size)	**Offer live music performance events**		**Name of the activity**	**Explanation of the activity**
	Prior to March 2020	In October 2021		
			Entertainment	moved to virtual online and/or cable-based programming
			Entertainment	Same as above, but note that we are now offering both online/cable and in-person hybrid options
Eastern/small	Yes	Yes	Lunchtime Concerts	
Eastern/small	No	No		
Southwestern/small	No	No		
Southwestern/small	Yes	No	Community Dances	Local musicians played live for two community dances per month
Southern/mid-sized	Yes	No	[Jazz] Big [Band]	
			Ball[room] Dancing	Night out with band and dancing
Southern/mid-sized	Yes	Yes	Music at Events	Live music is offered at events
Western/large	No	No		
Western/large	Yes	No	Vocalist Entertainer	Jazz singer performance
			Songwriter Producer	Eclectic/folk pianist, guitarist
Western/large	No	Yes	Choir Visiting Artists	Indoor singing
Western/large	Yes	No	Live Music Performance	Current music groups performed at agency-wide event
Western/large	Yes	Yes		
Western/large	Yes	Yes	Concerts	
North Central/large	Yes	No	Luncheon Field Trips	Entertainment

(cont.)

Senior center (US region/ city size)	Offer live music performance events		Name of the activity	Explanation of the activity
	Prior to March 2020	In October 2021		
North Central/ large	No	No		
North Central/ large	Yes	No	Special Events	
North Central/ large	Yes	No	Singer	After lunch entertainer
Northwest/ mid-sized	Yes	No	Weekly Dance Lunch Entertainment	
Northwest/ mid-sized	Yes	No	Party Performances	Monthly live bands during lunch
			School Performances	Monthly music performances by local school groups
			Voices of the Performing Arts	2x weekly theater arts school
Northwest/ mid-sized	Yes	No	Entertainment	Lunch entertainment
Northwest/ mid-sized	No	No		

Live music performance events

APPENDIX E

Center Management Survey

Q1. Please enter the **zip code** where this senior citizen center is located:

Q2. Please indicate whether this senior center is stand-alone or part of a multiage center.
- Stand-alone senior center
- Part of a multiage center

Q3. Check all that apply currently to the center you manage:
- ☐ Open for **in-person on-site activities** (e.g., classes, rehearsals or jams, concerts, wellness exercise, games, celebrations, social gatherings, special interest groups, etc.)
- ☐ Open for **in-person on-site services** (e.g., meals, tax help, legal or health consultation, support group, etc.)
- ☐ Currently scheduling and operating **off-site in-person outdoor activities** (e.g., trips, outdoor wellness activities, etc.)
- ☐ Currently scheduling **off-site services** (e.g., meals on wheels, social worker visits, etc.)
- ☐ Currently scheduling and operating **online activities** (e.g., classes, music meet-ups, games, celebrations, social gatherings, special interest groups, etc.)

None of the above

Q4. How many senior citizens are served on-site (including online) by this center **each week**?
Currently:

Q5. How many senior citizens are served on-site (including online) by this center **each week**?
Prior to March 2020:

Q6. How many senior citizens are served on-site (including online) by this center **each year**?
Currently:

Q7. How many senior citizens are served on-site (including online) by this center **each year**?
Prior to March 2020:

Q8. What are this center's **sources of funding**? Choose all that apply:
- ☐ Federal Government
- ☐ State Government
- ☐ County Government
- ☐ City Government
- ☐ Foundation
- ☐ Religious Organization(s)
- ☐ Donations
- ☐ Fees (class or membership)
- ☐ Other

Q9. What is the **minimum age** of attendees of this center?
[Pull down menu from "49 years and below," "50 years," "51 years," to "64 years," "65 years," "66 years and above."]

Q10. What is the age of **the oldest attendee** of this center?
[Pull down menu from "60 years," "61 years," "62 years," to "109 years," "110 years," "111 years or above."]

Q11. What is the **approximate age group** of **most center attendees**? Choose up to two groupings.
- ☐ 50–59
- ☐ 60–69
- ☐ 70–79
- ☐ 80–89
- ☐ 90–99
- ☐ 100 and over

Q12. What ethnicities are represented across center attendees? **Choose all that apply.** For ethnicities that represent approximately 30% or more of total attendees, estimate the percentage of each.
- ☐ American Indian and Alaska Native, estimate percentage if 30% or more:
- ☐ Asian, estimate percentage if 30% or more:
- ☐ Black, estimate percentage if 30% or more:
- ☐ Hispanic and Latino of any race, estimate percentage if 30% or more:
- ☐ Middle Eastern, estimate percentage if 30% or more:
- ☐ Native Hawaiian and Pacific Islander, estimate percentage if 30% or more:
- ☐ Non-Hispanic White and European, estimate percentage if 30% or more:
- ☐ Multiracial, estimate percentage if 30% or more:

Q13. Does your center offer an activity that involves singing, playing of instruments, musical improvisation, or musical composition?

	Yes	No
Currently	○	○
Prior to March 2020	○	○

Q14. List all music activities offered at your center that **involve singing, playing of instruments, musical improvisation, or musical composition**. Give the name and briefly explain what it is. Then indicate whether the activity is available for beginners, available for experienced attendees, requires a materials fee, led by a paid activity leader, and how the pandemic has affected this activity at the center.

	Name & explanation		Available for beginners		Available for experienced attendees		Materials or other fee required		Activity leader paid		How has the pandemic affected this activity at the center?
	Name	Explanation	Yes	No	Yes	No	Yes	No	Yes	No	
Music activity 1			○	○	○	○	○	○	○	○	[See note below]
Music activity 2			○	○	○	○	○	○	○	○	[See note below]
.	.	.	.	.	.	.	.	.	.	.	.
.	.	.	.	.	.	.	.	.	.	.	.
.	.	.	.	.	.	.	.	.	.	.	.
Music activity 14			○	○	○	○	○	○	○	○	[See note below]
Music activity 15			○	○	○	○	○	○	○	○	[See note below]

Note: Pulldown menu with the following choices for each music activity:

- Cancelled completely
- Cancelled for a time, then reinstated in person but less frequent
- Cancelled for a time, then reinstated online but less frequent
- Cancelled for a time, then reinstated in person resuming pre-pandemic schedule
- Cancelled for a time, then reinstated online resuming pre-pandemic schedule
- Not cancelled; moved online but less frequent
- Not cancelled; moved online continuing pre-pandemic schedule
- Not cancelled; continued to meet in person but less frequent
- Not cancelled; continued to meet in person on pre-pandemic schedule

Q15. Does your center offer an activity that **involves dance- or exercise-focused activities in which attendees move to music or exercise-focused activities with music in the background?**

	Yes	No
Currently	○	○
Prior to March 2020	○	○

Q16. List all music activities offered at your center that **involves dance- or exercise-focused activities in which attendees move to music or exercise-focused activities with music in the background**. Give the name and briefly explain what it is. Then indicate whether the activity is available for beginners, available for experienced attendees, requires a materials fee, led by a paid activity leader, and how the pandemic has affected this activity at the center.

Name & explanation		Available for beginners		Available for experienced attendees		Materials or other fee required		Activity leader paid		How has the pandemic affected this activity at the center?
Name	Explanation	Yes	No	Yes	No	Yes	No	Yes	No	
Music activity 1		○	○	○	○	○	○	○	○	[See note below]
Music activity 2		○	○	○	○	○	○	○	○	[See note below]
.	.	.	.	.	.	.	.	.	.	.
.	.	.	.	.	.	.	.	.	.	.
.	.	.	.	.	.	.	.	.	.	.
Music activity 14		○	○	○	○	○	○	○	○	[See note below]
Music activity 15		○	○	○	○	○	○	○	○	[See note below]

Note: Pulldown menu with the following choices for each music activity:

- Cancelled completely
- Cancelled for a time, then reinstated in person but less frequent
- Cancelled for a time, then reinstated online but less frequent
- Cancelled for a time, then reinstated in person resuming pre-pandemic schedule
- Cancelled for a time, then reinstated online resuming pre-pandemic schedule
- Not cancelled; moved online but less frequent
- Not cancelled; moved online continuing pre-pandemic schedule
- Not cancelled; continued to meet in person but less frequent
- Not cancelled; continued to meet in person on pre-pandemic schedule

Q17. Does your center offer **live music performances**?

	Yes	No
Currently	○	○
Prior to March 2020	○	○

Q18. List all music activities offered at your center that **involve listening to live musical performances**. Give the name and briefly explain what it is. Then indicate whether the activity is available for beginners, available for experienced attendees, requires a materials fee, led by a paid activity leader, and how the pandemic has affected this activity at the center.

	Name & explanation		Available for beginners		Available for experienced attendees		Materials or other fee required		Activity leader paid		How has the pandemic affected this activity at the center?
	Name	Explanation	Yes	No	Yes	No	Yes	No	Yes	No	
Music activity 1			○	○	○	○	○	○	○	○	[See note below]
Music activity 2			○	○	○	○	○	○	○	○	[See note below]
.	.	.	.	.	.	.	.	.	.	.	.
.	.	.	.	.	.	.	.	.	.	.	.
Music activity 14			○	○	○	○	○	○	○	○	[See note below]
Music activity 15			○	○	○	○	○	○	○	○	[See note below]

Note: Pulldown menu with the following choices for each music activity:

- Cancelled completely
- Cancelled for a time, then reinstated in person but less frequent
- Cancelled for a time, then reinstated online but less frequent
- Cancelled for a time, then reinstated in person resuming pre-pandemic schedule
- Cancelled for a time, then reinstated online resuming pre-pandemic schedule
- Not cancelled; moved online but less frequent
- Not cancelled; moved online continuing pre-pandemic schedule
- Not cancelled; continued to meet in person but less frequent
- Not cancelled; continued to meet in person on pre-pandemic schedule

Q19. What are your plans for center musical activities **after the pandemic is under control**?
○ Resume all musical activities to pre-pandemic in-person schedule
○ Resume a majority of musical activities to pre-pandemic in-person schedule
○ Resume a small portion of musical activities to pre-pandemic in-person schedule
○ Resume no musical activities
○ Other:

Q20. If some musical activities will be modified, how will they be modified?
○ On pre-pandemic schedule: combination of in-person and remote meetings
○ On pre-pandemic schedule: fully remote
○ Meet less frequently: in person with no remote meetings
○ Meet less frequently: combination of in-person and remote meetings
○ Meet less frequently: fully remote
○ Other:

Q21. What is your official position?
○ Executive Director
○ Director
○ Council on Aging Director
○ Assistant Director
○ Interim Director
○ Program Director/Coordinator
○ General Manager
○ Center Manager
○ Assistant Manager
○ Other:

Q22. How many years have you worked at the center?
○ [Pull down menu from "Less than 1," "1," "2," to "19," "20," "21 or more."]

Thank you for taking this survey!

Your participation will help us to learn more about the changes made in senior center musical activities during, and as we emerge from, the pandemic.

Your response has been recorded.

Take care.

References

Aday, R. H. (2003). *The evolving role of senior centers in the 21st century*. U.S. Senate Special Committee on Aging.

Aday, R. H., Kehoe, G. C., & Farney, L. A. (2006). Impact of senior center friendships on aging women who live alone. *Journal of Women & Aging*, 18(1), 57–73. https://doi.org/10.1300/J074v18n01_05

Ashida, S., & Heaney, C. A. (2008). Social networks and participation in social activities at a new senior center: Reaching out to older adults who could benefit the most. *Activities, Adaptation & Aging*, 32(1), 40–58.

Balsnes, A. H. (2017). The Silver Voices: A possible model for senior singing. *International Journal of Community Music*, 10(1), 59–69. https://doi.org/10.1386/ijcm.10.1.59_1

Barbeau, A-K., & Cossette, I. (2019). The effects of participating in a community concert band on senior citizens' quality of life, mental and physical health. *International Journal of Community Music*, 12(2), 269–288. https://doi.org/10.1386/ijcm.12.2.269_1

Barbeau, A-K., & Mantie, R. (2019). Music performance anxiety and perceived benefits of musical participation among older adults in community bands. *Journal of Research in Music Education*, 66(4), 408–427. https://doi.org/10.1177/0022429418799362

Beisgen, B. A., & Kraitchman, M. C. (2003). *Senior centers: Opportunities for successful aging*. Springer Publishing Company.

Blackburn, C. (2017). Young children's musical activities in the home. *Education 3–13*, 45(6), 674–688. https://doi.org/10.1080/03004279.2017.1342320

Bobitt, J., & Schwingel, A. (2017). Evidence-based programs for older adults: A disconnect between U.S. national strategy and local senior center implementation. *Journal of Aging & Social Policy*, 29(1), 3–19. https://doi.org/10.1080/08959420.2016.1186465

Brandler, S. (1985). The senior center: Informality in the social work function. *Journal of Gerontological Social Work*, 8(3–4), 195–210. https://doi.org/10.1300/J083V08N03_13

Bugos, J. (2014). Community music as a cognitive training programme for successful ageing. *International Journal of Community Music*, 7(3), 319–331. https://doi.org/10.1386/ijcm.7.3.319_1

Bugos, J., & Kochar, S. (2017). Efficacy of a short-term intense piano training program for cognitive aging: A pilot study. *Musicae Scientiae*, 21(2), 137–150. https://doi.org/10.1177/1029864917690020

Burckhardt, C. S., & Anderson, K. L. (2003). The Quality of Life Scale (QOLS): Reliability, validity, and utilization. *Health and Quality of Life Outcomes*, 1, 60. https://doi.org/10.1186/1477-7525-1-60

Calsyn, R. J., & Winter, J. P. (2000). Who attends senior centers? *Journal of Social Service Research*, 26(2), 53–69. https://doi.org/10.1300/J079v26n02_03

Cannon, M. L. (2015). Challenges, experiences, and future directions of senior centers serving the Portland metropolitan area [Doctoral dissertation, Portland State University]. PDX Scholar. https://pdxscholar.library.pdx.edu/open_access_etds/2317

Carstensen, L. L. (1991). Selectivity theory: Social activity in life-span context. *Annual Review of Gerontology and Geriatrics*, 11, 195–217.

Carstensen, L. L., Isaacowitz, D. M., & Charles, S. T. (1999). Taking time seriously: A theory of socioemotional selectivity. *American Psychologist*, 54(3), 165–181. https://doi.org/10.1037/0003-066X.54.3.165

Centers for Disease Control and Prevention. (2009, October 15). Healthy places terminology. https://www.cdc.gov/healthyplaces/terminology.htm

Clift, S., & Hancox, G. (2010). The significance of choral singing for sustaining psychological wellbeing: Findings from a survey of choristers in England, Australia, and Germany. *Music Performance Research*, 3(1), 79–96.

Coffman, D. D. (1996). Musical backgrounds and interests of active older adult band members. *Dialogue in Instrumental Music Education*, 20(1), 25–34.

(2009). Survey of New Horizons International Music Association musicians. *International Journal of Community Music*, 1(3), 375–390. https://doi.org/10.1386/ijcm.1.3.375_1

Coffman, D. D., & Adamek, M. S. (1999). The contributions of wind band participation to quality of life of senior adults. *Music Therapy Perspectives*, 17(1), 278–231. https://doi.org/10.1093/mtp/17.1.27

(2001). Perceived social support of New Horizons band members. *Contributions to Music Education*, 28(1), 27–40.

Cohen, G. D. (2000). *The creative age: Awakening human potential in the second half of life*. HarperCollins Publishers.

(2005). *The mature mind: The positive power of the aging brain*. Basic Books. https://doi.org/10.1080/01924788.2013.784944

(2006). Research on creativity and aging: The positive impact of the arts on health and illness. *Generations*, 30(1), 7–15.

Cohen, G. D., Perlstein, S., Chapline, J., Kelly, J., Firth, K. M., & Simmons, S. (2006). The impact of professionally conducted cultural programs on the physical health, mental health, and social functioning of older adults. *The Gerontologist*, 46(6), 726–734. https://doi.org/10.1093/geront/46.6.726

Cox, C., & Monk, A. (1990). Integrating the frail and well elderly: The experience of senior centers. *Journal of Gerontological Social Work*, 15(3–4), 131–147. https://doi.org/10.1300/J083v15n03_07

Creech, A. (2019). Using music technology creatively to enrich later-life: A literature review. *Frontiers in Psychology*, 10, article 117. https://doi.org/10.3389/fpsyg.2019.00117

Creech, A., Hallam, S., McQueen, H., & Varvarigou, M. (2013). The power of music in the lives of older adults. *Research Studies in Music Education*, 35(1), 87–102. https://doi.org/10.1177/1321103X13478862

Creech, A., Larouche, K., Generale, M., & Fortier, D. (2020). Creativity, music, and quality of later life: A systematic review. *Psychology of Music*, 1–21. https://doi.org/10.1177/0305735620948114

Dabback, W. M. (2008). Identity formation through participation in the Rochester New Horizons Band Programme. *International Journal of Community Music*, 1(2), 267–286. https://doi.org/10.1386/ijcm.1.2.267_1

Dal Santo, T. S. (2009). *Senior center literature review: Reflecting & responding to community needs*. California Commission on Aging. https://bit.ly/3tS1T6g

David, J., Yeung, M., Vu, J., Got, T., & Mackinnon, C. (2018). Connecting the young and the young at heart: An intergenerational music program. *Journal of International Relationships*, 16(3), 330–338. https://doi.org/10.1080/15350770.2018.1477436

Dingle, G. A. Brander, C., Ballantyne, J., & Baker, F. A. (2012). "To be heard": The social and mental health benefits of choir singing for disadvantaged adults. *Psychology of Music*, 41(4), 405–421. https://doi.org/10.1177/0305735611430081

Drummond, J. (2018). An international perspective on music education for adults. In G. E. McPherson & G. F. Welch (Eds.), *Special needs, community music, and adult learning: An Oxford handbook of music education* (Vol. 4, pp. 304–316). Oxford University Press.

Eaton, J., & Salari, S. (2005). Environments for lifelong learning in senior centers. *Educational Gerontology*, 31, 461–480. https://doi.org/10.1080/03601270590928189

Ekholm, O., Juel, K., & Bonde, L. O. (2016). Music and public health: An empirical study of the use of music in the daily life of adult Danes and the health implications of musical participation. *Arts & Health*, 8(2), 154–168. https://doi.org/10.1080/17533015.2015.1048696

Engen, R. L. (2005). The singer's breath: Implications for treatment of persons with emphysema. *Journal of Music Therapy*, 42(1), 20–48. https://doi.org/10.1093/jmt/42.1.20

Farone, D. W., Fitzpatrick, T. R., & Tran, T. V. (2005). Use of senior centers as a moderator of stress-related distress among Latino elders. *Journal of Gerontological Social Work*, 46(1), 65–83. https://doi.org/10.1300/J083v46n01_05

Felix, H. C., Adams, B., Cornell, C. E., Fausett, J. K., Krukowski, R. A., Love, S. J., Prewitt, T. E., & West, D. S. (2014). Barriers and facilitators to senior centers participating in translational research. *Research on Aging*, 36(1), 22–39. https://doi.org/10.1177/0164027512466874

Ferraro, K. F., & Cobb, C. (1987). Participation in multipurpose senior centers. *Journal of Applied Gerontology*, 6(4), 429–447. https://doi.org/10.1177/073346488700600406

Fitzpatrick, T. R., & McCabe, J. (2008). Future challenges for senior center programming to serve younger and more active baby boomers. *Activities, Adaptation & Aging*, 32(3–4), 198–213. https://doi.org/10.1080/01924780802563187

Fitzpatrick, T. R., McCabe, J., Gitelson, R., & Andereck, K. (2006). Factors that influence perceived social and health benefits of attendance at senior centers. *Activities, Adaptation & Aging*, 30(1), 23–45.

Flanagan, J. C. (1978). A research approach to improving our quality of life. *American Psychology*, 33, 138–147. https://doi.org/10.1037/0003-066X.33.2.138

(1982). Measurement of quality of life. *Archives of Physical Medicine and Rehabilitation*, 63, 56–59.

Friedman, D., Parikh, N. S., Giunta, N., Fahs, M. C., & Gallo, W. T. (2012). The influence of neighborhood factors on the quality of life of older adults attending New York City senior centers: Results from the Health Indicators Project. *Quality of Life Research*, 21, 123–131. https://doi.org/10.1007/s11136-011-9923-6

Fung, C. V. (2018). *A way of music education: Classic Chinese wisdoms*. Oxford University Press. https://doi.org/10.1093/oso/9780190234461.001.0001

Fung, C. V., & Lehmberg, L. J. (2016). *Music for life: Music participation and quality of life of senior citizens*. Oxford University Press. https://doi.org/10.1093/acprof:oso/9780199371686.001.0001

Fung, C. V., & Lehmberg, L. J. (Eds.) (2023). *Meanings of music participation: Scenarios from the United States*. Routledge.

Fung, H. H., Carstensen, L. L., & Lutz, A. M. (1999). Influence of time on social preferences: Implications for life-span development. *Psychology and Aging*, 14(4), 595–604. https://doi.org/10.1037/0882-7974.14.4.595

Gelfand, D. E. (1999). *The aging network: Programs and services*. 5th ed. Springer.

(2006). *The aging network: Programs and services*. 6th ed. Springer.

Gelfand, D. E., Bechill, W., & Chester, R. L. (1991). Core programs and services at senior centers. *Journal of Gerontological Social Work*, 17(1–2), 145–161. https://doi.org/10.1300/J083v17n01_12

Gembris, H. (2012). Music-making as a lifelong development and resource for health. In R. MacDonald, G. Kreutz, & L. Mitchell (Eds.) *Music, health, and wellbeing* (pp. 103–108). Oxford University Press. https://doi.org/10.1093/acprof:oso/9780199586974.001.0001

Giunta, N., Morano, C., Parikh, N. S., Friedman, D., Fahs, M. C., & Gallo, T. (2012). Racial and ethnic diversity in senior centers: Comparing participant characteristics in more and less multicultural settings. *Journal of Gerontological Social Work, 55*(6), 467–483.

Gordon, R. L., Fehd, H. M., & McCandliss, B. D. (2015). Does music training enhance literacy skills? A meta-analysis. *Frontiers in Psychology, 6*, article 1777. https://doi.org/10.3389/fpsyg.2015.01777

Grady, S. (1990). Senior centers. *Generations, 14*(1), 15–18.

Grau-Sánchez, J., Foley, M., Hlavová, R., Muukkonen, I., Ojinaga-Alfageme, O., Radukic, A., Spindler, M., & Hundevad, B. (2017). Exploring musical activities and their relationship to emotional well-being in elderly people across Europe: A study protocol. *Frontiers in Psychology, 8*, article 330. https://doi.org/10.3389/fpsyg.2017.00330

Guba, F. G. (1978). *Toward a methodology of naturalistic inquiry in educational evaluation*. University of California.

Guhn, M., Emerson, S. D., & Gouzouasis, P. (2020). A population-level analysis of associations between school music participation and academic achievement. *Journal of Educational Psychology, 112*(2), 308–328. http://dx.doi.org/10.1037/edu0000376

Hallam, S., Creech, A., Varvarigou, M., & McQueen, H. (2012). Perceived benefits of active engagement with making music in community settings. *International Journal of Community Music, 5*(2), 155–174. https://doi.org/10.1386/ijcm.5.2.155_1

Hallam, S., Creech, A., Varvarigou, M., McQueen, H., & Gaunt, H. (2014). Does active engagement in community music support the well-being of older people? *Arts and Health, 6*(2), 101–116. http://dx.doi.org/10.1080/17533015.2013.809369

Hanssen, A. M., Meima, N. J., Buckspan, L. K., Henderson, B. E., Helbig, T. L., & Zarit, S. H. (1978). Correlates of senior center participation. *The Gerontologist, 18*(2), 193–200. https://doi.org/10.1093/geront/30.1.72

Havir, L. (1991). Senior centers in rural communities: Potentials for serving. *Journal of Aging Studies, 5*(4), 359–374. https://doi.org/10.1016/0890-4065(91)90016-L

Hays, T. (2005). Well-being in later life through music. *Australasian Journal on Ageing, 24*(1), 28–32. https://doi.org/10.1111/j.1741-6612.2005.00059.x

Hays, T., & Minchiello, V. (2005). The meaning of music in the lives of older people: A qualitative study. *Psychology of Music, 33*(4), 437–451. https://doi.org/10.1177/0305735605056160

Hendricks, K. S., Smith, T. D., & Sanuch, J. (2014). Creating safe spaces for music learning. *Music Educators Journal, 101*(1), 35–40. https://doi.org/10.1177/0027432114540337

Hickey, M., & Schmidt, C. (2019). The effect of professional development on music teachers' improvisation and composition activities. *Bulletin of the Council for Research in Music Education, 222*, 27–43. https://doi.org/10.5406/bulcouresmusedu.222.0027

Hillman, S. (2002). Participatory singing for older people: A perception of benefit. *Health Education,* 102(4), 163–171. https://doi.org/10.1108/09654280210434237

Hudak, E. M., Bugos, J., Andel, R., Lister, J. J., Ji, M., & Edwards, J. D. (2019). Keys to staying sharp: A randomized clinical trial of piano training among older adults with and without mild cognitive impairment. *Contemporary Clinical Trials,* 84. https://doi.org/10.1016/j.cct.2019.06.003

Ishii-Kuntz, M. (1990). Formal activities for elderly women: Determinants of participation in voluntary and senior center activities. *Journal of Women & Aging,* 2(1), 79–97. https://doi.org/10.1300/J074v02n01_05

Janowitz, J. L. (1986). *Using a learning activity package for general music with older adults attending senior centers* [Doctoral dissertation, Temple University]. ProQuest Dissertations and Theses Global. https://bit.ly/3V2YM7y

Jenkins, B., Storie, S., & Purdy, S. (2017). Quality of life for individuals with a neurological condition, who participate in social/therapeutic choirs. *New Zealand Journal of Music Therapy,* 15, 59–94.

Jirovec, R. L., Erich, J. A., & Sanders, L. J. (1989). Patterns of senior center participation among low income urban elderly. *Journal of Gerontological Social Work,* 13(3–4), 115–132. https://doi.org/10.1300/J083V13N03_09

Johnson, J. K., Louhivuori, J., & Siljander, E. (2017). Comparison of well-being of older adult choir singers and the general population of Finland: A case-control study. *Musicae Scientae,* 21(2), 178–194. https://doi.org/10.1177/1029864916644486

Jorgensen, E. R. (2021). On values and life's journey through music reflections on the Eriksons' life stages and music education. In K. S. Hendricks and J. Boyce-Tillman (Eds.), *Authentic connection: Music, spirituality, and wellbeing.* Peter Lang.

Joseph, D. (2022). "The Potted Palms is bigger than each of us individually": Older musicians playing as community and for community. *Creative Industries Journal,* 15(1), 40–57. https://doi.org/10.1080/17510694.2021.1890378

Joseph, D., & Human, R. (2020). "It is more than just about music": Lifelong learning, social interaction and connection. *Muziki: Journal of Music Research in Africa,* 17(1), 72–93. https://doi.org/10.1080/18125980.2020.1855082

Joseph, D., & Southcott, J. (2018). Music participation for older people: Five choirs in Victoria, Australia. *Research Studies in Music Education,* 40(2), 176–190. https://doi.org/10.1177/1321103X18773096

Jutras, P. J. (2006). The benefits of adult piano study as self-reported by selected adult piano students. *Journal of Research in Music Education,* 54(2), 97–110. https://doi.org/10.1177/002242940605400202

(2011). The benefits of New Horizons band participation as self-reported by selected New Horizons band members. *Bulletin of the Council for Research in Music Education,* 187, 65–84.

Keller, M. J. (2017, January 1). Older adults: Exploring their changing demographics and health outlook. *Parks and Recreation Magazine.* https://bit.ly/3tWvtaE

Kim, W. (2000). The relationship between type of senior center and levels of utilization by the Korean elderly in New York City: A comparison of the utilization of ethnic-specific and mainstream senior centers [Doctoral dissertation, Fordham University]. ProQuest Dissertations and Theses Global. https://bit.ly/3EuVYJb

Kirk, A. B., & Alessi, H. D. (2000). Senior service centers: A comparison of affiliated and nonaffiliated participants. *Adultspan Journal,* 2(2), 89–100.

(2002). Rural senior service centers: A study of the impact on quality of life issues. *Activities, Adaptation & Aging,* 26(3), 51–64. https://doi.org/10.1300/J016v26n03_04

Knowles, M. S. (1980). *The modern practice of adult education: From pedagogy to andragogy.* Associated Press.

Krause, A. E., Davidson, J. W., & North, A. C. (2018). Musical activity and well-being: A new quantitative measurement instrument. *Music Perception,* 35(4), 454–474. https://doi.org/10.1525/mp.2018.35.4.454

Krause, A. E., North, A. C., & Davidson, J. W. (2019). Using self-determination theory to examine musical participation and well-being. *Frontiers in Psychology,* 10:405. https://doi.org/10.3389/fpsyg.2019.00405

Krout, J. A. (1983). Correlates of senior center utilization. *Research on Aging,* 5(3), 339-352. https://doi.org/10.1177/0164027583005003004

(1984). Knowledge of senior center activities among the elderly. *Journal of Applied Gerontology,* 3(1), 71–81. https://doi.org/10.1177/073346488400300108

(1985). Senior center activities and services: Findings from a national study. *Research on Aging,* 7(3), 455–471. https://doi.org/10.1177/0164027585007003008.

(1986). Senior center linkages in the community. *The Gerontologist,* 26(5), 510–515. https://doi.org/10.1093/geront/26.5.510

(1987). Rural-urban differences in senior center activities and services. *The Gerontologist,* 27(1), 92–97. https://doi.org/10.1093/geront/27.1.92

(1988a). Senior center linkages with community organizations. *Research on Aging,* 10(2), 258–274. https://doi.org/10.1177/0164027588102007

(1988b). The frequency, duration, and stability of senior center attendance. *Journal of Gerontological Social Work,* 13(1–2), 3–19. https://doi.org/10.1300/J083V13N01_02

(1989). *Senior centers in America.* Greenwood Press.

(1991). Senior center participation: Findings from a multidimensional analysis. *Journal of Applied Gerontology,* 10(3), 244–257. https://doi.org/10.1177/073346489101000302

(1994). Community size differences in senior center resources, programming, and participation: A longitudinal analysis. *Research on Aging*, 16(4), 440–462. https://doi.org/10.1177/0164027594164006

(1996). Senior centers and services for the frail elderly. *Journal of Aging & Social Policy*, 7(2), 59–76. https://doi.org/10.1300/j031v07n02_05

Krout, J. A., Cutler, S. J., & Coward, R. T. (1990). Correlates of senior center participation: A national analysis. *The Gerontologist*, 30(1), 72–79. https://doi.org/10.1093/geront/30.1.72

Kruse, B. B. (2013). "Without U it's just kulele": Expressions of leisure and 'ohana in an intergenerational ukulele club. *International Journal of Community Music*, 6(2), 153–167. https://doi.org/10.1386/ijcm.6.2.153_1

Laes, T. (2015). Empowering later adulthood music education: A case study of a rock band for third-age learners. *International Journal of Music Education*, 33(1), 51–65. https://doi.org/10.1177/0255761413515815

Lally, E. (2009). "The power to heal us with a smile and a song": Senior well-being, music-based participatory arts and the value of qualitative evidence. *Journal of Arts and Communities*, 1(1), 25–44. https://doi.org/10.1386/jaac.1.1.25/1

Lamont, A., Murray, M., Hale, R., & Wright-Bevans, K. (2018). Singing in later life: The anatomy of a community choir. *Psychology of Music*, 46(3), 424–239. https://doi.org/10.1177/0305735617715514

Lawler, K. (2011). *Transforming senior centers into 21st century wellness centers: A project made possible by a grant from AARP Foundation and Caesar's Foundation*. American Association of Retired Persons (AARP), Louisiana State Office. https://bit.ly/3EB2ZYS

Lee, J., Davidson, J. W., & Krause, A. (2016). Older people's motivations for participating in community singing in Australia. *International Journal of Community Music*, 9(2), 191–207. https://doi.org/10.1386/ijcm.9.2.191_1

Lehmberg, L. J. (2023). Participatory music making and quality of life of senior citizens. In C. V. Fung & L. J. Lehmberg (Eds.), *Meanings of music participation: Scenarios from the United States*. Routledge.

Lehmberg, L. J., & Fung, C. V. (2010). Benefits of music participation for senior citizens: A review of the literature. *Music Education Research International*, 4, 19–30. http://cmer.arts.usf.edu/content/articlefiles/3122-MERI04pp.19-30.pdf

Lehmberg, L. J., & Fung, C. V. (2023). Caring connection, music participation, and quality of life of older adults. In K. S. Hendricks (Ed.), *The Oxford Handbook of Care in Music Education*. Oxford University Press.

Lewis. H. (2021). A safe place to land: Music classes as safe havens for anxious and other youth. *The Canadian Music Educator*, 62(4), 35–40.

Li, S., & Southcott, J. (2012). A place for singing: Active music engagement by older Chinese Australians. *International Journal of Community Music*, 5(1), 59–78. https://doi.org/10.1386/ijcm.5.1.59_1

(2015). The meaning of learning piano keyboard in the lives of older Chinese people. *International Journal of Lifelong Education*, 34(3), 316–333. https://doi.org/10.1080/02601370.2014.999361

Litwin, H. (1999). Formal and informal network factors as sources of morale in a senior center population. *International Journal of Aging and Human Development*, 48(3), 241–256. https://doi.org/10.2190/6EAF-XKHL-FX93-EL3V

Livesey, L., Morrison, I., Clift, S., & Camic, P. (2012). Benefits of choral singing for social and mental wellbeing: Qualitative findings from a cross-national survey of choir members. *Journal of Public Mental Health*, 11(1), 10–26. https://doi.org/10.1108/17465721211207275

Lowy, L., & Doolin, J. (1990). Multipurpose senior centers. In A. Monk (Ed.), *Handbook of gerontological services* (pp. 342–376). Columbia University Press.

Macrotrends (2010–2021). [City] metro area population 1950–2021. [URL withheld to protect study participants' privacy.]

Marken, D. M. (2005). One step ahead: Preparing the senior center for 2030. *Activities, Adaptation & Aging*, 29(4), 69–84. https://doi.org/10.1300/J016v29n04_05

Mathieu, S. I. (2008). Happiness and humor group promotes life satisfaction for senior center participants. *Activities, Adaptation & Aging*, 32(2), 134–148. https://doi.org/10.1080/01924780802143089

McCaffrey, R. (2008). The lived experience of Haitian older adults' integration into a senior center in southeast Florida. *Journal of Transcultural Nursing*, 19(1), 33–39. https://doi.org/10.1177/1043659607309139

Merriam-Webster. (n.d.). Baby boomer. In *Merriam-Webster.com dictionary*. Retrieved August 5, 2022. https://www.merriam-webster.com/dictionary/baby%20boomer

(n.d.). Prevalent. In *Merriam-Webster.com dictionary*. Retrieved August 5, 2020. https://www.merriam-webster.com/dictionary/prevalent

Michalos, A. C. (2005). Arts and the quality of life: An exploratory study. *Social Indicators Research*, 71, 11–59. https://doi.org/10.1007/s11205-004-8013-3

Millett, G., & Fiocco, A. J. (2021). A pilot study implementing the JAVA Music Club in residential care: Impact on cognition and psychosocial health. *Aging & Mental Health*, 25(10), 1848–1856. https://doi.org/10.1080/13607863.2020.1758919

Miner, S., & Logan, J. R. (1993). Predicting the frequency of senior center attendance. *The Gerontologist*, 33(5), 650–657. https://doi.org/10.1093/geront/33.5.650

National Institute of Senior Centers. (n.d.). The National Institute of Senior Centers. Retrieved August 5, 2022. https://ncoa.org/page/the-national-institute-of-senior-centers

(1975). *Senior centers: Report of senior group programs in America*. National Council on Aging, Inc.

New Horizons International Music Association (NHIMA) (n.d.). *About Us*. New Horizons International Music Association. Retrieved August 5, 2022. https://newhorizonsmusic.org/about

Niles-Yokum, K., & Wagner, D. L. (2011). Senior centers and adult day services. In K. Niles-Yokum & D. L. Wagner, *The aging networks: A guide to programs and services*, 7th ed. (pp. 35–50). Springer Publishing Company.

(2015). *The aging networks: A guide to programs and services*. 8th ed. Springer.

(2019). *The aging networks: A guide to policy, programs, and services*. 9th ed. Springer.

Noice, T., Noice, H., & Kramer, A. F. (2014). Participatory arts for older adults: A review of benefits and challenges. *The Gerontologist*, 54(5), 741–753. https://doi.org/10.1093/geront/gnt138

O'Shea, H. (2012). "Get back to where you once belonged!" The positive creative impact of a refresher course for "baby-boomer" rock musicians. *Popular Music*, 31(2), 199–215. https://doi.org/10.1017/S0261143012000025

Pardasani, M. P. (2003). Senior centers: Patterns of programs and services [Doctoral dissertation, Yeshiva University, New York]. ProQuest Dissertations and Theses Global. https://bit.ly/3VjSwbd

(2004a). Senior centers: Focal points of community-based services for the elderly. *Activities, Adaptation & Aging*, 28(4), 27–44. https://doi.org/10.1300/J016v28n04_03

(2004b). Senior centers: Increasing minority participation through diversification. *Journal of Gerontological Social Work*, 43(2/3), 41–56. https://doi.org/10.1300/J083v43n02_04

(2010). Senior centers: Characteristics of participants and nonparticipants. *Activities, Adaptation & Aging*, 34(1), 48–70. https://doi.org/10.1080/01924780903552295

(2018). Motivation to volunteer among senior center participants. *Gerontological Social Work*, 61(3), 313–333. https://doi.org/10.1080/01634372.2018.1433259

Pardasani, M. P., & Goldkind, L. (2012). Senior centers and policy advocacy: Changing public perceptions. *Educational Gerontology*, 38(6), 375–390. http://dx.doi.org/10.1080/03601277.2010.544588

Pardasani, M. P., & Sackman, B. (2014). New York City senior centers: A unique, grassroots, collaborative advocacy effort. *Activities, Adaptation & Aging*, 38(3), 200–219. https://doi.org/10.1080/01924788.2014.935907

Pardasani, M. P., & Thompson, P. (2012). Senior centers: Innovative and emerging models. *Journal of Applied Gerontology*, 31(1), 52–77. https://doi.org/10.1177/0733464810380545

Patchen, J. H. (1986). The relationships among current musical activity level and selected musical and demographic variables within an elderly population [Doctoral dissertation, Indiana University]. ProQuest Dissertations and Theses Global. https://bit.ly/3uozyup

Patton, M. Q. (2015). *Qualitative research and evaluation methods*. 4th ed. Sage.

Pitts, S. (2012). *Chances and choices: Exploring the impact of music education.* Oxford University Press.

Pitts, S. E., & Robinson, K. (2016). Dropping in and dropping out: Experiences of sustaining and ceasing amateur participation in classical music. *British Journal of Music Education,* 33(3), 327–346. https://doi.org/10.1017/S0265051716000152

Pothoulaki, M., MacDonald, R. A. R., & Flowers, P. (2012). The use of music in chronic illness: Evidence and arguments. In R. MacDonald, G. Kreutz, & L. Mitchell (Eds.) *Music, health, and wellbeing* (pp. 239–256). Oxford University Press. https://doi.org/10.1093/acprof:oso/9780199586974.001.0001

Ralston, P. A. (1981). Educational needs and activities of older adults: Their relationship to senior center programs. *Educational Gerontology: An International Quarterly,* 7(2–3), 231–244. https://doi.org/10.1080/0360127810070214

——— (1984). Senior center utilization by Black elderly adults: Social, attitudinal and knowledge correlates. *Journal of Gerontology,* 39(2), 224–229. https://doi.org/10.1093/geronj/39.2.224

——— (1991a). Determinants of senior center attendance and participation. *Journal of Applied Gerontology,* 10(3), 258–273. https://doi.org/10.1177/073346489101000303

——— (1991b). Senior centers and minority elders: A critical review. *The Gerontologist,* 31(3), 325–331. https://doi.org/10.1093/geront/31.3.325

Ralston, P. A., & Griggs, M. B. (1985). Factors affecting utilization of senior centers: Race, sex, and socioeconomic differences. *Journal of Gerontological Social Work,* 9(1), 99–111. https://doi.org/10.1300/J083V09N01_08

Rhynes, L., Hayslip, B., Caballero, D., & Ingman, S. (2013). The beneficial effects of senior center attendance on grandparents raising grandchildren. *Journal of Intergenerational Relationships,* 11(2), 162–175. https://doi.org/10.1080/15350770.2013.782746

Rickard, N. S., & McFerran, K. (Eds.). (2012). *Lifelong engagement with music: Benefits for mental health and well-being.* Nova Science Publishers, Inc.

Rill, L. (2011). *An examination of senior center efficacy: Variation in participation & benefits.* [Doctoral dissertation, Florida State University]. ProQuest Dissertations and Theses Global. https://www.proquest.com/openview/e839cdc21da8d000def738926db61a85/1?pq-origsite=gscholar&cbl=18750

Rosenbaum, M., Sweeney, J. C., & Massiah, C. (2014). The restorative potential of senior centers. *Managing Service Quality,* 24(4), 363–383.

Roulston, K., Jutras, P., & Kim, S. (2015). Adult perspectives of learning musical instruments. *International Journal of Music Education,* 33(3), 325–335. https://doi.org/10.1177/0255761415584291

Sabin, E. P. (1993). Frequency of senior center use: A preliminary test of two models of senior center participation. *Journal of Gerontological Social Work,* 20(1–2), 97–114. https://doi.org/10.1300/J083V20N01_07

Sala, G., & Gobet, F. (2020). Cognitive and academic benefits of music training with children: A multilevel meta-analysis. *Memory & Cognition, 48,* 1429–1441. https://link.springer.com/article/10.3758/s13421-020-01060-2

Salamon, M. J., & Trubin, P. (1983). Difficulties in senior center life: Group behaviors. *Clinical Gerontologist, 2*(2), 23–37. https://doi.org/10.1300/J018v02n02_04

Schneider, A. E., Ralph, N., Olson, C., Flatley, A., & Thorpe, L. (2014). Predictors of senior center use among older adults in New York City public housing. *Journal of Urban Health: Bulletin of the New York Academy of Medicine, 91*(6), 1033–1047. https://doi.org/10.1007/s11524-014-9906-3

Shollenberger, D. (Ed.). (1995). *Senior centers in America: A blueprint for the future: Outcomes of a national meeting convened to develop recommendations for programs, policies, and funding of senior center programs of the future.* National Council on the Aging, Inc., National Eldercare Institute on Multipurpose Senior Center, and Community Focal Points.

Smith, D. S. (2012). A year with the senior center band: Facing aging head on. *International Journal of Community Music, 5*(3), 279–287. https://doi.org/10.1386/ijcm.5.3.279_1

Solé, C., Mercadal-Brotons, M., Galati, A., & De Castro, M. (2014). Effects of group music therapy on quality of life, affect, and participation in people with varying levels of dementia. *Journal of Music Therapy, 51*(1), 103–125. https://doi.org/10.1093/jmt/thu003

Southcott, J. (2009). And as I go, I love to sing: The Happy Wanderers, music and positive aging. *International Journal of Community Music, 2*(2–3), 143–156. https://doi.org/10.1386/ijcm.2.2-3.143_1

Southcott, J., & Li, S. (2018). "Something to live for": Weekly singing classes at a Chinese university for retirees. *International Journal of Music Education, 36*(2), 283–296. https://doi.org/10.1177/0255761417729548

Steinmayr, M., & Gritsch, B. (2019). Musical interaction with seniors: Music geragogic project of the Graz Music Pedagogy Institute. *Musikerziehung, 72*(1), 32–35.

Stige, B. (2012). Health musicking: A perspective on music and health as action and performance. In R. MacDonald, G. Kreutz, & L. Mitchell (Eds.) *Music, health, and wellbeing* (pp. 183–195). Oxford University Press. https://doi.org/10.1093/acprof:oso/9780199586974.001.0001

Taietz, P. (1976). Two conceptual models of the senior center. *Journal of Gerontology, 31*(2), 219–222. https://doi.org/10.1093/geronj/31.2.219

Tatum, M. E. (1985). *A descriptive analysis of the status of music programs in selected retirement residences and senior citizens' centers in the southeastern United States* [Unpublished doctoral dissertation, Indiana University].

Taylor, A., & Hallam, S. (2008). Understanding what it means for older students to learn basic musical skills on a keyboard instrument. *Music Education Research, 10*(2), 285–306. https://doi.org/10.1080/14613800802079148

Taylor-Harris, D. A. (2006). *Senior multipurpose facilities and quality of life among African American older adults: A case study.* [Master's thesis, Georgia State

University]. ScholarWorks @ Georgia State University. https://scholarworks.gsu.edu/gerontology_theses/1/

Taylor-Harris, D., & Zhan, H. J. (2011). The third-age African American seniors: Benefits of participating in senior multipurpose facilities. *Journal of Gerontological Social Work*, 54(4), 351–371. https://doi.org/10.1080/01634372.2010.539588

Tornstam, L. (1994). Gerotranscendence: A developmental theory of positive aging. In L. E. Thomas & S. A. Eisenhandler (Eds.), *Aging and the religious dimension* (pp. 203–225). Greenwood Publishing Group.

——— (2011). Maturing into gerotranscendence. *The Journal of Transpersonal Psychology*, 43(2), 166–180.

Travis, R., Rodwin, A. H., & Allcorn, A. (2019). Hip hop, empowerment, and clinical practice for homeless adults with severe mental illness. *Social Work with Groups*, 42(2), 83–100. https://doi.org/10.1080/01609513.2018.1486776

Turner, K. W. (2004). Senior citizens centers: What they offer, who participates, and what they gain. *Journal of Gerontological Social Work*, 43(1), 37–47. https://doi.org/10.1300/J083v43n01_04

United Nations. (2019). *World population prospects 2019: Highlights*. United Nations, Department of Economic and Social Affairs, Population Division. https://bit.ly/2MXgwm4

U.S. Census Bureau. (2019). United States Census Bureau quickfacts. [City, state, and URL withheld to protect study participants' privacy.]

Varvarigou, M., Hallam, S., Creech, A., & McQueen, H. (2012). Benefits experienced by older people in group music-making activities. *Journal of Applied Arts and Health*, 3(2), 183–198. https://doi.org/10.1386/jaah.3.2.183_1

Walker, J., Bisbee, C., Porter, R., & Flanders, J. (2004). Increasing practitioners' knowledge of participation among elderly adults in senior center activities. *Educational Gerontology*, 30(5), 353–366. https://doi.org/10.1080/03601270490433549

Weil, J. (2014). *The new neighborhood senior center: Redefining social and service roles for the baby boom generation*. Rutgers University Press.

Wick, J. (2012). Senior centers: Traditional and evolving roles. *The Consultant Pharmacist*, 27(9), 664–667. https://doi.org/10.4140/TCP.n.2012.664

Woody, R. H., Fraser, A., Nannen, B., & Yukevich, P. (2019). Musical identities of older adults are not easily changed: An exploratory study. *Music Education Research*, 21(3), 315–330. https://doi.org/10.1080/14613808.2019.1598346

Xaverius, P. K., Mathews, R. M. (1999). Attracting new participants to senior center activities: Publicly posted announcements. *Activities, Adaptation & Aging*, 24(1), 55–59. https://doi.org/10.1300/J016v24n01_06

Yeung, H. C., Baker, F., & Shoemark, H. (2014). Song preferences of Chinese older adults living in Australia. *The Australian Journal of Music Therapy*, 25, 103–121.

Index

AARP, 15
accessibility, 123, 126–129. *See also* entry points to activities
   expanding platforms for, 153
   financial, 127
   fluid activity entry points, 127–128
   physical, 126–127
activity formats
   beyond mid-pandemic, 147–148
   mid-pandemic, *142*, 142, 146–147, 149–150
activity leaders, 105–106, *145*, 151–152, 157–158, 168–173
activity participation, 24–27. *See also* music participation activities
advertising senior center activities, 24, 31. *See also* marketing senior centers
advocacy
   for programming change, 8–9
   social action, 32
age in place, 46
aging population demands, 7, 31–32
Alzheimer's disease, 46, 48, 59, 63, 115, 124. *See also* cognitive decline; mental health services
American Association of Retired Persons (AARP) Foundation, 15
attitude
   negative, 111–112
   positive, 132

baby boomers, 32–33, 48, 67, 122, 157
Better Living Senior Center, 49–51, 79, 83–85, 87–92

Caesar's Foundation, 15
The Center for Healthy Aging, 57–59, 69–71, 74–76
challenges and barriers
   for senior centers, 30–32, *30*, 55, 57, 59, 64
   for senior clientele, 112–113
choirs/choruses, 86–90

cognitive decline, 115, 150, 156. *See also* Alzheimer's disease
collaborations. *See* partnerships and collaborations
community music education, 9, 151–152, 158
community-based centers, 12, 31, 122–123, 158
concert bands, 69–73
conclusions and recommendations, 93–98, 152–153
connection with others, 25, 97–98, 115–117, 129–131, 149
continuing education. *See* lifelong learning

dance and movement, 132, 150–151, 158, *174–179*, 174
demographic statistics
   Better Living Senior Center, 48–50
   Center for Healthy Aging, 57–58
   ethnicity/race, 18, 95
   Good Hope Senior Center, 51–52
   mid-pandemic, 142, *143*
   Mountain View Senior Center, 55–57
   nationwide senior center count, 7
   The Senior Place, 59
   Sunnyside Senior Center, 44–45, 47–48
depression, 21–22, 24, 115
diversification of programs, 15
diversity
   categories of, 41
   cultural, 51, 61, 64, 78–79, 91, 122, 153
   ethnic/racial, 9, 47–55, 92
   lack of in research studies, 41
   mid-pandemic vs. pre-pandemic, 140–141
   in music audiences, 77
   in music-making groups, 71–74, 76, 78–79, 81, 83–84, 88–90, 92
   at The Senior Place, 61, 78–79, 92
   socioeconomic, 43

entry points to activities, 7, 108, 118, *145*, 152.
    See also fluid activity entry points

facility types and sizes, 13, 55, 124
fees, 51, 54, 57, 123, 140–143
fitness
    activities/classes, 14, 21, 53, 60, 63
    amenities, 52, 56
    senior center promotion of, 8, 50, 132
Flanagan's quality of life model, 135
fluid activity entry points, 94–95, 108, 118, 129, 152, 159
food insecurity, 63. See also nutrition services
funding sources
    for Better Living Senior Center, 48–51
    for Center for Healthy Aging, 58–59
    for Good Hope Senior Center, 48–55
    for Mountain View Senior Center, 57
    for The Senior Place, 61
    for Sunnyside Senior Center, 48
    current national status of, 13
    diversifying, 11, 157
    government, 124, 152
    lack of, 30–31, 48, 124
    mid-pandemic, 141–142, 149
Fung, C. Victor, 3, 5, 41, 98, 117

German and polka bands, 74–76
giving to others, 25, 117, 130
Good Hope Senior Center, 51–55, 76–78, 86–87
guitar
    classes, 78–79
    jam, 79

harmonica club, 76–78
health services, 32, 53, 63, 123
health-related
    benefits of music, 114–115, 156. See also music participation activities: benefits offered by
    challenges, 110–111
historical background
    evolution of model for, 7, 32–33
    origins of, 10–12
    role of socialization throughout, 18

identity and self-esteem, 132–135. See also self-worth
instrument accessibility/preferences, 104–105
instrumental activities
    concert bands, 69–73
    German and polka band, 74–76
    guitar classes, 78–79
    guitar jam, 79

harmonica club, 76–78
jazz bands, 73–74
overview, 68–69
ukulele classes/groups, 79–85
interviewee categories and numbers, 100
isolation, 5, 15, 25, 28, 151

jazz bands, 73–74

karaoke groups, 90–93

language barriers, 55, 64. See also challenges and barriers: for senior centers
Lehmberg, Lisa J., 3, 5, 41, 98, 117
life phases, 151
lifelong learning, 3, 8, 14, 18, 150
listening, passive and active, 65–67, 109–110, 179–181
literature reviews, 5–6, 41
loneliness, 115. See also social isolation

management, 139–142, *146*
marketing senior centers, 24, 30–31, 122–123, 157–160
meals. See nutrition services
mental health services, 17, 29, 55, 123–124. See also Alzheimer's disease
minority and underrepresented groups, 25–29. See also demographic statistics: ethnicity/race
Mountain View Senior Center, 55–57, 71–74, 89–90
multigenerational centers, 52, 158
multipurpose senior centers, 7, 33–34
music
    activity leaders. See music participation activities: group leaders
    benefits offered by, 3–6, 8, 114–115, 132. See also music participation activities: benefits offered by
    community, 3
    composition, 150–151, 155–156
    desired qualities in musical activities, 129–131
    older adults and, 132
    role of in senior centers, 37
music education, 151–152, 158. See also professional development
Music for Life: Music Participation and Quality of Life of Senior Citizens (Lehmberg; Fung) 4–5, 41, 98, 117
music participation activities. See also music-making; instrumental activities; singing activities
    at Better Living Senior Center, 50
    at Center for Healthy Aging, 58
    at Good Hope Senior Center, 53

music participation activities. (cont.)
  at Mountain View Senior Center, 56
  at The Senior Place, 50–60
  at Sunnyside Senior Center, 46–47
  benefits offered by, 3, 15, 113–120, 152, 156
  case studies of, 35–37
  community partnership opportunities and, 158–159
  defined, 3
  demand for, 14
  enjoyment of. *See* music participation activities: quality of life and
  forms and categories of, 65, 106–108. *See also* activity formats
  group leaders, 105–106, 151–152, 157
  groups, summary table of, *69*
  inventory of, 122–123
  listening, passive and active, 65–67, 109–110, 179–181
  mid-pandemic, *146*. *See also* pandemic-related
  movement and dance as, 67–68
  opportunities for, 8, 44, 158–159
  pleasure and, 113–114
  pre- vs. mid-pandemic, 140–143
  prevalence of, 95–96
  quality of life and, 35, 37, 119–120, 132, 159–160, 167
  research on, dearth of, 15, 35, 41
  research since 2000, 34–35
  socialization through, 115–117
  variables affecting, 35–36
  venue options for, 6–7, 166
  interview guides, 165–167
  methodology, 42, 163–164
  recommendations and study insights, 61–64, 93–98, 148–153
  study design, 162–163
musical development, 96–97, 129–130
musical genre preferences, 105
music-making
  activities, 125, *174*
  forms of participation in, 68–69, 101–102
  musical development and, 96–97, 129–130
  off-site, 108–109
  research since 2000, 125

National Council on Aging, 13
National Institute of Senior Centers, 12, 33, 60
negativity, 111–112
New Horizons International Music Association (NHIMA), 71

New Models Task Force (NMTF), 33
non-participants in senior centers, 13–14, 21–24, 100, 164
nutrition services
  education, 21
  gleaning program, 46, 63
  Meals on Wheels, 64, 142
  not provided, 50
  provided by centers, 7, 29, 32, 51–61, 123

offsite services, 30
Older Americans Act (OAA), 11, 48, 61
operation models
  center for voluntary participation, 11, 15–18
  community-based centers, 11–13, 31
  evolving nature of, 12, 32–33
  multipurpose senior centers, 7, 33–34
  New Models Task Force (NMTF), 33
  pandemic-related, 10
  primary models (8), 12
  social services agency, 11, 15–18

pandemic-related
  activity schedules, 146
  clientele age groups, 143
  lifelong learning, 150
  mid-pandemic plans for future action, 147–148
  operation models, 10
  pre- vs. post-pandemic data, 140–143
participants, *16*, 16–18. *See also* demographic statistics
  with music backgrounds, 101
participation variables, 24–27
partnerships and collaborations
  Better Living Senior Center, 51
  Center for Healthy Aging, 59
  Good Hope Senior Center, 55
  Mountain View Senior Center, 57
  opportunities for, 153
  reasons for partnering, 11
  Sunnyside Senior Center, 48
patience, 112
policy makers, 159
professional development, 32, 153, 158
programs
  diversification of, 14–15
  offered by senior centers, 8, 14–15, 50, 53
  variety and choice of, 94–95
promotional materials, 24, 31. *See also* marketing senior centers
public image of senior centers. *See* senior centers: public image of

quality of life
  connection with others, 25, 97–98, 115–117, 129–131, 149
  elements of, 37, 162
  Flanagan's model of, *135*
  music's contribution to, 35, 37, 97, 119–120, 132, *135*, 159–160, 167
  wellness consciousness and, 35

recommendations and study insights, 93–98, 148–153
recreational opportunities, 14, 32–33, 46, 54, 56, 123, 134
recruitment of senior center clientele, 48, 55
research on music participation. *See also* studies; surveys
  dearth of, 35, 37, 41
  future subjects for, 160–161
  lack of participant diversity, 21, 41
  limited research sample for, 43–44
  since 2000, 34–35
  since 2015, 129
research, empirical, 43–44, 47, 64, 124, 149, 152, 159, 161
resources, 124–125. *See also* challenges and barriers: for senior centers
rural centers, 30

safe space, 113, 118, 129, 151
self-worth, 117–118, 151
senior centers. *See also* multigenerational centers
  atmosphere at, 93–94
  benefits offered by, 27–30
  Better Living Senior Center, 49–51, 79, 83–85, 87–92
  Center for Healthy Aging, 57–59, 69–71
  clientele, 16–18, *16*, 122
  common elements across research sample, 61–64. *See also* recommendations and study insights
  demographics relating to. *See* demographic statistics
  functions of, 13, *15–18*
  Good Hope Senior Center, 51–55, 78, 86–87
  history of. *See* historical background
  motivations for participation in, 13–14
  Mountain View Senior Center, 55–57, 71–74, 89–90
  operation models for. *See* operation models
  programs offered by, 8, 14–15, 50, 53
  public image of, 7–8, 11, 30–31, 34, 122–123, 158–160. *See also* marketing senior centers
  representative sampling of, 42–44
  sustainability of, 32–33, 122
The Senior Place, 59–61, 78–79, 92–93
singing activities
  choirs/choruses, 86–90
  karaoke groups, 90–93
social isolation, 5, 15, 25, 28, 151
social-environmental issues, 32
socialization
  as senior center core function, 18
  music participation central to, 97–98, 115–117, 156
  senior centers' role in, 21
spiritual uplift, 119
spirituality, 4, 15, 37, 129
staff continuity, 31, 157. *See also* challenges and barriers: for senior centers
stick-to-itiveness, 112
studies
  aspects of activity participation, 24–27
  challenges and barriers for senior centers, 30
  functions of senior centers, 16
  literature reviews, 5–6, 41
  minority and underrepresented groups, 25–29
  of operation models, 11
  senior center clients compared with nonparticipants, 21–24
  since 2000 34–35
  since 2015 129
  stability of activity participation, 24
Sunnyside Senior Center, 44–49, 79–83
surveys
  live music performances, 179–181
  of management personnel, 182–190
  mid-pandemic music activities, 149
  mid-pandemic plans for future action, 147–148
  of music activities, 6, 36
  operation models, 13
  of partnerships and collaborations, 11
  pre- vs. mid-pandemic activities, 140–143
  pre- vs. mid-pandemic music activities, 140–143, 174

ukulele classes/groups, 79–85

volunteerism programs, 14, 25
volunteers
  as activity leaders, 75
  center staffing by, 47, 50, 54, 56, 60–61
  recruitment challenges, 48, 64, 124
  staff continuity, 31, 157. *See also* challenges and barriers: for senior centers

well-being
    elements of, 4–5
    and music activities mid-pandemic, 149
    role of music in, 3, 5, 35, 132, 135, 152, 154, 156
    senior center promotion of, 8, 18, 27, 47

wellness consciousness
    dimensions of, 15
    and music activities, 15
    quality of life and, 34
    targeted outcomes, 15

For EU product safety concerns, contact us at Calle de José Abascal, 56–1°,
28003 Madrid, Spain or eugpsr@cambridge.org.